THE
HORSE ANGELS

BY MARK NEIHART

The Horse Angels by Mark Neihart

Edited by Becky Harding
Proofreading by Ken Passarella
Layout by Lucy Jordan, Jordan Communications
Cover Art by Mark Neihart

© Copyright 2014 Dancing Deer, LLC

Published by Dancing Deer, LLC. Sandy, UT

www.TheHorseAngels.com

ISBN 978-0-9860315-1-9

First Edition 2014

Printed in China

To my wife Heidi

You were the inspiration, the creative spark,
and the muse needed to keep me writing for three years.
Without you, this book would not be.

~ AUTHOR'S NOTE ~

It is my belief that mankind owes a huge debt of gratitude to the horse. Though this book will interest all people whether horse lovers or not, it did come to life from the idea that mankind owes much of our cultural advancement to the horse.

Through my creative professional life I have been über-fortunate to work with some of the top horsemen in the world. The German dressage master Walter Zettl, Pat Parelli, *the* natural horseman, Linda Parelli who has brought natural horsemen principles to dressage, Brad Anderson, the guy who actually got me on a horse, Gary Rockwell, Lilo Fore, Janet Brown... the list is getting longer every year. These people have inspired me and informed me, each one uncovering a bit more understanding of how important the horse has been in the progress of mankind through the millennia.

This story, The Horse Angels, started out as that epic tale about the history of horse and man. Though the somewhat boring historical details were shed in favor of something much more interesting for the common reader, the seeds of that original thought are still contained herein. It is what motivates many of the characters in The Horse Angels.

This book would not have been possible without the tireless efforts of my beautiful wife Heidi Zorn, who shares the writing credit. When the storyline was stuck, Heidi would breathe fresh life into my creative reservoir. She was the inspiration, the muse who kept me writing. If you see her, thank her!

One hundred and fifty years ago it was the horse pulling the cart. Today we see the Chevy Suburban pulling the horse, within the trailer. This is the perfect symbol of our collective love and appreciation of the horse as well as an apt symbol of our gratitude.

Mark Neihart
Wellington, Florida
February 2014

FOREWORD

by Linda Parelli

I first met Mark Neihart about 10 years ago through Walter Zettl, a master of dressage with whom I had the privilege to study for five illuminating years. Mark and his wife Heidi produced Walter's video series "A Matter of Trust" and we instantly became friends. Personally, I love how passionate they are about spreading the message of thoughtful training and the ethical, loving treatment of horses.

When Mark said he was writing a book I was curious to see what it would be about and let me say that it is not at all what I expected!

The Horse Angels is a work of fiction but there is an underlying arc to the story as Mark artfully weaves in messages of the important role horses have played in our past and present humanity. Touching on the need to create a better world for horses and humans, a mission very close to my heart, The Horse Angels tells the tale of our ancient bonds and the vast array of cultures impacted and developed because of mankind's relationship with horses.

The subtle messages sent and received by our equine companions is something I have spent a lifetime learning and teaching, but the mystical elements are the creative twist to the book that I did not expect. The Horse Angels is surprising, compelling, a romance, a drama, historical, ethical... a fabulous ride that captures wholeheartedly the unexplainable, magical passion we have for our blessed horses.

Somewhere around 6,000 years ago humans domesticated the horse. At one point in history, the first man crawled up on the back of that first horse and a bond was forged. That bond, which still exists today, is responsible for a remarkable history of innovation, evolution, and growth. Mankind rode into modernity on the back of a horse.

It all started on that vast plain we call the Russian Steppe. From there, very slowly over thousands of years, horse culture spread, first south, then west and east. In the mountains of modern-day Armenia there are 5,000-year-old petroglyphs showing horses pulling chariots, plows, and wagons. Move forward 1,000 years and the Celts ride into Europe carrying in their hearts the Goddess Aponia giving us the word "pony." Two hundred years later horsemen enter Asia Minor and bring horse culture to ancient Persia, the Middle East, and Egypt. Skip ahead 500 years and we find horses entering India. Another 500 and horses arrive in China.

Breeding starts. New horses are developed in Central Asia, the Lusitans are developing the great Spanish bloodlines, the Arab is brought into being, and throughout Europe new breeds appear. This epoch sees a growth of specialization, as the horse is valued for everything from agriculture and transportation to war. It will still be 1,500 years until the New World is discovered and horses are reintroduced to the Americas.

All through this very long history we find a similar thread, a common story. It appears as a kaleidoscope with the pieces of the narrative splayed out in countless and endless variations on the theme. That theme, that common thread, is the bond—the enduring bond between horse and man. That is the theme of this story.

From the foggy mists of ancient history, mankind has had a faithful partner. This partnership has resulted in propelling our race beyond the scope of any one man's reckoning; beyond the collective abilities of any one group of human beings. It has brought us to a place that transcends the very vehicle that delivered us here. As we move forward into our technology-driven world, into the future, the question must be asked: What will become of our ancient bond with our evolutionary partner? For 6,000 years we have relied on our relationship with this animal to clothe, to feed, and to protect us. Now what? How do we move forward? How do we preserve one of our deepest commitments? If we merely move on and shed off the past, one must ask the question:

What will become of the horse?

THE HORSE ANGELS

CHAPTER ONE

Anne Harper quickly rode her dressage horse out of the competition arena. She moved past the small group of people gathered near the gate and continued until she was in a quiet place between the warmup and the main competition arenas. There she slid off the back of her horse and threw the reins at the waiting groom.

"Get this worthless loser out of my sight!" The man blinked but he knew the rules: Say nothing, do what you're told. He led the horse away. Anne stood motionless in the morning sun oblivious to the horse show thrumming all around her. Anne hated losing. Inside she was fuming; outside the fine features of her face were screwed up into a tempest. She snatched a cell phone from her riding jacket. After fumbling a few times to enter the number, she pushed the phone to her face. She was shaking with rage.

"Tammy?" Anne's voice cracked as she yelled into the phone. "How did it go? You know how it went!" Now Anne was shrieking. "I told you we needed to train harder. I told you we needed the rollkur. I could have scored 10 points higher, but now I have missed the class. I'm out for the season and it's all your fault." Anne let Tammy get a few words in just for the chance to catch her breath. A moment later she furiously interrupted.

"I am not interested in your theories, I am interested in winning! Obviously you are not. Oh, forget it! You're fired!" Anne threw her phone into the sand. Her anger always left her impotent, consuming her very will; and typical of those people not in control of their passions, always left her with regrets.

She huffed off toward the show manager's office. She would blame the arena footing for her horrible ride. She would have her score expunged. She could salvage this. Unexpectedly, she heard a small voice.

"Mommy?" Anne stopped abruptly and turned around. Her six-year-old daughter was standing close by with her shoulders hunched and hands tucked deep into the pockets of her jeans. Anne, completely absorbed in her anger, had forgotten that her daughter was watching her ride.

"Oh …Samantha …there you are!" Anne tried to calm down as she saw the frightened look in her daughter's eyes.

Samantha knew her mother's ride had not gone well; she understood how important winning was to her mother's career. She also knew the best strategy to avoid her mother's wrath was not to mention it. At the moment, her mother's ride really didn't matter to the young girl. She was thinking about her father and his cross-country competition. Simon and his horse Henley were favored to win the cross-country portion of the event competition. Samantha wanted nothing more than to see him run his race. But she needed her mother to take her there.

"Mommy, when does daddy run? I really want to see him go." Samantha was not begging, just speaking plainly, safely. Anne rolled her eyes and heaved a deliberate sigh. She knew she needed to take Sam to see her father before he started his race. She had promised, but in her current state of mind, had been hoping to blow it off. She flashed her daughter a fake smile.

"Okay, sweetie," her voice was strained, "Of course we are going. He starts in about an hour. I only need to change my clothes, okay?" Samantha mustered a smile. Anne reached out and took her daughter's hand. "Come with me first, then we'll go up to the starting gate."

The two walked away from the dressage competition arenas toward the center of the horse show grounds where the sprawling complex of horse stalls was situated. Anne was a tall, fit woman with long, dark hair. Samantha, favoring her father's genes had a much fairer complexion. With her short blond hair and skinny frame, Sam, as she was called, looked like a miniature version of Simon. She also shared her father's calm demeanor. In contrast to her mother, he was easy going, solid, and not prone to emotional outbreaks.

Anne and Sam walked hand-in-hand, not out of affection but for safety's sake amid the inherent danger of walking through a crowded horse show at the height of the morning action. Everything was in mo-

2

tion around them, a giant scramble of movement—people, horses, scooters, golf carts, utility trucks—all zooming around like cars in an Italian roundabout. Controlled chaos, balanced in a way that could, at any moment, fall apart, unleashing the potential for disaster and serious harm. Anne and Samantha joined the participants and made their way slowly toward the horse stalls.

They were at the Kentucky Horse Park for one of the largest horse shows in the world. It was a competition of all equestrian disciplines; the biggest of its kind, attended by top athletes worldwide. All disciplines were represented, from English to Western and all styles in between. It was like the Olympics of the horse world. Anne and Simon were making their mark in this world—Anne as a dressage rider while Simon competed at eventing.

The morning had risen bright and clear over the 5,000-acre equestrian park. The April air was crisp but warming quickly with bright sunlight streaming through the budding springtime foliage. It was the third day of the weeklong competition and the excitement of the show was gaining momentum.

A main road separated the show rings from the stalls and it was growling with the daily horse show traffic. Anne and Samantha stepped cautiously onto the road and made their way to the other side, the dust puffing from beneath their shoes with every step. With an estimated 200,000 people attending the show, swarms of equestrian devotees were everywhere. Crowds of folks were milling around the vendor booths set up along the sprawling midway. Others were queued up in front of food trailers waiting for their morning breakfast. Anne and Sam walked alongside the crowd.

The traffic and noise grated on Anne's already-frazzled nerves. She was still fuming as the two walked past the first rows of horse stalls and moved deeper into the complex. The chaos of the main road subsided and the relative quiet took the edge off Anne's irritation. All she'd wanted was to score high enough to make it to the next level of competition; she had worked so hard, so intently. Expectations always die such a cruel death. Obsessing on her loss, she searched for someone to blame.

Tammy Powell, her current trainer, used the old-fashioned techniques of classical dressage training. Anne had reluctantly decided to submit to Tammy's antiquated training methods at the urging of her husband. Simon's views on training were at odds with her own. He was always going on about gentleness and about not pushing the horse too far when training. He was at the top of his game. A real winner. A real horseman. Of course the thought of Simon's success right now made Anne even angrier. Simon was a more talented rider; he always had been. That is why he could get away with those long-term training methods. But Anne needed shortcuts, some quick-fix techniques to get her horse to submit. She had accepted Tammy into her barn on Simon's insistence. Now she was walking away from the competition season a loser. The word was burning in her mind. Tammy was a mistake; Anne didn't need her. Anne knew how to win.

"Damn it!" she said out loud. Samantha looked up at her mother. She saw the

far-away stare, the detachment, the aloneness. She let go of her mother's hand and ran ahead to their show stall where the support crew would be gathered, where she would be noticed, where she would be welcomed.

Far across the show grounds—far away from the dust, noise, and hustle of the main road, the food trailers and vendor booths. Out across acres of rolling green hills up into the very corner of the sprawling horse park—was the starting gate for the cross-country course. Simon Harper held a cell phone to his ear listening to the ringing on the other end, then a click, then his wife's recorded voice asking the caller to leave a message. Simon closed his phone and frowned. He knew Anne was done with her ride, she should be answering. He opened the phone and punched in another number. Immediately a vibrant and friendly voice answered.

"Hi, Simon!" It was Grace, his wife's barn manager.

"Hi, Grace. How's the morning?"

"Oh, I don't think you want to hear," Grace said with a bit of sarcasm.

"Not good, huh?" Simon figured Anne must have scored poorly.

"Well, there's always next year," Grace answered.

"Damn." He paused. "Okay …is she there? I've tried to call her but it goes right to voice mail."

"She's just walking up," said Grace. "Hang on a sec."

Simon waited. He could hear the conversation taking place at the show stall. It didn't sound good; he was glad he was on the other side of the park. He listened while Grace told Anne she had a call. Simon braced for impact.

"Hello." Anne's voice was plainly perturbed.

"Hey, are you okay? I heard about your ride. Sorry." Simon tried to sound calm and understanding. There was a long silence on the other end. "Anne?"

"Yeah, I'm here. Just trying to hold it together. The judges weren't very kind to me this morning."

"Oh, sorry," Simon said. "I want to hear all about it after I get through with my run. I am starting in about 40 minutes. Are you bringing Sammy out?"

"Yes," Anne said. "I have to change and we will be on our way."

"Great!" said Simon trying to sound positive. "See you soon. Oh, by the way, why aren't you answering your phone?" Anne suddenly remembered her phone lying on the ground back at the show ring, a new round of anger sweeping through.

"Oh, I guess my battery died," she lied. She was ashamed of her violent temper and didn't want to be reminded of it.

"Hmm," said Simon, sensing something different. "Well, I'll see both of you soon."

Anne handed the phone back to Grace and said, "Send someone back to the show ring. I think I dropped my phone. Have someone go find it."

"No problem," said Grace. "I'll take care of it."

Simon was an eventer. Eventing, one of the most aggressive and dangerous equestrian sports, is a three-day triathlon comprised of dressage, endurance, and show jumping. Simply known as the three-day event, it is rooted in the old cavalry and grew from the comprehensive testing required of cavalry officers way back when horses were still used in war. The testing was to demonstrate mastery over several riding styles. From the parade ground to the battlefield, the demands on the military horse and rider were severe. The testing was just as severe in its scope and demands on the competitors.

It was the endurance phase of the three-day event, commonly referred to as the cross country, that Simon loved most. He loved the full gallop, the obstacles, and the wide-open spaces. He knew the dressage phase was necessary to demonstrate that the horse was capable of performing in a graceful, relaxed and precise manner. But dressage, ridden in a relatively small and confining ring, was not at all exciting to Simon. Show jumping, which demonstrates the fitness of the horse after completing the endurance phase, was held in a bigger arena and was fun but still a bit restrictive. Simon excelled at all three disciplines, but it was the cross country he loved most.

The cross-country course covered several miles with 25-plus obstacles, including ponds and streams, ditches, drops, and banks. Such a course allowed as much freedom as one could expect from a staged and controlled competitive race. Simon craved the cross country even though it was extremely dangerous and not uncommon for riders to crash over one of the jumps and become seriously injured, or even die. Simon knew several riders who had landed on the other side of the jump with an injured horse on top of them. But Simon was skilled at putting this danger out of his mind and pushing his horses safely to maximum effort. Today would be no different. Today was his day—the day he has been training for. Win this one and it was off to the Olympic team, no questions asked. There would be a great ceremony tonight as his friends and colleagues gathered to congratulate him and send him on his way to worldwide triumph. This was the day—his moment had finally come. He checked the clock; his starting time was 30 minutes out. He scanned the crowd around him; each face seemed to be beaming with the same expectation—today was his day.

Of course the day would be nothing without Simon's talented and most favorite horse, Henley. The stallion was of the Hanoverian breed, a giant at 17 hands with deep brown coloring and a perfectly symmetrical white blaze covering the front of his head. The horse had a willing spirit; he could run, jump, and turn almost effortlessly. He was supple with a brave, bold heart and a love for Simon that made the two a formidable team. They were made for each other. Simon knew it and Henley knew it.

Simon had picked him up for cheap from a small farm in Utah. The owners hit the skids and couldn't afford to keep the animals they had. Henley was one of several horses all but abandoned to an unkempt field. When Simon first met the horse, the animal was underfed, shaggy, and still quite wild. But when Simon saw how the horse moved, he could tell right away there was something special there, a raw talent that needed only to be developed, brought out, and encouraged. Simon bought him on the spot and started training right away. That was four years ago. Now Henley was a top athlete. A horse that was keen to run, a horse that could jump anything without fear, a horse that could move through the graces of dressage, and be at home in the jumping ring. Simon had many horses over his long career, but never had he bonded with one as he did with Henley. When he was on this horse they truly were one being, one heart, and one mind. It was complete unity in the dance.

Simon, at six feet tall, had an athlete's build, fit, trim, and muscular. His light brown hair was cropped close giving his ruggedly sharp features an air of intensity. If he wasn't smiling, one would swear he was in a deep concentration. That was the look he had in sober moments. Sharp blue eyes reflected a soul of great depth, kindness, and confidence.

He was finishing the fine points of readying Henley for the run when Anne and Samantha rolled up in their rented golf cart. Anne parked near a tree next to the other rented carts. There were about 30 altogether creating an impromptu parking lot. Samantha spied her father and jumped from the cart, running full gallop into his arms. Anne came up behind trying to disguise how she was really feeling. She wouldn't get over her loss quickly. Simon grabbed his little girl and swung her up into the saddle on top of Henley.

"Hello, sweetheart! Are you ready to watch your dad win this thing?"

"Uh, huh!" Samantha cheered. The sparkle in her eyes declared her absolute love for her father. Samantha leaned over and wrapped her arms around Henley's thick powerful neck. Simon turned to Anne.

"Hi," he said tentatively.

"Hi," Anne replied in an undertone that belied her straining smile.

"So ...not too good in the ring this morning?"

"I scored a 62! One of the worst rides I've ever had. It was ridiculous! I just couldn't get her engaged. She missed every one of the tempis, and she was completely downhill. I could strangle Tammy..."

"Tammy?" Simon could see where this was going and he didn't have the time to defend the first-class trainer he had encouraged Anne to engage.

"Yeah, Tammy!" The fire returned to Anne's eyes as her anger began to push its way back into the red zone. "I don't know why I listened to you. She is the absolute worst! I could have scored higher with no trainer. I was completely humiliated and ...."

She went on but Simon tuned her out. He had to concentrate on his ride and his preparation. Anne never did have the capacity to feel for other people; she couldn't see that all he needed was a bit of support, some tranquility, and a tender kiss for good luck. He was irritated by his wife's selfishness.

"Uh, look," he cut her off mid-sentence. "I really have to get ready here. I would love to hear all about it but right now is just not the time. You understand that, right?"

Anne stopped talking and frowned. She knew he was right but her anger overrode this knowledge. "You asshole!" she was stage whispering so as not to draw too much attention. "If you hadn't forced that freak trainer of yours on me I could have at least gone on to the next class but NO! I have to lose to that other stupid freak Lisa Brainer. This is all your fault!"

Simon was silent. He was stunned by his wife's angry tirade and wondered why she would push this argument right here, right now.

"Okay, off you go," he said firmly shaking his head. "We'll pick this up later."

Simon pulled Samantha down from Henley's back and gave her a gentle hug. The horse looked back at the tiny human girl and nickered.

"Good luck, Daddy!" Sam's voice was all high expectations and confidence.

"Thanks sweetie! I think Henley needs a hug too. There ya go."

Simon turned to his wife. As he handed the girl over to her his tone grew much colder. "Number 25 will be a good place to watch from." He pressed his lips together into a slight frown.

"Yeah," Anne answered, feeling the shame of knowing she should be supporting her husband right now, but her anger carried her away. She was simply too proud to apologize. It always felt like submission and that didn't suit Anne Harper. "Don't worry about us. Just make sure you win this one." Her tone was unintentionally condescending. "Oh, and be careful over number 12; that is my biggest nightmare."

Simon looked at the ground with grim determination. He wasn't going to let Anne's anger ruin his morning or his race.

"Yeah, I have my strides worked out, no problem with number 12. Henley here knows the way." Simon put his hand on the stallion's neck and gave a caring pat.

"I know," Anne said. She felt bad but didn't know how to unwind the situation now. Rigidly she blurted out a forced "I love you. See you at the finish line." Simon just looked at her, speechless for the moment.

Anne and Sam walked over to the golf cart and climbed in. Before they started off to join the other spectators, Anne smiled sheepishly at her husband, gave a wink, and blew him a kiss. She would make it up to him later that night, after the celebrations.

Simon shook his head and then tried to put the distraction out of his mind. He needed to focus. Turning to the task at hand, he continued the ritual of dressing for the competition. He already had on his jodh-purs and a long-sleeved, blue- and yellow-striped riding shirt. From his equipment bag, he pulled out his Kevlar cross-country vest and a two-point air vest. The Kevlar was designed to take full impact from front and back while the air vest acted like an air bag, inflating instantly if the rider left the saddle during a fall.

Safety was always a top concern in the cross country phase. The obstacles are designed to be solid and unmovable, which encourages the horse to make a clean jump, out of sheer survival instinct. Yet if a horse refuses a jump or stumbles and falls into the obstacle, the result can be severe. It was not all that uncommon to have a fatality during this phase of the three-day competition.

Next out of the truck was Simon's lucky helmet. He used this same helmet for several years with never a fall. Of course his sponsors had outfitted him with many helmets since but Simon was not interested in the latest designs or features, not as long as his lucky helmet was in usable shape. Once a rider did take a fall, the helmet had to be replaced. But Simon's lucky helmet was as fit as the first time he wore it during a winning competition in Brazil. He retrieved his gloves from the bag along with his large-faced racing timer and his medical armband. The armband held relevant medical information for attending paramedics, and all riders were required to wear one in case of an accident. It wasn't long before Simon was suited up; his horse was ready. He was ready. Simon mounted the stallion with the familiar surge of adrenaline.

Buzzing slowly along in the golf cart, Anne and Samantha plodded forward through the throngs of spectators. Cross country was probably the most popular of the equestrian competitions, and crowds of people swarmed along the route, which was marked off by two bright yellow ropes that formed a lane. The riders would proceed down the lane through the course in 10-minute intervals. Along the route were the course stewards whose job it was to assure a clear lane for the riders. Each steward had a whistle that was blown when the next horse was approaching. The spectators would hear the whistle, which would signal lane crossings to be closed, and would cause a hush to fall on the audience. As soon as the rider passed, an almost frenetic mood would sweep over the crowd and the sounds of cheers, wild applause, and encouragement would ring out across the course.

Anne drove carefully so as not to run anyone down. People were everywhere. She drove the cart straight across the field and bypassed the first part of the course. As they approached the remaining jumps, Anne still marveled at the size and girth of the obstacles. She had seen this course countless times, watched her husband race across the turf, literally sailing over these jumps. Still, when seen up close they were more than a little terrifying.

The jumps were designed and built to resemble the natural obstacles that were encountered on the battlefield by yesteryear's cavalry. Each obstacle may have one or more jump routes giving the rider flexibility depending upon the training of his mount. Each jump had a name, and each had combinations of differing elements such as brush, water, ditch, log and so on.

Jump number 9, the *Trakehner*, a five-foot diameter log set astride a deep pit with brush on either side. Nine feet wide and four feet high, it took quite an athlete to get over this one without losing stride. Number 10 was a set of five jump rails, down the slope to a ditch, and then back up another slope to the big curved brush at the top. Number 11 was just over the hill and out of site. Number 12, the *Oxer*, was a long stretch up another hill to a set of two tall jumps at the top. The jumps, set at four feet apart, had to be cleared in one leap. Then it was back down the hill to jump 13 called *Creek Challenge*. This was a multi-obstacle jump starting with a large brush oxer, followed by a ditch, then a four-foot palisade, then another brush oxer, all on a turn.

Anne took in all of these obstacles one by one. When she heard the steward's whistle, she would stop her golf cart and with a rush of exhilaration watch the next rider fly by in full gallop on up to the obstacle. Then the rider would disappear, the crowd would go wild and she would continue on. She was heading for jump number 25 across the small creek directly in front of her. When the stewards gave the "all clear," she continued over the bridge and parked her cart next to the lane in front of the jump. There she waited. At that vantage point she could view jumps 9, 10, 11, 12, 13, 14, 22, and 24. Though the course spanned acres, her vantage point on the hill overlooked this particular part of the course. Samantha got out of the cart and went to play on a large wooden sculpture made to look like a duck. Anne kept her eyes on both Samantha and the course alternately as she waited nervously to see her husband run the course.

At the starting gate, Simon was done with the soundness check where veterinarians inspected each horse before the run. He sat high in the saddle, regal in his riding gear. In his mind he was running the course. The first 10 obstacles were no real concern; they were designed to allow the horse and rider to gain confidence and get into a rhythm. Just keep the timing up, make clean jumps, and move ahead. The large distance between 10 and 11 was where he could make up any time lost. His horse was a fast runner and throughout the training season he had been increasing his speed, moving faster than the previous year. Jump 11, no problem. Jump 12 is where his mind faltered. Jump 12 was the place where the course sloped upward, slowing the horse down when speed was most needed. To clear the oxer, a double-fenced obstacle spread out to four feet, he needed to reach the top in the right stride, make the jump then turn slightly down the hill into jump 13, the challenging oxer/ditch/palisade combo. These two jumps were the most challenging. He worked the movement though his mind stopped and did it again. The three-minute buzzer startled him out of his daydream. Three minutes before his green light.

Out on the course Anne watched as the next rider, a woman, rounded the corner and took jumps 9 and 10 without a hitch. Jump 11 came up and the rider slowed a bit, made the jump, then raced down the hill and up the slope. Right before jump 12, that huge oxer, the horse stopped dead, throwing the rider headfirst into the log railing. The pop of the air-jacket was heard across the course as the rider slammed the railing and tumbled up and over the top. A groan went through the crowd as the course emergency team scrambled over to fetch the horse and retrieve the rider. Anne watched breathlessly. She knew of the real danger, the broken necks and snapped spines, the internal injuries. The rider came up from the ditch. At her side were two members of the course team. The rider seemed to be okay. Applause broke out and spread through the crowd. And when she waved to the spectators, the crowd roared its approval. Anne felt an uneasiness growing in her gut. Jump 12 really should be redesigned. It was notorious for disaster.

Back at the starting gate, Simon watched the clock tick down the seconds. Thirty seconds remaining until green light. He checked his racing watch, a large-faced timepiece strapped to his wrist. This was his tool to measure his progress through the course. All was well. He took a deep breath and relaxed his entire body, which cleared his mind and focused his thoughts. He clearly perceived the oneness between himself and Henley. He could feel the same anticipation in the life beneath him. His horse was ready, he was ready, the world was ready and waiting. The buzzer sounded, the light flashed green, and in the blink of an eye he and Henley were off.

Running at full gallop was the best feeling Simon knew. The sound of the hooves on raw turf hammered out a soothing, rhythmic, thudding pulse. The horse was free and gliding smoothly toward the first obstacle. The wind whistled in his ears as the horse's breath was keeping time with the gallop. Jump 1, up and over.

"Good boy," Simon cooed to his horse. "Come on!" He gave the signal to run free and fast and the horse responded. Picking up speed, he ran down a small hill and through a stand of trees. On either side of him were the course lane ropes keeping the people out of harm's way. On either side of the lane, the crowds were thick but respectfully quiet. Jump 2, no problem. After the jumps the people signaled their approval with hoots, hollers, and congratulatory screams. Simon felt great, his horse felt great. Henley was running in a fluid, seemingly effortless gait.

The obstacles flew by one by one. Simon was completely present in each moment, his full concentration focused on each stride taken. Every second of the race was an eternal critique of his position on the course, his horse's response, the condition of the ground, the taste in the air. Simon was in that zone where warriors go in the heat of battle. That place where time stops and extrasensory abilities rise up to command absolute control of mind and body. His brain was analyzing each step the horse took, each ripple in the course and each obstacle as it came rushing forward at 40 miles per hour. His body was reacting to every needed correction. His horse was responding perfectly, the two melded into one form singing along in the glory of the April sun.

Anne was perched on top of the golf cart watching over the course with a bird's-eye view. Samantha had joined her and the two sat side by side watching over the spectacle. The crowd gathered along the course buzzed and seemed to sway to the rhythm of some inaudible cosmic music. They were all waiting anxiously for the next rider to appear. Again, the sound of the stewards' whistles began to sound up and down the course. The course crossings were pulled up and the crowd stopped their movement. All heads were turned up-course waiting to catch the first glimpse of the approaching horse and rider.

Across the course Anne and Samantha saw Simon bounding over the hill.

"Look Mommy!" Sam cried out. "There's Daddy!" Anne smiled

nervously and nodded her head. From this distance Simon looked like a toy. Anne watched as he rode down the hill in a straight beeline to jump 11. Even at this distance Henley looked regal, his mane flowing in rhythmic bounces as the pair rode up to the obstacle and effortlessly cleared all seven feet. Up and over. The pair was now heading up the hill to jump number 12. Anne thought about closing her eyes. Something had roused true fear in her heart. Her eyes closed involuntary and she forced them open. She had to see. Simon and Henley closed in fast on the infamous jump. Just before the oxer, Anne thought she saw something out of place. Did the horse slip? Her mind raced; in that split second her eyes registered horror. Her heart skipped as Simon raced up the hill, and without missing a beat went up and over jump 12, down in the ditch to jump 13, up and out, over the palisade and the remaining oxer and was clear. Anne swallowed hard, then let out a long sigh.

"Shit!" she whispered under her breath. Samantha was cheering loudly along with the rest of the crowd. Anne looked at her little girl and gave her a weak smile. They watched as Simon cleared number 14 and disappeared over a hill.

"Daddy's winning, isn't he, Mommy?" Sammy's voice was cheerful and full of confidence.

"Yes, I think you're right, Sammy. I think you're right."

The course took a long arc to the right, more jumps, and then back to the left where it circled around through some water obstacles, up another long sloping hill and then down to the finish line. Simon's mind was focused, yet the stress of the run was starting to wear on him. Henley was breathing hard and the lather was thick along his shoulders and neck.

"Come on, buddy." Simon whispered in his horse's ear, "Just a few more of these bad boys." They were running headlong, breathing hard, muscles straining under the pressure of the long endurance. Jump number 24 in view now, coming up fast. The two went up and over, no problem. Simon glanced at his race watch. Great timing so far, just like he had practiced. Five more jumps, about a mile to go. Simon felt a rush of exuberance. Focus, he needed to focus. Directly ahead was jump 25, a straightforward set of rails, a galloping jump.

The stewards' whistles were blowing now. The crowd was settling into their spots as the course crossing ropes were drawn tight. Anne and Samantha sat on top of the golf cart looking down the course. A hush fell over the crowd as the sound of the gallop came rushing up from the hill just in front of them.

The sunshine was warm; the clear light illuminated the day's details with a crispness and contrast that would stay in Anne's mind forever. She watched with pride as her husband approached the jump. Being right on the running lane, she could see the yellow ropes on either side of the lane narrowing together towards the vanishing point off in the distance. In between, Simon and Henley were visibly straining. The white lather on the horse was gleaming as it foamed and was brushed away in the wind of the run. Simon's face was determined and set in a grimace of stress and concentration. All watched as two great athletes in full glory, in the form of champions, raced past in full gallop. They were in the last stretch of a great run, minutes away from winning it all.

It happened very fast—almost in the blink of an eye. So fast that no one really could tell what happened. The cause of the accident was not at all evident. One moment Simon and Henley were in full gallop, one in form and rhythm. The next moment Anne was watching in shock as Henley seemed to stumble before the jump. His canter lost its stride and the pair hit the jump at full speed. The tremendous force of impact caused a sickening sound as the inertia of the run carried the duo up and over the static fence into a cartwheel of outstretched arms and flailing legs. There was a loud pop as Simon's two-point air jacket puffed out in a vain attempt to save his life.

Over in a mere three seconds, to Anne the time shift in her perception caused the action to slow to a crawling horror scene as she absorbed every possible detail of that moment in time. The horse's stumble …the look on the face of a man across the lane who was eating a hotdog and was in mid-bite …the impact of the horse against the immovable fence …the glint of light reflecting off the saddle buckles as Simon and Henley tumbled through the gleaming daylight …that horrid sound of flesh and bone on impact …a bird soaring up in the distance but in line sight of the catastrophe unfolding before her …all this in slow motion. There was that terrible sound of the safety vest as it exploded its lifesaving air to inflate a safety barrier around the man she loved. There was the vision of the falling, tumbling pair as they disappeared over the jump only to bounce back up into view and disappear again ...flailing horse legs and the blunt force of sharp hooves on Simon's crushed body. The scene unfolded all in super slow motion, and when it was over the crowd stood still, shocked into immobility for a ticking moment, standing there in the bright April springtime sunlight looking on, not quite believing what they had just seen.

After that brief stunning second, the rescue action kicked into high gear and the rush of men and women, both lay and professional, converged onto the crippled horse and the dying man.

Anne and Samantha sat paralyzed on top of the golf cart. Samantha was the first to scream—a blood-curdling primal sound that came from the very pit of despair. Anne grabbed her little girl and pulled her tight into her bosom shielding those tender eyes from seeing any more of the carnage that was her father. Anne blinked, her head twitched from one face in the crowd to another. They all had the same look, the look of complete devastation and bewilderment. As the reality of what had taken place streamed into her now-rising consciousness, she let out an uncontrollable sob, a gulp. As her whole body convulsed, a pitiful noise was forced out, the sound of total surrender, then another and another until the misery of reality cascaded into full-on tears of pain. Those tears wouldn't stop for two full weeks.

SIX YEARS LATER...

CHAPTER TWO

S amantha sat upright and rigid in her dressage saddle. Through the earpiece she could hear her mother screaming at her to kick the horse to get his attention. Somehow this didn't feel right to the gentle-hearted twelve-year-old girl. She could feel the horse. She could feel his heart, his life beat, his caring attitude. She could also feel his confusion and didn't want to punish him. She wanted to help him understand. She could feel all of this, but in her inexperienced mind and with her undermined self confidence, she couldn't exactly verbalize these feelings. Instinctively she knew that a kick was not the right way to get his cooperation, she knew that. With some hesitation she raised her boot and half-heartedly stabbed her spur into the side of the animal.

"Are you listening?" her mother moaned. "KICK HIM!"

Samantha frowned; she hated training with her mother. She hated dressage. She hated the competition, the horse show, and the show ring. With a renewed determination, she jabbed the poor animal hard and swift getting his attention and mistrust at the same time. The horse snapped into gear, swishing his tail violently and trotted forward in a medium gait.

"Again!" snapped her mother.

Once again Samantha put aside her intuition and gave in to the nagging voice coming through her earpiece. She kicked again and the horse firmed up its frame and trotted ahead in a steady uphill rhythm.

"Okay! Now keep him that way ...good ...turn left at the corner ..."

This was the daily routine now that Samantha was old enough to start in the lower levels of dressage competition. Her mother kept her in training almost four hours a day. They had six horses that were rotated through the two-hour sessions. During the morning session, Sam rode three of the lower-level "schooling horses." In the afternoon she was tasked with three upper-level horses. All of the horses had different skills and were supposed to help Sam learn faster and therefore win faster. Four days a week she was in training, one day off, and then a horse show on most of the weekends. The pressure was constant. Up at dawn for two hours of training. Then six hours in the classroom where she sat with her private tutor and learned the three Rs, plus history, science, and art. An hour off, then another two hours of training before dinner and reading time. Then it was off to bed by 10:00 pm. Expectations were impossibly high. This was the daily routine and in the six months that she had under her belt, Samantha was almost completely at odds with the whole thing. Such was the fate of the daughter of a once-promising dressage champion.

Sally Bateman was hired to train Sam after her mother had been forced, due to financial strains, to get a day job. Most days Sally would be the one to run Sam and the horses through the paces, but once a week Samantha's mother would be home and always insisted on conducting the training sessions. Today was one of those days and Samantha hated it. Sally was a tough and serious trainer, but at least she was a bit more thoughtful of Samantha's feelings. Sally was just as tough on the horses too, which always bothered Sam, but there was a safe distance kept between them that was not possible with her mother.

Again the screeching woman's voice came high-pitched through the earpiece, "You're posting on the wrong leg!" Samantha bounced once and got into the correct rhythm. The horse she was on was a small six-year-old quarter horse, jet-black with four white socks. His name was Concord and he was steady, confident, and willing. He was trained up to second-level movements, which gave Sam the opportunity to learn how to ride shoulder-in and to start sitting the trot. Sam was a good rider for her age; she had practically grown up on horses. Ever since her father died and her mother had bought this farm, Sam was able to spend many hours with the horses—grooming and feeding them, talking to them, and riding them. She was a natural and had the desire to be a great eventer like her dad. Of course that was out of the question, as her mother wouldn't even let her jump. Dressage was the only equestrian sport Sam was allowed to pursue. It was safer, a higher art than mere jumping, and more prestigious. Sam hated the restrictions, and sometimes when her mother was gone she would take one of the big horses out to the fields and jump any obstacle she could find. Never anything really big that scared her, but she would find a log that had fallen, or a short hedge and pretend she was at the Three-Day racing for big money. She would run across the fields in a full canter and fly over the small obstacles, then turn, circle back and do it again. This is what she loved. She loved being free, letting the horse carry her with confidence, letting go of restraint and having fun. This was the world in her head, but in the real world—the world of her mother's making—she was being trained to be a dressage champion.

"Samantha!" her mother's voice was shrieking again. "He's losing his hind end. You've got to keep him up. Come on, give him a good kick!"

Concord's tail was swishing violently back and forth. Samantha was angry and kicked him hard again. The result was temporary but effective. And so the training went for another 15 minutes—Samantha working to keep her mother happy and her mother working to keep the pressure up. The two were locked into a dangerous dance of power and submission—completely based on Anne's secret desires and lost dreams—and on her desire to see Samantha succeed where she had failed.

On the other side of the wireless, Anne held the microphone close to her lips. She was barking out orders trying to get Samantha to engage the horse. She couldn't understand why her daughter was being so unresponsive today.

"Okay …now walk …take a rest …give him the reins," she said into the small black microphone. Anne was sitting on the trainer's stool at the side of the arena. The morning sunshine was brushing against the back of her black hair, pushing a shadow onto her aging, but still beautiful, face. The morning was rising all around the farm, illuminating the two white stucco barns with a glowing warmth. Brilliant white fencing that surrounded the arenas, lined the drives, and enclosed the pastures was reflecting the growing sunshine with stabs of harsh light in very sharp contrast to the verdant green grass that lay dewy in the morning air. Anne loved this time of day: the fresh chill of the air, the quiet of the countryside before the farm workers started their morning chores, the smell of wet grass.

She looked out across the arena. Her daughter was perched on the black gelding with a natural grace that few possessed. With a little work Anne knew she could get Sam to second level by the end of the year. With a little work she could be riding third level the next. The plan was set and the wheels were turning. Anne had it all laid out in detail right down to the weekly lesson plans. In four short years her daughter would be riding on the Young Riders team, traveling the world in high-level competition. The horses she would ride were purchased and were in training with the best of the best. The pieces were falling into place one by one, just as planned. There was one unexpected turn though; Anne had been forced to return to work. After the last stock market crash, Anne lost most of her nest egg. She invested her fortunes into a series of highly risky private investments that she was assured were safe. All of her moneyed friends climbed on board and for a while they were all making serious dough. But when the time came to pull the money out, Anne stalled, mostly out of sheer laziness, and one by one she saw her investments decline precipitously. By the time she took the necessary action to protect what she had left, it was too late.

She was never very good with money and her advisors were typically driven by self-interests. When Simon died and she received the large insurance settlement, plus the money from the U.S. Team's private fund, she had enough to last her a lifetime. She was set. She bought this farm on the outskirts of Sacramento, paid in full. She hired the best trainers, acquired some very competent horses, and set out to make her daughter the champion that Anne herself had almost become. The plan was working perfectly until the market crash. The panic she felt upon the grim realization of her loss sent her to the hospital more than once. The panic embraced by the thought of losing everything was too much for her already battered nervous system. If it wasn't for Samantha and the dream of Olympic gold, Anne would have lay down and died, shriveled up, turned to dust to be carried away by the western wind. It was this dream that made it possible to get up, get back on the horse, so to speak, and keep moving forward. It was this dream that kept her whole world in place, the focus of her life. With this dream, Anne could do anything, like dust off her resume, call some old contacts, and land a great-paying job at the region's biggest television station. It was this dream that made it possible for her to get up five days a week and make the drive into the city, spend the droning hours producing some of the biggest news stories of the day, and then make the long, traffic-snarled drive back to her refuge which was this farm.

Anne sat in the rising sunshine and watched her daughter on top of the horse slowly walking around the arena.

"Okay, Sam," she said into the microphone, "That will do for this session." Sam looked up at her mother and without smiling turned the horse toward the arena gate. Anne took off her headset and walked over to open the gate. Sam came up and took out her earpiece and handed it and the receiver to her waiting mother. The ritual had been practiced countless times over the last six months. Sam walked her horse through the gate and toward the nearest barn where her groom was waiting to take the horse in.

As Sam dismounted, her mother was standing nearby. "Okay, sweetie, you did well, but you have to learn to keep the horse engaged. If you let him think he can do whatever he wants, then you will be fighting him forever. You have to be the leader. You have to force him to do what you ask."

Sam looked at the ground and in a weak voice replied, "Okay, I know, I know." Anne was frustrated by her daughter's lack of enthusiasm but decided not to press it now.

"So go get your breakfast then we can start your second hour," Anne was trying to sound sweet, it came across as condescending. "I have to go to the station for a couple of hours today so Sally will be taking over from here. Make sure you follow her instruction; you need to learn engagement."

Sam's spirits lifted slightly. She looked up at her mother and said, "I thought you were training me all day."

"I was planning on it," said Anne, "but there is this thing that came up and I told Matthew I would come in and help him put it together. Is that going to be okay?"

Sam smiled slightly, "Sure, Mom, I'll be okay." She ran off toward the house and her waiting morning meal. Anne watched her go, then turned to the groom.

"Get Belmont ready to go. Sally will be here in about 15 minutes.

You know she runs on time so don't make her wait."

Anne turned away and walked up to the house to get what she needed for her drive in to the station. As she moved toward the house, a slight wind pushed through the tall trees encircling the farm and gently rustled the leaves. Anne looked up at the velvet sky—light blue and very clear. She loved this time of day.

When Anne finally made it to the television station, things were as normal. The creative guys were holed up in the conference room going over mock-ups of some new kid's show they were producing. The sales cubicles were buzzing with phone chat. The 25 televisions hanging on almost any available surface were showing the current programming run, and the tech geeks, interns, and engineers were milling around unpurposefully. Anne wondered why they were the ones that always seemed at ease in this frantic atmosphere. The tech people were the ones who had the time to chat at the coffee bar, the time to give a courteous hello, the ones who didn't look like they were on fire every time you saw them.

"I guess things must be running smoothly," Anne thought to herself as she watched Bob Stiller, the head engineer dressed in Levi's with suspenders, slowly walking up the hall toward the engineering complex.

Anne threw her things into her office and headed directly across the hall into the station manager's office. His name was Matthew Clark. He had been running things at this show for over 15 years and had a knack for keeping a large market share with great local programming mixed in with the necessary network feeds. Matthew was sitting behind his modest desk munching a doughnut and going through the weekly Arbitrons. He looked up and smiled when Anne walked into the room.

"Have a seat," he said. "Thanks for coming in on your day off. I really think you will be perfect for this crazy thing going on out in Nevada."

"Nevada?" the word surprised Anne. Without taking time to think about it, she protested, "You know I don't work the remotes."

"Oh, calm down," said Matthew. He knew Anne well and had the patience and the skill to let her rant before bringing her back from the edge.

"This is something I want to see," he said. "This one is a real tearjerker. A heart-string puller." Anne sat down and remained silent. Matthew was a talker and she knew better than to interrupt.

"Listen," he continued, "I have a problem. You know Jason Strom, right? Well he was working this thing for me when his car was hit from behind by one of those produce trucks. You know the ones? Big-ass flatbed plowed right into his Camry. Bam!" Matthew liked sound effects to punctuate his stories.

"Is he alright?" Anne asked.

"Well, he will be, but right now he is laid up out at Mercy with a broken pelvis. Poor bastard. He was going to be married next week and honeymoon down in Cabo. Now he will be lucky to be up and at it by next month."

"Oh, no," Anne's disposition sunk as the trauma of her own loss rushed into her memory.

"I know," said Matthew, sensing her sinking feelings. "He'll be alright, he will. But what I really want to do is get you involved in his project," Matthew said trying to change the subject. "You see, there is this ranch out in Nevada . . ."

"A ranch?" Anne repeated suspiciously.

"Yeah, a ranch …in Nevada," Matthew said. "There is this ranch in Nevada that sits next to BLM land, you know, the Bureau of Land Management. The folks up there are kinda peculiar I'm told. Jason was on his way up there when he got…" Matthew paused not wanting to bring Anne down again.

" …When he was in that accident."

"Why was Jason going to Nevada? Isn't that a bit far out of your local area? And what does the BLM have to do with anything?" Anne didn't like the sound of this.

"Jason was headed up to the ranch to do a story on a few angles. First, the ranch sits next to BLM land. Apparently there are a couple hundred wild horses that run up there…"

Anne cut him off. "Just stop! Are you talking about a roundup story? Right? Are you kidding me?" Anne was exasperated. "I am not going to do a damn roundup story. First of all, every one of those cowboys out there are all a bunch of numbnut hicks who know nothing about real riding. Second, I am not going to drive out to the middle of nowhere to watch a bunch of good-for-nothing mustangs get penned up and tortured. Third…"

"Now hold on a second," Matthew raised his arms to deflect the tirade. "Hold on. This is NOT a roundup story," Matthew was lying, but he needed a minute to spin his sales pitch. "Look, this is a complex, multi-layered piece. There are nuances here that not just anybody can pick out. There are some strange stories coming out from that region that can't be explained. There is some real news up there. A strong story, really."

Anne settled back in her chair. She had stated her boundaries and now could listen to the details. Although she would never drive out to a BLM mustang roundup, she was curious as to what the bigger picture might be.

"Okay, go on," she conceded.

"Okay," Matthew was glad she was listening. "There is a ranch out there in Nevada, next to BLM land. The ranch happens to be a horse rescue operation. You know, an animal rescue place where they take in unwanted and abused animals. This one specializes in horses. Apparently it is one of the larger places of its kind. Well-funded with donations from all over the country."

"What's the name of the place?" Anne asked.

"It's called the Angel Ridge Rescue Ranch," Matthew said plainly. "They have been there for years and they bring in millions of dollars every year."

"Yeah, typical." Anne said sourly. "People will spend more money on a dying animal than their own dying family sometimes. So anyway, what's the story, why the BLM?"

"Umm," Matthew hesitated, "okay, it IS a roundup story."

"Oh crap!" Anne gasped. "Come on, Matthew. Don't do this with me."

Matthew wasn't at all apologetic. "It's a roundup story with a great twist. See, the wild herd used to run far from where they are now, way out past Tonopah. But recently the entire herd has moved up to the Angel Ridge Mountains, still on the BLM land, but much closer to civilization. Anyway, you probably know the BLM guys are mandated to clean up the range and get rid of most of the wild horse herds out there in Nevada."

"I really don't follow it, Matthew," said Anne.

Matthew didn't let that slow him down. "Well, now that the herd has moved up to Angel Ridge, the ranch is getting involved in messing up the BLM's work. What would you expect from a bunch of animal crazies? There's a huge fight going on between the ranch and the BLM. Some say it has come to blows, but I don't have any evidence of that. Anyway, last week when the BLM took their operations out to Angel Ridge, the damned people at the ranch apparently ran the herd onto their private land and stopped the BLM from getting to them."

Anne perked up. "Really? Yeah, I could see why that might cause a bit of friction with the BLM."

"Well, more than that. After the BLM folks went home, the ranch let the herd back out onto public lands. Their ranch is plenty big, but not enough to graze 200 wild horses."

"So what's the big deal?" Anne asked.

"The big deal is that the Angel Ridge range land is owned by a certain Nevada senator who controls the pocket strings of the BLM."

"Senator Ruud?" Anne guessed.

"Yes, Senator Ruud. He has a grazing operation out there that runs about 1,000 head of top breed Angus cattle. Of course the wild horses run havoc over the place and they compete with the cows for rangeland and water resource. Ruud wants the horses gone—yesterday—but the Angel Ridge Rescue folks keep fowling up the plan. So it's come to kind of a showdown between the two groups."

"Hmm," Anne was thinking about the story. "Well, I can see why you would want to go after that story; corrupt public official using government resources to protect his private interests from wild mustangs." She shook her head, "Yes it has all the makings of a great big story."

"There's more," said Matthew, with an unreadable look in his eye.

Anne wrinkled her brow, "What?"

"There is this guy, this cowboy. He works at the ranch and he has some kind of special horse power."

"Horse power?" Anne echoed.

"Well, I don't know what you call it. I don't know the first thing about horses. But I've been told about this guy at the ranch who can …well, he can talk to horses."

"Oh, you mean a horse whisperer?" Anne said.

"Yeah, maybe. But I think even more."

"What's more than a horse whisperer" Anne asked. "I mean," she paused, "how do you know all this?"

"From my sister Rosie; she's worked up at the ranch for years. She runs the place with her husband, Joe."

"Oh, now I get it," Anne's light went on. "You need this story to come out to help your sister keep the place from being overrun by Ruud and his group."

"Well, I do have a slight personal interest in this one, yes. That's why I need you! I need someone who can take this story on and really make it big, make it sing. With Jason out of the picture, you are all I have; I need you. You know all about horses and can really tell a heart-wrenching story about how Ruud and the BLM are not playing nice with the poor wild horses. You can get this thing off the ground. All Rosie needs is a little public support and she thinks Ruud will back off."

"Why not just allow the horses to be rounded up? Problem solved."

"I need you to find that out. Rosie says the horses will be sent to holding pens somewhere in Utah, then it's off to slaughter. They try to adopt them out, but who the hell wants to adopt a wild horse? Rosie won't hear of it."

"Oh, they don't slaughter horses anymore. We all know that," Anne said bullheadedly.

"Well …again," cajoled Matthew, "I need you to find out all those details and make a story, a big story."

"Okay," said Anne with more interest, "so who's the magic cow-boy?"

"I don't know. Rosie tells me he's real special. Showed up one day and wanted to join the crew at the ranch. She calls him a horse angel, whatever that is."

"Horse angel? A cowboy?" Anne laughed. "Does he have wings?"

"Rosie tells me there is something extra special about this guy. I want you to go up there and put the pieces together. Really, I actually need you to go up there. I have promised Rosie I would help in any way I can. Please tell me you will do it. You need some time away any-way. How long has it been since you've been out of town?"

"I live in the country, Matthew. I leave town every day. Trust me, I don't need to get out of town."

"Well, whatever. How soon can you get your butt up there to see what's going on?"

Anne sat still with the thoughts of this puzzle buzzing around in her mind. "A horse angel, huh? Yeah, I can go. I want to see what a horse angel looks like." She was smirking.

On the drive home, Anne was thinking about Samantha. Anne's daughter had been working very hard on her riding lessons but she seemed to be less and less willing as the months drew on. Samantha was starting to withdraw; she almost seemed hollow, sometimes with nothing to say. The thought crossed Anne's mind that maybe she was pushing too hard. Of course, Sam was moving into her teenage years. Anne was told by many acquaintances to expect trouble, especially with girls this age. It wasn't uncommon for tensions to rise between mother and daughter. Teenage girls were notorious for becoming little screaming bitches at the drop of a hat, especially toward their mothers. Anne's heart sank. Sam used to be such a caring little girl, always quick with a smile and a hug. She was playful and generous, at least up until recently. Maybe she needed a break; maybe Anne was driving her too hard in the quest to get to the junior Olympic team. But Sam had seemed excited about the plan; she had almost begged her mother to put her into training. They talked about it in excited tones, dreamed about the places they would go—Brazil, Germany, Spain, and, of course, all over the U.S. Sam had really been all in, a willing participant. But now Anne could feel Sam slipping away, retreating into her own self, and sharing nothing about her feelings. Anne wondered if Sally knew anything about this recent change in Samantha. She tried to put it out of her mind.

Anne pushed the small button on her cellular wireless headset. After hearing the beep, she voice-dialed the number Matthew gave her to get in touch with his sister, Rosie, the general manager of Angel Ridge Rescue Ranch. After a pause, Anne heard a busy signal. "Busy signal?" Anne thought. "Don't these people have call waiting? Or voice mail?" She ended the call with the touch of a button and wondered what kind of operation wouldn't have the simplest of technology.

The heavy traffic on Interstate 80 was beginning to thin as she moved farther away from the city. Now only the long-haul trucks, RVs, and cross-country tourists headed for Nevada remained on the east-bound lanes, as well as a few local farmers and the truckloads of migrant farm workers who seemed to be everywhere. Anne turned off the interstate onto the highway heading south leading to her farm.

Maybe Samantha was missing her father, Anne thought. Maybe this was the time of life where girls really need their dads. Anne thought back to her own father and her budding teenage years spent in the foothills of the Sierra Nevadas up in Grass Valley. She remembered the long afternoons when she and her dad would take a couple of the horses and ride for hours up into the mountain trails, where the solitude of the pine forests surrounded grassy meadows, where the wildflowers blazed their dazzling hues across the verdant background pallet. She could still remember the smell of mountain air mixed with the pungent tones of the rotting forest floor. She could almost see her father riding along at her side talking away, glibly telling stories of his youth, his family, his work. Her father loved to talk and Anne loved to listen. His gentle voice made her feel safe. She felt loved, and like she belonged. Maybe this was what Samantha was missing. Maybe she needed a father figure in her life. Anne had not dated anybody since Simon had died. Sure, there'd been several men vying for her attention, but her heart wouldn't let her love for Simon go. She wasn't available for romance. Period. As a consequence she buried herself in her work and in her dreams for Samantha. These thoughts lingered in Anne's mind, stirring up a poignant nostalgia for her long-gone youth.

She pushed the button on her headset and again voice-dialed the number to the Angel Ridge Rescue Ranch. This time the phone was ringing.

"Hello? This is Angel Ridge, can I help you?" It was a man's voice. By the staccato cadence and flat accent, Anne could discern he was probably Native American.

"Hello!" she responded in her professional work voice. "This is Anne Harper from KTVX in Sacramento. How are you?"

The voice on the other end sounded pensive and questioning.

"Well, I am doing well. What can I do for you, Ms. Harper?"

"I am trying to reach Rosie Whitehorse. Her brother Matthew Clark asked me to call. Is she available?"

"Well, no, she is out right now. There are some new horses coming in today and she is probably out at the corral. Can I give her a message?"

Anne didn't want to play phone tag all day. "Um, does she have a cell number I can reach her at? I really would rather speak to her as soon as I can."

"A cell number?" the voice sounded amused. "No, she doesn't have a cell number. I can take a message if you like."

Anne was perplexed. No voice mail, no cell phones. How could a business operate like that?

"Okay, I guess that's okay. Have her call me at 817-399-2938. If you don't mind, please tell her it's urgent. Matthew wanted me to talk to her as soon as I could."

"Okay, you probably will talk to her as soon as you can," the man said.

"Um," Anne didn't know how to respond to his comment. "Okay, again, my name is Anne Harper, and did you get my number?"

"Got it." Silence.

"Well, thank you. Do you know when I can expect her call?"

"Probably as soon as she gets back."

Anne felt this man was playing a game. She decided not to push it. In her current dark mood she could definitely go bitch on the guy and scold him for his unprofessional tone, but for Matthew's sake she held her tongue.

"Thank you for your help." She said with a shrug.

"No problem, I will give Rosie your message."

Anne poked the "end call" button. A feeling of wonder unexpectedly came over her all in a rush. "What was that?" she said aloud. She had a feeling that Matthew hadn't told her all the details of what kind of mess he was sending her into.

The highway forked and she took the small right turn. Across the land were rolling hills of green fields. It wouldn't be long until summer came and the fields would dry up into the wheat-brown tones so common in Central California. A few miles down, she again turned right and entered her farm. She was still thinking about Samantha when she pulled up in front of her house. Right away she could tell something was not right.

Anne looked through the line of Goldenrain trees that surrounded the main training arena. Through the afternoon shade she could see no movement. She looked at her watch: 5:45 p.m. A flare of anger swelled in her chest.

"Where's Samantha?" she thought to herself. "Why is she not training?" Anne quickly got out of the car and headed straight for the barn. This was not acceptable. There was a schedule to keep. The farm was strangely quiet as she walked through the double doors into the cool barn. No one.

"Hello?" Anne called into the distance. One of the horses poked his head out from his stall, looked at Anne and snorted. Anne frowned, then turned and headed for the house. Opening the front door, Anne stepped into the foyer and heard some noises coming from the main living room. She entered the main room and the sight made her roll her eyes in disgust. Samantha was collapsed on the floor, sobbing with her head in her arms. Sally was kneeling beside with her hand on the girl's back in an apparent attempt of comfort. Anne was exasperated. She let out a deep sigh, and pursed her lips. Sally looked up with an expression of helplessness.

"What's going on?" Anne demanded. "Samantha! Are you all right? What happened?" Anne had little sympathy for drama and even less for losers.

"She's okay," said Sally. "She is just having a little meltdown. I guess I was pushing her too hard in the arena."

"What?" Anne snapped back. "That's your job …that's HER job. Samantha! Get up right now." Anne's blood pressure was rising. She was used to giving orders and even more used to people following them.

Samantha laid there, her shoulders rhythmically bouncing to her sobbing cries.

"It's okay, sweetie," Sally cooed. "Come on, get up and tell us what's going on."

Samantha was insolent. "Leave me alone!" she shouted. She sniffed hard and the gurgling noise made Anne shudder.

"Come on," said Sally in a gentle mother's voice. "Let's talk about it. We can talk about it, okay?"

Anne looked at Sally. "What happened?" Sally had a confused look on her face. "Well, we were going through the warmup on Bally-hoo," Sally explained, "and Sam burst out into tears, jumped off the horse and ran into the house. I really don't know what happened."

In a tone of resignation, she said, "Give us a minute, Sally. Let me talk to her alone." Sally got up from the sobbing girl and after shooting Anne a puzzled look, left the room and returned to the barn.

Anne sat down on a large red leather chair and looked down at her girl. She had never seen her like this. Sam had always been very eager to talk, to take direction, to be a good kid. This was new and Anne didn't quite know what to do. She was pretty sure yelling wasn't the right tactic at this point. She tried to calm herself; she tried to relax.

"Okay. Samantha …are you okay?" Anne's voice was plainly different and actually sounded like she was concerned. Samantha just lay there with her head buried in the carpet. "What's the matter, honey? I hate to see you like this. Please tell me what's going on."

Anne really had no idea what was happening in her daughter's mind. "Is it Sally? You don't like her? Tell me. I don't know what to do if you don't tell me." Anne was reaching. Samantha was silent. "Come on, come here, and let me give you a hug."

"Leave me alone!" Sam bawled. "Just leave me alone!"

"Oh, for heaven's sake," said Anne, as she knelt down next to her daughter and gently rubbed her shoulders.

"I don't want to do it anymore!" sputtered Sam.

Anne was surprised. "Do what?"

"Training, dressage training, I don't like it!"

Now Anne was really shocked. She had always assumed that Sam had really liked the life she had. She obviously really loved her horse. She was a natural, graceful rider. This news came as a cold splash of water to the face.

"You don't like training?" Anne asked slowly. "Or you don't like Sally?"

"It's not Sally," said Sam, speaking to the floor. "It's not Sally; It's YOU!"

"Oh, God," Anne said out loud. "What did I do?" Her defenses were rising, even though she was talking with a twelve-year-old. "What did I do? I am the one who's giving all of this to you."

"Well, stop it!" Sam said. "I don't like it."

Anne paused. "I don't understand. I wasn't even out there today. You were with Sally. You have to help me understand."

"All you do is make me kick the horse. Sally too. You both make me hurt them and they don't like it." Sam was letting it all out now. Between sobs she continued, "All you want is for me to win; you don't even care about the horses. You just want me to hurt them." She trailed off into a new round of sobbing.

Anne knelt there by the girl with no clue as to what she was saying. "I don't want you to hurt the horses. Where did you get that idea? You know I love those horses. You know that."

"Then why do you always make me hurt them; every time?"

"Horses are animals, honey. This is the way I trained. I don't hurt horses. They just need a little extra to learn. That is not hurting them. I am teaching you how to be the best rider you can be. Once you get to understand it, then you don't have to be so rough. Really, you are not hurting the horses."

"It hurts them, I know it." Sam snapped back. "Don't tell me it doesn't, I can tell!"

Anne let out a sigh. She wasn't getting anywhere with this line of reasoning. She got up and sat back in the chair. Looking down at her daughter distressed on the floor made Anne think back to her own childhood. Her father was the one who would always come to her rescue when she was down. Her father was always there to say the right thing, to lift her spirits, to make it all better. Anne didn't know what to do. She couldn't be the father and the mother to Sam. She was doing the only thing she knew how to do.

Suddenly without thinking, she said, "Hey, do you want to go see a horse angel?"

Sam stopped sobbing. Anne had her attention.

"What?" Sam asked

"A horse angel. I have to go see a horse angel for my job. You should come with me."

"What's a horse angel?" Sam was captivated.

"He's a man …who helps horses. They call him a horse angel."

Sam turned over and looked at her mom. Her face was puffy and red and her nose and mouth were dripping with gooey tears. "What does he do?"

"Well, that is what I get to go find out." Anne was stuck now, no way to back out. She would rather go up to the Rescue Ranch by herself. Sam would be a major inconvenience, but she was stuck. "You can come with me," she said to Sam. "Just me and you. It will be fun and we can see what a horse angel really is. You obviously need a break."

Sam thought for a second. "Where? Where are we going?"

Just then Anne's phone rang. She picked it up and looked at the number. "Oh, this is them calling right now," she said to Sam. "Let me talk to them and I'll tell you all about it. Why don't you go and get yourself cleaned up, and then we can talk." The phone continued to ring. Sam slowly got up, but didn't leave. Anne pushed the call button.

"Hello? Anne Harper speaking."

"Hello, Anne? This is Rosie Whitehorse calling from Angel Ridge. I understand you want to come and see me."

CHAPTER THREE

I t was about a five-hour drive out to the Angel Ridge Rescue Ranch. The route took Anne and Samantha up and over the Sierra Nevadas into Reno and then due south for 150 miles. They started out early morning and watched the sun rise into their eastbound faces. The mountains were glorious as usual; the day cloudless, clear, and bright. Traffic was moving in its typical fashion along I-80 as the vehicles trudged up the steep slopes to Donner Pass.

Anne was driving her own car; Samantha was in the passenger seat. On any other assignment, Anne would have been in a news team van accompanied by a cameraman, reporter, and maybe one assistant. But Matthew insisted that she go alone on the first round and just gather information, put the pieces together. Because of his personal interest in the story, Matthew was willing to spend the extra money to cover this unusual protocol. Once Anne had the basics, Matthew would send up a crew to formalize the interviews, get some B-roll, and put the piece together.

Anne had some idea of what she would do upon arrival. She wanted to interview Rosie, of course, and talk to some of the others who helped on the ranch. She had a short conversation with Rosie the day before when they finally connected on the phone. Rosie didn't tell her much, just that she had a place for Anne and Sam to stay, that she was looking forward to meeting them, that Matthew talked very favorably about Anne, and that she was anxious to get the story out about what was happening to the wild horses that surrounded her property.

Anne also wanted to talk to the cowboy, this horse angel, and see how she might work him into the story. Anne asked Rosie about the man and Rosie told her his name was Nolan Powell and assured Anne that she would be able to meet him and ask him all the questions her heart desired. Anne knew she would have to befriend this guy, get him to open up. It would be a challenge for her because the truth was she hated cowboys. To her, guys who rode western style were a bunch of hayseeds, hicks, and rednecks. Their big saddles, with the horns used for roping, were an eyesore. The horses they chose were nothing more than ponies, puny quarter horses that stood no more than 14 hands. Put a 220-pound cowboy on one of those small horses and the picture was that of a big-hatted, asymmetrical, clown parade. That is how she saw it anyway. And there was nothing more amusing than seeing a cowboy trying to ride dressage, with their stupid boots and western-cut shirts. Anne went to one clinic where a dressage master was trying to teach Reiners how to ride in the style of dressage. Reining was a proud tradition of the western rider based on the work of moving and managing cattle herds. To see them trying to ride dressage was pathetic to her, not worth the time or trouble. The joke in the dressage community was, "Real men don't have room for a saddle horn." It always made Anne laugh, that stupid joke. Of course, many male dressage riders were gay, so the cowboys laughed about that as well; a sport for pussies they called it. She felt some trepidation in having to go to these people and take them seriously. She would have to keep her feelings to herself, something that always came hard for her.

The easy part of the job was to embrace the rescue part of the story. Anne loved horses and she always thought the people who spent their time and money rescuing abandoned and neglected horses were a noble lot. She understood the need for rescue farms; there were so many horses that needed help. Some people just ran out of money and couldn't afford to care for their animals. Some horses came off the racetrack, careers finished, with no more economic value to their owners. Some horses were just plain neglected, left in the field with no proper shelter, vet care, or food. There were literally thousands of operations across the country that specialized in caring for these unwanted horses. They would take them in, vet them, give them training, feed them, and if possible, adopt these unwanted horses out to caring families that could both afford and love them. Anne knew this part of the story would very much appeal to the general public.

Then there was the story of the wild horses, the feral descendants of domesticated animals either escaping from or being intentionally released by the early European explorers and later settlers of the area. The origin of many of the earliest explorers was Spanish, generally resulting in a strong Iberian influence remaining in some of the wild horse populations. These Spanish breeds were sometimes mixed with other escaped or released horses from the military and early frontiersmen who favored Thoroughbred, Morgan, and Quarter Horse breeds. These wild-horse populations of mixed ancestry increased over the years to inhabit large areas of U.S. western rangelands mostly owned by the U.S. federal government and managed by the Bureau of Land Management, the BLM. Anne knew less about this part of the story. Most of what she knew came from the seasonal news stories about the BLM roundups. The management of the herds became a daunting task as their numbers continued to swell. It was compounded by the outright ban on the slaughter of horses for disposal. The slaughter was used to regulate the number of unwanted horses, but since the ban, the numbers have swelled. So about every three years the BLM was sent out to "gather" the herds and cull the younger ones out to be shipped off to the BLM holding pens to wait for adoption. Most of the horses ended up spending the rest of their lives in the pens—a grim existence. Each roundup was a clash between the BLM trying to carry out its federal mandate, and the animal rights people trying to protect the wild horse herds. In the age of instant information, it was very easy for wild-horse advocacy groups like Respect4horses to gather and disseminate heart-wrenching video footage showing government helicopters chasing majestic herds of wild horses across the western rangeland, eventually to capture them in chaotic holding pens where the babies would be pulled out, loaded on a truck, and shipped off, never to be seen again. This was the extent of Anne's knowledge about the BLM versus the Wild Horse story. She was hoping to get a more intimate look at what was really going on.

Anne was also thinking about Samantha. The girl had been unusually quiet during the first few hours in the car. Anne hoped this break would be a good bonding time for both of them, but Samantha remained obstinate. Anne tried talking with her—girl talk really—and

Sam was just distant. Anne was a bit worried by this new display of behavior.

The hours drew on and the scenery changed from mountain stream, forest, and meadow to the high desert of Nevada. Along the eastern side of the Sierra Nevadas, the forests spilled down from the mountainside onto the dry foothills that rose up from the most western reaches of the great deserts of Nevada. The road took a southeasterly direction and soon the forests were left behind and the land fanned out into a grey and brown color palette, flat with low shrubs and stunted trees. This was the Nevada rangeland, all but completely owned by the federal government. For years this land was the source of many feuds and political battles ever since the early settlers came to graze their cattle, mine the hills, and draw water from the scarce supplies flowing in the small number of rivers.

Over the past 50 years, the area saw a growing disconnect between the ranchers who actually lived and worked in the area and the bureaucrats in Washington, D.C. charged, by mandate, to manage the land and resources. The government was ostensibly trying to placate environmental activists, wild-horse protectors, and recreational enthusiasts wanting more and more access to wide-open spaces. The local cattle ranchers gained some ground in the '60s and '70s with what became known as the Sagebrush Rebellion. The rebellion came about when ranchers, farmers, and mining companies joined together politically and demanded the federal government relinquish control of local resources. This gave more power to the local interests but it had to be pried from the hands of the faceless federal government. It also caused a lingering resentment among those whose interests fell on the federal government side.

The interests of the federal government were now being shouldered by a new growing cadre of environmental lawyers. They filed lawsuit after lawsuit in a sort of federal government proxy trying to lock up the resources of large tracts of land. Using wilderness arguments and threats of endangered species, their goal was always the same—to run the cattle business off federal lands and to put the control of the land and resources back into federal hands. They claimed that cows harmed the sensitive balance of nature, promoted non-native plant species, endangered wild animals such as sage grouse, and disturbed the soils causing runoff destruction. There grew a vicious political fight between the environmentalists, who used state and federal law along with regulations, and the men and women who for generations had lived on the land, raised cattle, and built economic empires in an area of the country that few people would find even semi-livable. These two interests were battling it out in court, on the ground, and most importantly in the press.

Ironically, the wild horse herds found themselves in the middle of these two battling factions, the environmentalists on one side and the cattle ranchers on the other. In these modern times the horses were all but native to the land. Having lived and thrived for hundreds of years, the herds were a fixture in these parts. A heritage. A national treasure. Groups of well-meaning people formed into associations dedicated to the preservation of the wild horse. These groups were sandwiched between the federal government proxy lawyers and the old-family cattle ranchers. The modern politics created by the mere presence of the wild horses created strange alliances among all of the parties. The BLM was mandated to manage the herds, which was in the best interest of the cattle ranchers who worked with the feds to protect their grazing rights. The environmentalists, who wanted the cattle gone, also wanted the wild horses gone in an effort to return the land to the native species of plants and animals. The wild horse community stood against both rancher and environmentalist in protest of the BLM and the actions taken against the wild horse herds in concert with federal law.

Both the environmental lawyers and the ranchers pointed to the wild horses and their over-population, which leads to starvation and suffering, as a reason for the BLM to continue to step up management tactics such as the roundup. Of course the wild horse community was dead against any roundup measures and would protest any BLM action. The horses themselves became the pawns in the decades-long struggle between the ranchers, the environmental groups, the BLM and the wild horse community, with the rangeland setting the stage.

Anne pulled her car onto the long dirt road that led into the Angel Ridge Rescue Ranch. Angel Ridge was a high outcrop of land that jutted up from the basin floor. The ranch enveloped the entire ridge and stretched out to the east some two miles. Sprawled across 2,500 acres, it was a large operation that was owned by the same family for four generations. The dirt road wound around the northern edge of the ridge and came to a series of barns, outbuildings, and a modest-sized house that served as the main lodge. Away in the distance Anne could see several pastures and a long, high fence that seemed to encircle the entire property. She pulled up in front of the house and parked her car. Several dogs were scampering about barking, alerting the ranch to the strangers' arrival—not threatening in any way—just doing their job.

Anne and Samantha stepped out of the car into mid-afternoon sun. The air was still and warm. The front door of the house swung open and a robust middle-age woman stepped out onto the covered porch. She had thick auburn hair pulled back into a flowing pony tail. Her face was friendly and showed evidence of years in the sun.

"Howdy!" she called out to her new guests. "You must be Anne."

Anne was walking up to the porch. "Hello. Yes, I'm Anne and this is my daughter, Samantha," she said, extending her hand toward the woman.

"Hi, Anne, I'm Rosie Whitehorse, Matthew's sister. It's mighty good to meet ya." Anne and Rosie shook hands and Rosie turned to Samantha. "Hello, young lady. My, you are a beauty. I love your hair."

Samantha smiled and shook Rosie's hand, not saying anything.

"Well, come on in. You probably both need to freshen up a bit. You drove in from Sacramento, right? Well, come on in and get settled. We can talk after I get back. I need to run down to the barn and check on one of the ponies. Won't take but a few minutes."

Rosie showed the two into the house, pointed out the facilities, and promptly left them alone, promising to return shortly.

The house was quiet, with the smell of fresh baked bread wafting through the air. Somewhere a clock ticked out the seconds with a pulsating rhythm that seemed to amplify the quietness. The main room featured two large leather couches facing a giant coffee table that held stacks of books, papers, and magazines. A large Persian carpet covered the timeworn, heart-pine floor and was nearly invisible underneath the assorted side tables, lamps, statuary, and other furniture. The walls were lined with shelves and stuffed with books and magazines. Each shelf also had assorted knick-knacks randomly placed along any surface that was available. The room seemed full—over-full—with years of cumulative possessions, useful and not useful, lying where they had first been placed upon being brought into the house.

"Cluttered but clean," thought Anne as she moved past the couches, through the main room into the kitchen and dining area. Here she found the house in similar condition—a large, cluttered, well-lit modern kitchen with every surface covered by some gadget, cookbook, knick-knack, or stack of dishes. There was a sturdy dining table with a bowl of oranges in the center, surrounded haphazardly with piles of magazines, important-looking papers, and an old electronic calculator. The house was inviting, and Anne felt instantly welcome. She resisted her urge to straighten up the books on the table.

"Look, Mom. Cute!" said Samantha, picking up a small stuffed horse from one of the side chairs. "I like this house."

"Me too," said Anne. "Very homey."

The two were sitting at the dining table when Rosie came bursting through the back door leading off the kitchen. She came over and sat down.

"So? Where do you want to start?" she asked with enthusiasm. "I've got as much time as you need, and with the story we've got to tell, it may take some!"

Anne kicked into professional mode. "Well, first I would like to tour the ranch and see what you are doing out here. Then I would like to interview you and your husband. Joe, is it? Yes, and I very much want to talk to Nolan Powell, the…" she trailed off. "What is he exactly?"

Rosie smiled, "He is one of our trainers."

"Okay," continued Anne. "I want to meet him and then maybe some of the other people you think may have something to contribute to the story. As soon as we get the facts together, Matthew will send up a camera crew and we will get the footage we need."

Rosie looked at Samantha, "And you, young lady, what part are you playing in this?"

Samantha liked Rosie right off. "I am going to be my mother's assistant and help with the interviews," Sam said, trying to pull off her grown-up act.

Rosie smiled again and said, "Well, Anne, you are lucky to have a daughter who takes on responsibility so easily. Okay, we'll start with the tour. Let me warn you, some of these horses have been beat up pretty bad. It's not a pretty sight, some of them. People can be so cruel. I have never understood it. Anyway, we can start down at the main barn and go from there."

Anne agreed, and the three rose from the table and left the house through the back door. There was a small landing alongside the road that led down the hill to a large wooden structure that served as the main barn. As they walked, Rosie continued to talk.

"This place was originally settled by my great-great grandfather. It used to be a working cattle operation. I have been here now for 30 years. After my dad retired, I was the only one left that wanted anything to do with it. All my brothers are city folk now. Sometimes they come out and visit, but mostly I don't see much of 'em."

"Did your family grow up here?" asked Anne.

"No, we all grew up in Reno. My dad was in politics and when he inherited this ranch it was just a weed patch—leased land, cattle, sheep …that kind of thing. After college I used to come out here to get away and grew to love it. When Joe and I decided to marry, we thought it would be a good place to live, work and raise the kids. They're all gone now, growed up and moved away."

"How many kids do you have?"

"Oh, Joe and I had five altogether, three boys and two girls. They come and visit pretty regularly. Most of 'em live up in Reno."

They came up to the main barn. It was obviously old but well maintained. Constructed from wood, the old building stood two stories tall and 60 feet wide. The great double sliding doors were spread apart revealing a row of horse stalls down either side with a wide path in the middle. Two grooms, dressed in black pants and red shirts, were at the far end sweeping up some stall bedding into a wheelbarrow.

"This is our main barn," Rosie said, as she led the two inside. "These are the horses we have groomed for adoption. They're the lucky ones."

Samantha ran up to the first stall. A grey thoroughbred stuck her head through the gate expecting some kind of treat. Sam stroked the muzzle of the mare.

"It looks like you aren't afraid of horses," Rosie remarked.

"Oh, not me. I've been riding since I was six," said Sam.

"Oh!" Rosie arched her eyebrows in approval. "Really? What kind of horses do you ride?"

"Well, we have some Hanoverians, some Morgans, and a couple Andalusians," said Sam casually. Rosie turned to Anne.

"Matthew didn't tell me he was sending an equestrian up to talk to me."

Anne smiled, "Yes, we are both riders. Sam just started her dressage training. I am retired from it, help in training mostly."

"Dressage …I love dressage," said Rosie to Sam. "It is so precise and so beautiful to watch. Do you have a favorite horse?"

"I really like a horse named Spirit. He's old, but I think he's my favorite."

"Well, anytime you want to ride here you let me know and I'll put you in the saddle."

"That would be fun," Sam said with a smile.

"I don't think there will be time for that," said Anne, trying to head off any false expectations Sam may be developing.

"Oh, sure, you got plenty of time," said Rosie, not taking the hint.

The three spent what remained of the afternoon touring the entire rescue operation. Anne was making mental notes about shot angles, content, and light. The main barn, which stood between the house and the rest of the ranch, held the horses that had been fully rehabilitated and were ready for adoption. It was adjacent to five large paddocks where the horses went for their daily turnout. Rosie had many contacts though the horse community near and far and was semi-successful in getting the horses adopted out. Anne learned that over 50 horses a year came and went through the process. At any one time the ranch supported over 150 head of unwanted animals. The costs were staggering.

Farther down the hill was the training center, which was a set of two barns and four large arenas, eight paddocks, and a turnout pasture. This complex held the horses that were recovering from abuse and abandonment or starvation, or coming from auctions that were stalked by the kill-buyers. Kill-buyers were those people who purchased unwanted horses and then resold them to rendering plants where the horses were slaughtered and processed into a variety of products. The horses at the rehab center were being trained to be around humans again and learning to trust. They also were being worked daily in the arenas to build their atrophied muscles and their equally atrophied spirits. Rosie had a staff of five that worked the rehab section.

Farther away, standing alone out on the flats, was the quarantine barn. Here they brought the new horses, the damaged and broken animals that were sloughed off by the world. Here the heartache was truly evident, as this barn was filled with horses that had lost their trust, their spirit, and their health. A full-time vet, along with three trainers and five grooms, worked this herd with loving care. The quarantine was necessary to protect the entire operation from unknown disease that may be carried in with the new arrivals. There were no paddocks or arenas here; just 30 large stalls with plenty of bedding, light, warmth, and love. Anne and Samantha had never seen anything like this before, even in all their years around horses. The cruelty was plain to see in both body and spirit of these once-regal animals reduced to skin and bones. The fear emanating from the horses was palpable as was their misery. Most of the horses here would be cared for in a way they'd never experienced. But the transition from literally horse hell to the world of life wasn't an easy one. This is where the heart of the ranch was, where the healing began. To think that people could be so cruel was beyond the scope of a twelve-year-old girl. Sam didn't understand; Anne was appalled. Both of them developed a deeper respect and admiration for Rosie who spent her resources, time and money doing what she could for these poor animals. They left the quarantine in a somber mood.

Past the quarantine, out to the edge of the property, was open rangeland. This part of the ranch was fenced off and rarely used. It bordered the vast open spaces of BLM land that stretched to the horizon; the land where Senator Ruud ran his cattle.

Other areas of the rescue ranch contained a dozen houses scattered here and there that were used by the staff for living quarters. In the center of the ranch was a large building used as a commons for the ranch's human occupants. It featured a large dining hall, an industrial kitchen, and a library. Outdoors there was a swimming pool ringed by a patio complete with a fire pit. This is where the residents gathered during mealtimes to eat, catch up on the day's news, and gossip.

After the tour, Rosie took the two back to the main house. There they sat on the front porch and watched the late afternoon light as it faded into twilight. Anne wanted to get into the story she had to write, but Rosie told her it would all be discussed at the dinner table when Anne would meet the others who operated the ranch. This delay was frustrating to Anne, but she decided to just go along with the slow pace of the western desert. She could wait another hour. Dinner would start at 6:30.

CHAPTER FOUR

The dining hall was a large structure made from wide metal trusses and corrugated sheet metal walls, although because of the stone finish, the metallic nature of the building wasn't evident to the casual observer. The interior of the building was covered with knotty wood paneling with a rich, glossy light brown finish. It didn't look cheap. The high ceiling vaults were also covered with wood and there were several ceiling fans keeping the air moving. Photos and paintings hung along the walls—mostly of the favorite horses that passed through the ranch over the years. Big, colorful ceramic pots sat in the corners containing different types of cactus native to the area. The overhead lights flooded the room with a warm yellow hue.

The room was loud with the chatter from the voices of those gathered for the evening meal. Anne and Samantha sat at a table with Rosie, her husband Joe; Tyler and Marsha Jebson, who were on the board of directors; Cindy Dixon, the main trainer, and Max Gray, the main vet. Anne found herself straining to hear the conversation across the round table as the noise from the crowd gathered steam. They were discussing Senator Ruud and his recent activities to rid his leased rangeland of the mustang herd that had just appeared.

"They showed up one day," said Rosie to Anne. "We think they came from the Robertson-Hewitt herd up north, but no one really knows."

Anne knew embarrassingly little about the wild horses that roamed the deserts of Nevada, Oregon, California, and Utah. Until now, they were another annoying cowboy factoid that deserved little attention. She listened attentively.

"They don't really have that large of a footprint, and tend to stay in a general area, although that area may be quite large. But these horses just showed up one day, a herd of more than 200 head. Quite remarkable, really."

Anne nodded in agreement. Joe was looking at Anne intently. He was a large man, a Native American with long graying hair, a huge twisted nose, and small, but bright and intense black eyes. To Anne he looked like he knew exactly what she was thinking.

She looked into his eyes, "What do you think, Joe? Where'd those horses come from?"

"They came with the horse angel," he said, very calmly and deliberately.

Sam looked up from her potato. "Horse angel?" She looked at her mom who had asked her the day before if she wanted to see a horse angel.

"That's what we sometimes call Nolan," explained Rosie with a smile. "Our newest trainer, we sometimes call him the horse angel, 'cause he's so good with horses."

"The horses came with him," said Joe again.

"Is he ...um ...Nolan ...is he here?" asked Anne scanning the room.

Rosie looked around and frowned. "No, not yet. I guess he's still out at the quarantine looking after that colt that just came in. Nolan likes to work that part of the operation best."

Anne was disappointed.

"Anne," it was Marsha Jebson speaking, "do you know what the senator is up to out there? He is trying to remove those beautiful mustangs off that land, all of them. He is using his connections to get a special BLM roundup to come out and take those horses away."

"That's because of his cattle operation right?" asked Anne.

"Yes. His family recently received grazing rights to about 5,000 acres next to the ranch. He put his cousin's son in charge of the operation. They must have 1,200 head of cattle out there. It's already fouled one of the rivers. Just a shame when those greenhorns get into a business they don't understand. These areas are sensitive—plant life, wildlife, water sources. It's all a bit more delicate in the desert because of the heat and lack of water. Cattle are hardest on the land because there aren't any natural grazers that evolved out here. So you bring in cattle and sheep and you end up with problems."

"He has tried to round them up twice now," said Rosie.

"What do you mean, tried?" asked Anne.

"Well, both times the BLM came out we got a heads-up, enough advanced notice to be able to help," said Marsha

"Help? How?"

"We open up the gates out there at the BLM border and run the herd onto our land. The BLM can only operate on government land," Marsha explained.

"Then what? You let them back out?"

"Well, it *is* against the law to confine a wild horse. And the herd is much too big for a long-term stay here, but for a few days we take 'em in," said Marsha.

"The BLM guys will only stay around for a few days," said Rosie. "When they move on, we let the herd back out into the range. It is all we can do for now. But Ruud is not going to roll over. I think he's figured out why his guys can't find the herd when they're out here. He's starting to come after us. That's why we need you to tell the world our story."

Anne nodded in understanding.

Just then the main door opened. Anne looked up. A man stepped into the light of the room, looking to be around 40 years old, with a face that was both kind and a bit foreboding. He was dressed in denim, stained from the day's work on the farm, and wearing a cowboy hat badly faded from the sun. As he scanned the room, Anne was shocked by how much he looked like Simon. The similarity was uncanny and made her uneasy.

"Oh, there's Nolan now," said Rosie with a smile as she waved him over. The man approached the table and smiled at the group.

"Nolan, I would like you to meet Anne Harper. She is with the news station Matthew runs. She's here to do the story."

Nolan looked down at Anne. There was a familiar look to his smile as Anne said hello.

"Nice to meet you, Anne," he said, shaking her hand. "I'd sit down with you, but I promised Becky I would go over tomorrow's schedule. We'll have to catch up in the morning, if that's all right."

Rosie looked annoyed. "Well, okay, but we really need to get you two together. Anne wants to interview you for the story."

"No problem. I will be around first thing, okay?" said Nolan to Anne.

"Yes, okay," Anne replied. "First thing tomorrow."

Nolan left the group and took a seat on the other side of the hall. Anne watched him as he sat talking with two rather tough-looking women. Occasionally Nolan would look up and catch Anne's eye. There was something curious about the man. Anne couldn't quite place it.

After dinner ended, Joe invited Anne and Samantha to join the group around the fire pit. Anne would rather go to her room to read and be alone, but Samantha insisted and so the two found themselves out in the cool evening air sitting around a large stone fire pit with several of the ranch hands, Rosie, Joe, and the Jebsons. They all sat in old time-worn rocking chairs, big and comfortable. The high clouds in the sky covered most of the emerging starlight as the fire in the pit raged bright and warm.

Samantha was sitting next to Joe captivated by the dance of the rising flames. The conversation started up again about the wild horses.

"Sam, do you know about the wild horses?" asked Joe in his clear monotone voice.

Sam nodded, "I know a little bit. They are leftovers, right?"

Joe smiled. "Leftovers. Yes, I guess you could say that. Did you know that there were horses here millions of years ago? Before the … " he paused, "leftovers."

"Really?" Sam said. "I thought they all came from Europe with the Spanish explorers. I did a report on them last year at school."

"Well, I'm talking about before that time. Long ago, before men walked the earth, before my people rose up from the deserts, there were horses; many horses. They lived in this country, in the plains and in the forests. Ancient relatives of the horses we know today. These early ancestors were the first horses, the first horse spirit. They were smaller and different from the horses we know today, but the spirit is the same."

"Horse spirit?" Sam asked.

"Oh yes, the spirit of the horse has been with us since the beginning. It is a strong force, a willing partner to man. It is a helper spirit.

Let me tell you, some spirits are helpers, some are protectors, some are destroyers, and some just come to play. The horse has the helper spirit. The horse is our partner, a match for man, to help us."

Anne grew a bit uncomfortable. "We're Christians," she blurted out. She immediately regretted her interruption, as all looked at her curiously.

Joe smiled, "Yes, as am I. I mean no disrespect to you, Ms. Harper. I too am a Christian, for it is clear that Christ is the master spirit. The leader. The unifier. The one."

"So why do you talk about these other spirits?" asked Sam.

"Because the Great Spirit is like a kaleidoscope with many beautiful facets, all of them part of the whole. Horses have a great spirit about them, a helper spirit. They are willing partners of men. They have helped us throughout the ages, they have been a huge part of our development. They have helped man, and so we, as men, in their honor, choose to help them."

"Is that why you have a rescue farm?" Sam asked.

"Exactly," said Joe. "We have this farm to help the horses as they have helped us. They deserve it; we owe it to them."

"So what happened to the horses that used to live here? Where did they go?"

Joe sat back and looked into the fire. "No one really knows. Some say the climate changed and the food sources disappeared, like a terrible winter lasting for thousands of years. Others say they were hunted to extinction; killed by the very men who were sent here to help."

"But why would men hunt and kill something that was a help to them?" asked Sam.

Joe looked at the girl. With a sad smile, he said, "Samantha, the wisdom of men is deep, but it gets cut short by hunger, fear, and survival. Whatever the reason, it is clear there were millions of them living throughout this country. And not just one kind—many kinds. Some of them were as small as a dog, some were bigger. Some had three toes, some had two toes, and some had hooves like our horses today. They lived in the forests, they lived on the grass plains, and they ate leaves, grass, and shrubs."

"So they all died?" asked Sam again.

"Well, they are extinct now," said Joe. "The changing climate, the ice ages—there are many theories, but they all died out. The world changed, the spirit receded, and the land lost these creatures for centuries."

"Well, they couldn't have all died out. We still have horses," said Sam.

"That is true. There were some horses that lived through the changes, but not here, not in this land. The horses of today are much different than those early brothers and sisters. The horses of today have a different history, a different story."

Joe kept speaking. "In a land far away, in what we now call Asia, there lived a people known as the Butai. They lived on the steppes—vast open stretches of grasslands, much like what we call the prairie in this country. There were few trees, apart from those that grew near the lakes and rivers. But there was plenty of grass, and that is where the horse survived. The Butai people were the first people to start the long process of domestication. There is a story my grandfather used to tell me about the Butai people and the first boy to make friends with a horse. Would you like to hear it?"

Anne felt a wave of incredulity pass through her gut. "That was over 5,000 years ago!" she said, a bit too loudly.

Joe laughed. It was a deep laugh from his belly, gentle, knowing, caring. He looked at Anne. "It is just a story," he said with a glint in his eye.

Anne backed down. She saw something in Joe's eye that moved to the center of her doubt, something that made her logic melt, something that she couldn't express—an intuition, a feeling, a longing. Her mind went blank and she felt ashamed.

"I want to hear it," said Samantha. "Tell us the story."

"Okay, Samantha, I will tell you the story," Joe said.

"A very long time ago, when the first men were given life and the spirit of the horse ran free and wild across the grasslands, there lived a people known as Butai. Life was hard for the Butai, for not much grew on the plains but grass and small shrubs. The Butai were hunters and the tribe came to this spot to live near the large herds of wild horses that ran the plains. They got water from the creek and food from the horse herds.

"Now Xa, the chief of the tribe, had three sons. The eldest, Si, was a great leader and was destined to one day become chief. The second boy, Sun, was skilled at hunting. The third boy's name was Xu. He had no discernable talents. He was smaller than the rest, sickly and weak. He could never go on the hunt because he always ran out of strength. The other boys of the tribe made fun of Xu and would sometimes beat him for sport. The chief was ashamed of this boy and would rarely talk to him. Xu grew up alone and lonely.

"When Xu was in his 12th season, he was sent by his mother down to the creek to get as much water as he could carry, which wasn't much because of his small size and diminished strength. But he would obediently go and do his best. This day was the first day of spring and the sun was bright and warm, the air cool and fresh. Xu carried his small bucket down to the creek, which was running fast with winter's runoff. The banks of the creek were muddy and steep keeping Xu from the water. He walked much farther down the creek to find a place that was flat and more easily accessible.

"Xu came to such a place and was surprised to find a horse deeply mired in the springtime mud. The horse, buried up to its chest, was unable to free himself and was lathered with exhaustion. Xu was overcome with pity and couldn't stand to see this animal suffering. He committed himself to freeing the animal, but being so small and weak, his confidence was undermined. If only the Great Spirit could show him a way. Just then a small beam of light was reflected off the top of a large crystalline boulder that rested near the banks of the creek. That beam of light hit Xu in his face and suddenly he understood.

"Xu took some deadwood from underneath one of the few trees that stood near the creek and with that stick started to dig the earth from underneath the boulder. Being so near the creek, the digging was easy as the earth was saturated with water from the springtime runoff. Within minutes the boulder was undermined and with a swift splash fell into the creek. The water now had no choice but to change course around the boulder. The stream was diverted and started to flow into the mud around the trapped horse. As the water flowed around the horse, the mud washed away and eventually the horse pulled itself from the creekside and walked up onto the dry bank.

"Now, up to this point it was known to all that Xu had no special talents and no one seemed to pay much attention to him. So it was a shock to Xu when the horse looked over at him and spoke clearly in a low, majestic voice.

"'You have set me free,' the horse said, not so much in a human voice but like a voice in the heart or mind. 'For this I am grateful. No other man has ever been so kind to the horse. Please, tell me your name.'

"Xu could hardly believe his circumstance, but he heard the voice of the horse plainly and clearly. 'My name is Xu,' he said out loud. 'I am from the Butai village that sits on this creek further down the way.'

"The horse looked at the boy. 'Xu, my name is Amrit. I am the leader of the horses that run on these grasslands. My life I owe to you; my debt is eternal.' And Amrit the Great knelt down in front of Xu. Meekly, Xu climbed upon the back of the great horse. It was the first time any man had been permitted to ride the back of a horse. When Amrit stood up, Xu could hear him say, 'Xu, I am forever at your service; you are an angel sent to help my kind. Ride with me across the plains and feel the winds of freedom upon your face.' With that, Amrit turned toward the plains and ran cantering toward the rest of the herd.

"Now the rest of the men from the village were out hunting on the plains. It was Chief Xa that first spotted his son riding swiftly upon the back of the great horse. Chief Xa first thought it was an angel from God, as no one had ever seen a man riding a horse. Soon the others saw it too and stood in stunned amazement. Chief Xa, being an old and wise man, knew that he was seeing the world changing forever. A new world was emerging, one in which horse and man would live together and not as enemies. A world where the horse would be a help to man, a help to ease the harsh burdens of daily life. A world where man would help the horse in a partnership, in an eternal bond. It was Chief Xa that first called Xu by a new name, a name that would last his lifetime. The name was Sen Li, which means Horse Angel."

Samantha was wide-eyed. She looked up at Joe who was smiling. "The first horse angel!" she exclaimed.

"Yes, Sam," Joe agreed. "The first horse angel."

CHAPTER FIVE

E arly the next morning, Anne sat at a small desk in her bedroom. It was 5:30 a.m. She slept well enough but awoke early and refused to go back to sleep. Samantha was still sleeping soundly in one of the twin beds. She was always hard to wake. Anne sat quietly under the dim light of the reading lamp attached to the top of the desk. In front of her was a small note pad. She was thinking over what she had to accomplish in the coming day. The story was pretty straightforward it seemed: high government official uses his power to illegally remove wild horses from his Nevada cattle ranch. The heroes of the story were the good people at Angel Ridge, fighting the good fight on behalf of the horse, against profit, greed, and government corruption. The story had all of the drama and conflict to capture the attention of the public. There was something else though, a part of the story that wasn't so clear, this horse angel thing. Anne wondered how she could work that part into the story. She needed more information. This obviously was a myth, a child's story, grown a bit out of proportion. Yet, still, there was some faintly romantic notion about the term: *horse angel*. She wrote the two words across the top of her empty note pad. If she could work this into the story, it would bring the piece to life. A personal savior for horses, a cosmic equine guardian, some higher power working as mediator between man and beast. She saw the pieces faintly glimmering in the back of her imagination but she couldn't connect them to anything real, anything solid. However, her intuition told her there was some power in that part of this story.

Out on the range, far out past the quarantine barn, a man stood in the stillness of the rising dawn. The last stars were fading in the growing light, but the sky remained dark. This lone figure was unnoticed by all but a single horse that stood 50 feet in front of the man. The two faced each other in silence.

Anne looked at the note pad in front of her. She needed a plan. She had one day to gather the necessary information and then get the camera crew on their way up. She wrote down the names of interest: Joe Whitehorse, Rosie Whitehorse, Marsha Jebson, Cindy Dixon, Nolan Powell. These people would give her Angel Ridge's side of the story. Then she reached in her planner and flipped through the pages where she found the name she was looking for and wrote it onto her note pad: Vicki Pearson, the Nevada State Director the BLM. She would have to get Pearson on camera; that might be tricky. She also wrote down the name of Senator Ruud. No way he would consent to this interview but with a little digging she could find someone affiliated with the cattle ranch to go after. She also needed to explore any connections between Ruud and Vicki Pearson. There had to be some influence Ruud had over the regional BLM office; there had to be some angle there. She would make a call to Ruud's office later that morning. She would wait for the camera crew and drive out to the BLM office and, if necessary, ambush Ms. Pearson for her statement. That would be a last-ditch effort. Anne hoped that she could get Pearson on camera willingly, but she would get her one way or another. The final piece was how to get someone from Ruud's cattle ranch to talk. She had to play this one by ear.

From below, Anne heard the rumblings of someone stirring downstairs. She looked at her clock. It was 6:00 a.m. A small chat over breakfast would be a perfect way to start the interviews. Anne quietly stood up from the desk and slipped into her clothes, covering her morning hair with a feminine ball cap. She left Samantha sleeping in the room and made her way downstairs.

The creaking floorboards alerted Joe to Anne's presence. He was standing at the sink looking out the kitchen window. The quiet of the house seemed to shatter when he gave Anne a warm "good morning." Anne returned the greeting and made her way to the kitchen table and sat down.

"How did you sleep?" asked Joe as he grabbed for the coffee pot.

"I slept well. It's very quiet here," Anne answered.

"Yeah, that is one thing we have going for us," Joe said. He opened the lid on the clear pot and started filling it with water. Anne watched as he went through the routine. Joe counted the scoops of coffee, placed each one in the filter basket, closed up the basket, and flipped the switch to on. The red light flickered and the coffee pot made a low gurgling noise.

"Not long now," Joe said as he joined Anne at the table. "Help yourself to whatever it is you eat for breakfast. There is a fridge full of goodies and the pantry." He pointed down the hall at a closed door.

"I may have some fruit in a while, but right now I would really like to hear your story about the senator and what he is doing. That is, if you don't mind talking right now."

"Oh, I don't mind," said Joe. "I have always been a morning person. Rosie's a bit different though. Don't try to talk to her until about 10:00 and you two will get along fine." He smiled a big goofy grin that made Anne feel at ease.

"So what's the deal?" asked Anne. "How did this conflict start?"

Joe raised his eyebrows. "You don't know?" He paused while Anne shook her head. "Oh, well, I guess you don't." The coffee pot gurgled and sent a shot of steam rising up to the cupboards.

"This started a long time ago, even before Rosie was born. See, Rosie's father, Gary, was a state senator." Joe smiled fondly as he remembered his father-in-law. "Gary was a great man. Everybody loved him. He was a man of the people and when he went to Carson City to do the people's business, he was as straight up as anyone could have hoped for."

Anne looked thoughtful, "Senator Clark? Yes, I guess Matthew had mentioned that before."

"You work for Matt, right?" asked Joe.

"Yes, that's right," said Anne.

"And he didn't tell you?" Joe looked surprised.

"Why don't you tell me?" said Anne in a friendly soothing voice. Really, she was thinking the same thing. What had Matt left out of the story when he sent her up here?

"Well, in short, there's been a family feud between the Ruuds and the Clarks going back about 50 years now. I'm surprised you didn't know that, working at the station and all." Joe got up and grabbed for the coffee pot.

"Coffee?" he asked.

"Yes, please," Anne said. "So tell me about this ...feud. It obviously started between Senator Clark and Senator Ruud. Am I right?"

"Yeah, back in the '60s, Gary and LaVar Ruud worked together in the state senate, way before Ruud ran for the national office. The two grew up together, not but a mile apart ...were friends for years, some say best friends. I dunno ...that was before I met the family." Joe paused to pour two large mugs of coffee. He snatched a small bottle of cream from the fridge and sat back down at the table.

"Sugar is there in the bowl if you'd like," Joe said casually. "Anyway, the story I always heard was there was some state-owned mineral rights up for bid."

"What kind of mineral rights?" asked Anne.

"Gold. It was gold. The mine is still operating; I think it's owned by a company called Newburgh, or something like that. Anyway, back then it was called the Sinem Ridge Mine. Gary and LaVar were in the senate and sat on the committee overseeing the Natural Resources Bureau, the department that grants mineral rights. The way I heard it was the committee had settled on a bid submitted by a group of local businessmen. The deal was all but signed. Then in some midnight swindle, LaVar, who was the committee chair, threw the deal out and gave the rights to a couple of fellas from Colorado. It turned out that these guys had given LaVar a big payoff—a bribe—and he ended up with a rather large share of stock from the company operating the mine."

Anne started to see the bigger picture. "So, let me guess," she said. "Gary found out about the deal and that started the whole mess between the two families?"

"Yes," said Joe. "Gary found out. He was furious and tried to stop the deal. He went to the press; he went to the ethics board. He did everything he could to expose Ruud and his corruption."

"What happened?" asked Anne. "How is Ruud in congress now?"

Joe shrugged. "Ruud's family owned the newspaper. In the end there was a smear campaign against Gary and he was run out of the senate. The two families have been at odds ever since."

Anne now understood why Matt sent her up here. It wasn't about wild horses or horse angels. It was about trying to get even with Ruud, to expose his continued corruption. She had a sinking feeling as a cloud of doubt swirled into her mind. She shouldn't be here; she should be back on her farm with Samantha in training. The cloud darkened quickly as her heart sank into a strange misty feeling of worthlessness.

"Huh," Anne said looking into her coffee cup. "Interesting."

Joe noticed Anne's change in consciousness. "What is it?" he asked.

Anne looked up, "Oh, well, I was wondering why I was sent up here. I like the story and all, but now it seems maybe I've been sent into the middle of something that just isn't my business."

Joe nodded his understanding. "It has been my experience that nothing happens by accident. The true reason you are here has not yet been revealed."

Anne shook her head dismissively. "My experience is different. There are accidents and they change our lives forever." Her mind took her back to the day Simon was killed. That terrible sound, the smell of the crowd, the horse violently struggling, writhing on its back, the piercing, flesh-tearing hooves, the horrible sense of helplessness. Tears welled up in her hazel eyes.

Joe sat in silence inwardly chanting a soft prayer of solace. He could see the woman's utter pain. He could feel her disappear into some far-off trauma, reliving the scene imprinted on her soul. He drew in a deep breath and with it all of the angst in the room, all of the fear and memories. With his breath he drew all of that sorrow into his lungs, into his heart. After blessing it he slowly let the breath out with a steady sound of rushing wind, a quiet raspy intonation, as he pushed all of those feelings down to the bottom of his spine, out and into the vast, unquantifiable energy of the earth.

Anne felt her energy shift. Suddenly she was back in the kitchen, at the table with this big Indian named Joe. Her memories flashed white and were gone in an instant. Suddenly she was present, in the moment. The instant change confused her. With wide eyes she looked at Joe. He was sitting calmly with a soft look of compassion on his face.

"What was that?" she asked with hesitation.

Joe raised his eyebrows and shrugged with a smile.

"No, what just happened?" she insisted.

"Listen," he said with a quiet authority. "We all have our reasons for being here. Right now yours is to help us tell our story, to help us assist these wild horses, to help us keep them safe. Ruud has got the BLM in his pocket and will stop at nothing to roundup this herd and send them off to the holding pens. We can't let that happen. There is too much at stake. It is important that you are here."

Anne felt a strange familiarity with this man. She felt his love and honor, his gentleness, his inward beauty. She felt his undying love for the horses. Her muscles relaxed and something within told her everything was okay, everything was right. She knew she could trust this man Joe. Her skeptical mind released all her suspicions she took a deep breath and smiled.

"Okay," she said with conviction. "Okay, you're right. I do have a job to do and I will give it my all." She smiled and took a sip of coffee. It was bitter and too strong, but she felt at ease.

Rosie was up and came into the kitchen heading straight for the coffee pot. She gave a weak "good morning" to Joe and Anne, took her coffee and disappeared into the living room where she sat in silence and read the morning paper.

Out on the range the sun was now just below the horizon. The light grew delicate but determined. The man and the horse stood on the range facing each other in silent communion. The man was Nolan Powell, the stranger ranch hand that showed up three months earlier asking for a job. The horse was Cloud Runner, a bay mustang stallion with a black mane and tail and a clear white blaze on his face, the lead stallion of the Angel Ridge herd. The herd had migrated to the area just before Nolan arrived. This man and this herd were connected by an ancient bond. It was that same bond Xu had forged with Amrit, the sacred bond between man and horse some 6,000 years ago. The bond that swore love and protection, aid and forgiveness. The bond that was honored by a few select humans and a few select horses for millennia. At this place, at this time, the two creatures—man and horse—were renewing this bond. They stood in silence but in the secret whispers of the soul they spoke aloud, with purpose, with complete understanding. The unspoken language of the horse was clearly understood by Nolan. He heard the music of Cloud Runner's inner voice, his horse song. He was enveloped by the vibrations of equine color and nuance. He knew what the sounds meant. He could also impart his own vibrations and inner language to his horse companion. He could communicate the deep language of soul, love, and compassion. This language was passed down through the ages like an invisible thread, carried in the hearts of certain men and certain animals. Through the ages this communion thrived though secreted away for all practicality.

At this time Nolan and Cloud Runner were immersed in a conversation of grave importance. The time was approaching when Cloud Runner would need the assistance of men to save the herd from total annihilation. The danger was growing each day. Several members of the herd were gunned down by men from the cattle ranch. Then Cloud Runner said something that scalded Nolan's heart, "The last of the last." Nolan heard these words and did not understand.

"What does that mean?" he probed.

"The last of the last," said Cloud Runner. "This herd is the last of the last, all others have gone."

"The last what?" asked Nolan, not sure if he wanted to hear the truth.

"The last of those who remember, those who understand the sacred bond. We are the last of the horse kind that have the memory of Xu."

Nolan was shocked. He had always thought that all horses remembered. He never once thought that the horses would forget. Only man would forget; that was what he had been taught. This news came as an electric jolt through his nervous system. He now understood the position the herd was in.

"How many are you?" he asked the stallion. "How many remember?"

"All of us remember. All of us hold the sacred bond in our hearts and minds. Each time one of us is taken, we get closer to losing the bond forever. Our numbers have dwindled over the years. This place is our last stand. If we win our freedom, our numbers will grow and we can bring the message back to horse-kind. It will take many years, but it can be done. If we die then the bond of Xu dies with us and our ability to help our man-brothers will die as well. We cannot let this happen; that is why I come to you now."

The brave stallion had come to fulfill the ancient pact made so long ago. Nolan stood in silence and listened to the pleading. He understood the importance of this time, this day, this hour. He swore loyalty to the herd and promised his undying allegiance. He told Cloud Runner there were others at the ranch who understood. He told Cloud Runner they would and could help save the herd.

Joe and Anne had finished their coffee and their conversation had waned. Anne was thinking about her next move …maybe talk to Rosie …but the timing didn't seem right. Joe stood up. He walked over to the sink and looked out the window at the rising dawn.

"I have to meet with Nolan," he said. "You should come along."

"Right now?" Anne asked, moving her hand up to the back of her head. She had not showered, cleaned up or even washed her face. She hated being unprepared and instinctively wanted to say no. However, a bigger part of her natural intuition told her it was an opportunity she couldn't miss. "Give me five minutes," she said as she rose from the table and headed upstairs for a quick brush of her teeth. She passed Rosie in the living room. Rosie didn't even raise her head from the newspaper. Anne took no offense and made her way up the stairs.

Ten minutes later Joe and Anne were in an old green Chevy pickup slowly rolling down a dirt road toward the quarantine. Joe was silent now and Anne watched the land open up in a radiance of color as the sun came sliding up over the far mountain range. A long, wide valley gently sloped down and away to the south while Angel Ridge provided a firm border to the right. Out ahead and to the left a few small trees struggled against the backdrop of sagebrush and creosote bushes. It wasn't long until Joe turned off the road and the truck creaked to a stop in front of the quarantine building. The building was a low wood-framed structure with beige siding and a flat roof. The few windows that faced the front were clouded with years of dust. The two left the truck and entered through the front door.

Inside the quarantine were a few small offices with a water cooler and some old pictures hanging on the walls. The place was as dusty on the inside as it was on the outside. The musty smell of barn mold hung heavy in the air.

Joe didn't stop at the offices but went directly to the back where the stables held the new arrivals at the ranch. Following him, Anne looked down the center aisle to see eight stalls on either side. Two workers in jeans and red shirts were busy with the morning feeding. The sounds of stamping horses, impatient for their food, echoed through the rafters. Joe kept walking through the stables, and at the far end, pushed open a door and stepped out into the morning light. Anne followed as he made his way past the four large paddocks all the way to the end where the facility ended and the rangeland began. Joe set his gaze out to the range.

"There he is," said Joe pointing.

Anne looked out and saw Nolan walking up some invisible path cutting its way through the thick sagebrush. She wondered what this man was doing so far out from the quarantine. Though she couldn't pinpoint it, there seemed to be an ever-so-slight mystery to the way he walked—confident and with purpose, but relaxed and detached. As he got closer, she could see he appeared deep in thought, lost in some otherworld puzzlement. Nolan was a man of medium build and stood just less than six feet tall. His large-brimmed Stetson shaded a handsome, gentle, fine-featured face. Dressed in jeans and a denim work shirt, he gave the aura of all-American cowboy. Anne hated cowboys.

He approached Anne and Joe without smiling and forced a quiet "hello." Anne could see in his dark brown eyes some burden, some heaviness. They exchanged greetings and she noticed that he seemed to be distracted. Turning to Joe, he said, "It's worse than we thought."

"Tell me what you found out," Joe asked, obviously disturbed.

Nolan eyed Anne suspiciously, then back to Joe as if to ask why the woman was here. The silent communication was not lost on Anne. She disliked cowboys but was starting to dislike this one even more. She bristled.

"I am here at the request of Rosie's brother Matt," Anne said. "He wants me to do a story to expose what the senator is doing to the mustang herd. I am here to help."

Even though she was trying to be accommodating, her tone came out icy and accusatory. Nolan looked at her with a long, unemotional gaze. She could feel his strange power break through her crusty shell and work its way to her core, as if trying to plumb the depths of her character and honesty. The look threw Anne's confidence off-balance. Suddenly she felt exposed and vulnerable; inexplicably she heard a strange voice, deep inside her head, whispering, "Do you even know why you are here?"

Anne broke eye contact and looked away. She felt embarrassed but didn't know why. Something about this man rattled her. "I am here to help," she repeated in a quieter tone.

"Anne is here to help," assured Joe. He understood what Nolan was doing. Nolan needed to be confident the people around this horse herd had the right intentions. There was much at stake and Nolan's first priority, in fact his only priority, was to see to the safety of the herd. Joe knew why; one day Anne may know as well.

"Anne is a friend," said Joe to the cowboy. "She comes at the right time and can help get the public on our side. She will play a major role in getting things sorted out up here."

Nolan was still looking at Anne trying to get a read on just who she was. He didn't look convinced, but finally broke his gaze and turned his attention to Joe. Anne stood by, feeling like a child, an outsider.

"It's worse than we thought," Nolan repeated. "Seven horses have been shot dead; three are missing. It seems Ruud's men have been ordered to get the herd off the land by any means. They are a bunch of heartless bastards."

"They are killing the horses?" Anne asked. She was shocked. Although she was feeling a bit out of place, she wasn't going to back out completely.

"Yes. Four yesterday, three last night," confirmed Nolan.

Anne was amazed at his accurate figures. "How do you know this? Did you find the animals' bodies?" Nolan didn't answer, but kept his attention on Joe. Anne was not amused.

"Look, Joe," he said, "there's more …something I didn't know. These horses …" He paused and looked at Anne pondering how to say what needed to be said. "These horses are the last of their kind. They are the last ones."

"The last ones, what?" Anne asked not too eloquently.

Nolan grew impatient. He turned to Anne, his face grim. He was direct and spoke with purpose and authority. "Please! Miss Anne—"

"Just call me Anne, thank you!" Anne shot back, interrupting.

Nolan continued, "Please …Anne …it will be best if you just observe for a while, calmly. We are in the middle of a situation here; a little bigger than you will understand at first. Give it some time and you may learn what we're doing. But for right now, it will be best for you to be a quiet observer."

Anne's eyes narrowed, "Well, that certainly is a circuitous way to tell me to shut up."

"Should I be more direct?" asked Nolan, his voice getting a bit edgy.

Joe raised his hands. "Come on, you two, we need to work together on this thing." He turned to Anne with a warm smile. "Would you excuse us for a minute? I think Nolan needs a word alone with me."

"Sure," said Anne curtly, "but you were the one who asked me to come along. I didn't know there were going to be secrets."

"No secrets," Joe lied. "Just a delicate matter than needs some strategizing."

"Fine," said Anne, "I'll be in the barn." She looked at Nolan and scowled. She remembered why she never liked cowboys, such macho jerks. They all thought they were kings.

Nolan looked at her. His dark eyes had a sense of purpose, no malice, just confident purpose. Again the look rattled Anne as she turned away and headed to the barn.

When she was out of earshot, Joe turned back to Nolan. "We are going to need her on our side, Nolan. Not a good idea to get off on the wrong foot."

"Why did you bring her here?" asked Nolan. "I needed to meet with you, not the whole damn public."

"Yeah, sorry," said Joe. "But we need her. You'll see."

Nolan looked at the lady as she walked past the paddocks and disappeared into the barn. "I'll trust you on that one. I couldn't tell."

"Okay," said Joe, directing his attention back to Nolan. "Tell me, what did you find?"

Nolan's face dropped. "These are the last of the horses that remember. It has been confirmed."

Joe frowned. He immediately knew what Nolan was talking about. "I knew they were getting scarce; you know all that breeding does away with the ancient shared memories."

Nolan nodded. "The lead stallion, his name is Cloud Runner."

Joe's eyebrows raised curiously. "Cloud Runner? I remember that name from somewhere. He's their leader?"

Nolan nodded.

Joe slightly smiled. "Hmm, Cloud Runner. I seem to remember my grandfather talking about a horse named Cloud Runner." Joe's memories faded back into the distant past when he was a boy. He and his grandfather sat near a small creek, the watery sounds of tinkling china, the tall range grass turned brown and hot, the cobalt sky. Joe remembered. "It couldn't be the same horse, but it's the same name, hmm," he said.

"Cloud Runner is here. He tells me that this is the last of the memory herds. The pressure is on from Ruud's men. They are hunting the herd day and night. We need to act fast if we want to help save them."

"Well, we have room for some of them here, but not the whole herd," said Joe. "We need to get the public informed; we need pictures of the kill. We need Anne to get this out. Then the people will come in droves. This we know."

Nolan looked worried. "Okay, I guess you're right. I hate to bring too much attention to this, but I guess you're right. Get Miss Prissy Primo ready and I'll take her into Ruud's operation. We'll have to go by foot so I hope she's in shape. She'll need a camera."

"I think you would be better off on horseback," said Joe.

"She can ride?" asked Nolan, somewhat surprised.

"Oh yeah! She was in line for the U.S. Olympic Equestrian Team," said Joe.

"Oh," Nolan sighed, "Now I remember. I knew she looked familiar."

"You know her?" asked Joe.

"No, but I have met her. She was Simon's wife. Remember Simon? The guy that died at the Kentucky three-day about five or six years ago?"

"Not really," said Joe, shaking his head.

Nolan lowered eyes. "A dressage queen. Now I get it. That explains the attitude."

Joe smiled, "Give her a chance. I feel she is here at the right time. I think you will find that too."

"We'll see," said Nolan, not convinced.

The two men walked up to the barn and entered the stables. Anne was leaning into one of the stalls cooing at the equine occupant. She turned towards them when she heard the door open. They converged in the middle of the aisle. Anne's attitude was brittle as she felt snubbed. Nolan wanted nothing more than to get as far away from this woman as soon as possible. He knew, however, that wasn't possible. Joe played the peacemaker, deciding to take the direct approach.

"Anne," said Joe, "here's the deal. Ruud's guys aren't going to wait for the BLM. They have started hunting the horses and have already killed seven. We have word that they are out there today looking to kill more. If we can prove that they are killing wild horses, we can cause some real trouble for Ruud and his cattle ranch. Enough trouble to get him to leave the herd alone."

Anne's face showed her feelings. She took the news hard. Even though her exterior was stoic, her heart was tender and compassionate at its deepest levels. The thought of seven dead horses out on the range seemed unreal. Killed by men. That was outrageous.

"I want you and Nolan here to ride out and find the kill site. Take your camera and get the story on film. Nolan can take you to the spot, but we need you to get the evidence, to get the story. The sooner you two can get out there, the better."

Anne looked at Nolan, "You and me?" she asked him with surprise.

"Look," Nolan responding. "I mean no disrespect to you, Anne. Maybe I can fill you in on what's happening as we ride out. But facts are, we do need you. Things are getting critical for the herd and we need to act fast."

The look on his face was urgent and sincere, even though Anne still thought he was a big jerk. But in her mind there was another growing apprehension. She hadn't been on a horse for over 10 years. After Simon's death, she thought it best not to risk any more accidents for Samantha's sake. She made the decision to end her riding career and focus on training Samantha to take her place in the world of high-level dressage competition. She hadn't come out here to ride. Besides, all this farm could offer were some old beat-down trail horses. What would she wear? She had no riding clothes, no boots. The thought bothered her, a shadow of old panic.

She thought for a few seconds. Not wanting to appear weak, she turned to Joe, "What can I do with Samantha?"

"Rosie will watch over her, give her some chores and keep her occupied. She'll be all right. Should only take you two a couple of hours to go in, get the shots, and get back here."

"But I didn't bring any farm clothes," Anne protested. "I didn't think we would be needing anything like that. I'm afraid I am a bit unprepared." She was looking for a way out.

Joe discerned her hesitation, and saw straight to the heart of the matter. No gentle coaxing here. He cut straight to the chase. "Oh, we have plenty of clothes for you and for Sam. Don't forget, we raised five children out here. There are plenty of resources we can draw from."

He looked at her feet. "Size 8½?" he asked.

Anne was impressed. "Why, yes." She knew she was trapped. There was no graceful way out of this one. She had to submit. She needed the story and this was a chance to get some real impact.

"Okay," said Anne. "I'll do it. I can't believe someone would actually shoot a wild horse. I'll do it," she committed herself to the gory task.

The three left the barn and piled in the truck, all three across the front bench seat. Joe called ahead on some ancient CB radio and requested two horses be tacked up immediately. He wanted Jasper and he wanted Mickey. He ordered the person to roundup some clothes and boots for Anne, and he asked that some water and sack lunches be brought down from the kitchen. Anne noticed Joe's change in demeanor as he took charge of the situation and went from gentle Indian to commanding warrior. The truck chugged on up the dusty road.

They were soon back at the main complex. The two horses, Jasper and Mickey, a paint mare and a quarter horse gelding, were in the last stages of being tacked up and were almost ready to ride. A girl named Jan had a stack of clothes for Anne as well as some boots that seemed to be just the right size. Anne winced when she saw the boots. For the past twenty-five years she had worn nothing but custom DerDau riding boots at $2,500 a pop. These worn-out Tony Lamas were not her thing. She gave a condescending smile as she took the clothes and boots from Jan.

"Thanks, I think." she said sarcastically.

Joe smiled at her.

"You can change in the bathroom over there," he said pointing to a door at the end of the barn.

At that moment Samantha ran into the barn. She was dressed in Levis, Tony Lamas, and an old work shirt that Rosie had brought out from some overstuffed closet in the house. Anne swore under her breath.

"What's this?" Anne asked her daughter as she came within earshot.

"Hi, Mom!" said Sam, obviously excited and not registering her mother's disapproval.

"Rosie found me these clothes and I am going to help her with the horses. She said she would even give me a riding lesson today." Samantha's voice echoed with joy. She felt free from the constraints of dressage training. She felt free and wild in her "cowboy" clothes.

"Really?" Anne strained to control her revulsion. She didn't want to cause a scene in front of all these people. Equally, she didn't want her daughter getting a potentially destructive riding lesson from the cowpoke, let alone dress like one.

"Are you sure that's what you want?" she asked through her teeth.

Sam noticed her mother's reaction and it put a damper on her enthusiasm. She could feel the disapproval; she knew what the consequences would be. But she also had another feeling, one that was new, and one that she didn't quite understand. She felt safe with these new people around her.

Rosie was walking up, following at a distance from Sam. She was watching the mother and daughter and could intuit the feelings between them. Never one to shy away, she just started talking as she approached the two.

"Oh, we have a great day planned for Samantha. Don't you worry about a thing, Anne. You and Nolan have some work to do. We'll be all right. Sam here knows how to handle herself. She knows horses.

You've taught her well Anne."

Anne was disarmed and decided to let it go. One lesson couldn't possible destroy the years of expert training she had invested in her daughter. Although she still had an uneasy feeling, she let it go.

"Fine," she said, a bit too abruptly. "I mean …thank you."

Anne turned to Sam. "Would you go grab my camera bag for me, please? You know, the one that's a backpack? It's in the back seat of the car."

Sam ran off. Anne looked over and saw Nolan strapping a gun belt to his waist. An imposing Colt 45 was lodged in the holster. The scene shocked her and she finally registered the reality that this situation could easily get out of hand.

"You think that's necessary?" she asked.

Nolan looked over at Anne, then down to his holster. "I hope not," he answered. "I hope not."

Anne felt a shiver run down her back. A slight tinge of fear was rising in her gut, a wariness that she needed to be careful here, needed to keep awake and aware. Shooting horses was crazy and outrageous to her, but the thought of needing a gun out there changed the game in frightening ways. She turned to Joe.

"Joe, is this safe?"

Joe could see the turnings of her mind. He didn't want to lie but neither did he want to infuse undue fear into the situation.

"Look," he said sternly. "Ruud plays for keeps. He's willing to destroy that entire herd of horses for his own pocketbook. Is it safe? Hell no! It's not safe. But is it necessary? You have to decide that, Anne. I don't want any harm to come to you, and you need to know that Nolan is one of the best at moving through the range unnoticed. Trust me on that. It's not like a war is going on out there, but if you run into Ruud's men, they're going to be mighty territorial. The pistol is a precaution …I think a wise one."

Anne looked into his black eyes. She could see the urgency in his mind. She could feel the extent to which he cared about these horses.

"Okay," she said. "I just don't want to be walking into a bear trap."

"We'll be fine." said Nolan assuringly.

Anne disappeared into the bathroom to change her clothes. She soon emerged a transformed woman. Gone was the stuffy business attire of the high society diva. Gucci and Anne Taylor had given way to Wrangler and Sears.

Nolan looked over and did a double take. "Wow!" he thought to himself. "Now that's more like it."

Anne felt like a fool. She never wore a pair of Wrangler jeans in her life.

Joe gave her the once-over. "You look great!" he said with a genuine smile.

Anne glowered.

"Thanks," she replied without conviction.

They led the two horses out of the barn and into the morning sun. Anne looked up at the house and saw Samantha running down the lane holding the camera bag. Her intuition told her that her daughter would be fine, no need to worry. She looked over at Nolan and grimaced. A day with the cowboy would feel like years. What would they talk about? What could they possibly have in common? His dusty clothes were worn and hung loosely on his frame. She couldn't find the first words to say. Maybe something about wardrobe tips? She put her foot in the stirrup and lifted herself up into the saddle. The western saddle with its large horn felt constricting and wrong. "Whatever," she said to herself. Her dressage sensibilities were straining as she settled into her seat. The horse was patient and held still under her slight weight.

Samantha arrived and handed the bag up to her mom. Anne swung the bag around and slipped her arms through the straps. The backpack carried a Canon EOS-1D with four different lenses and all the gear. Samantha was trying to suppress a laugh.

"What are you laughing about?" Anne asked her daughter.

"You," Sam said. "You look funny dressed up like a cowgirl."

"What?" Anne blushed, but knew she would have to take the joke. "And what do you think YOU look like, young lady?" Anne said with a playful smile. Inside she was mortified, but she knew Sam meant no harm, just a girl's fun.

"I like it!" exclaimed Sam. "I like being a cowgirl!"

Anne genuinely chuckled. She hadn't seen her daughter this happy for some time and it warmed her heart. "Well, don't get too used to it.

We have to go home sometime." Sam was smiling. The morning light reflected off her fresh young face. Anne gazed at the visage of her young daughter and saw herself. In that short glimpse, Anne saw herself and all of her youthful dreams, the freedom of childhood, the innocence of youth. For a second she felt that carefree feeling of being young, being cared for, no worries, no thought of the future. For that split second, Anne felt the moment. No past, no future, just the now. She smiled back at her daughter.

"All set?" asked Nolan with an ingratiating smile.

"All set," replied Anne. She looked down at her daughter. "Be a good girl, Sam. I'll see you this afternoon."

Anne instinctively sat up straight, drew in the reins, and pressed her heels in slightly, urging the horse to step into the walk. Immediately the horse's head raised up sharply, his tail gave a violent twitch, and he took one step back. Anne's eyebrows furrowed. She drew in her reins even more and gave the horse more pressure from her heels. The horse shook his head, the heavy bit being a stranger to its mouth. The horse made a few stammering passage-like steps and turned around toward the barn. Anne was mortified as the group watched her and this horse do the dance of denial.

Nolan saw the horse in distress. He wanted to scold Anne, but knew it would be inappropriate in front of the group.

"Just relax," he said calmly to Anne. "Mickey there is a trail horse, he knows how to follow. Relax and he'll do the work."

Anne frowned. She looked down at Samantha who was hiding a smirk. Anne let the reins go loose and the horse relaxed. Nolan took a few steps forward on Jasper and Mickey turned and started to follow. This was why Anne hated cowboys, untrained trail horses, stupid clothes, and...

"Here, you might need this," Joe said as he held out a light straw cowboy hat.

"Oh!" Anne said, slightly shocked. "No thanks, Joe. I've got a hat in my bag if I need one."

"It can get awfully hot out there, even this time of year," he said waving the hat at her as the horses moved by.

"I'll be fine. See you guys later."

"Bye, Mom," Sam called out as Nolan and Anne stepped out onto the trail and headed south toward the High Star Ranch, Ruud's ranch.

The trail—an old dirt road that grew thinner through years of neglect—was wide enough for two horses. On this side of the ranch the ridge was between them and Ruud's operation, jutting from the desert floor and rising abruptly on their right. The sun was up now and the morning was growing hot on this east side of the ridge.

Anne continued trying to shape the horse with her hands and legs, pulling on the reins, squeezing her legs into the horse's sides. Mickey continued to resist the forceful riding technique and began to speed up, only to get pulled back by his rider. The horse's nerves were flaring. Anne's nerves followed, and the horse and rider found themselves in a battle of wills.

Nolan watched the jigging horse in quiet amusement. He knew Anne thought she was a great rider and was secretly enjoying her display of complete detachment from her mount. He had seen many of these so-called "great riders" over the years, torturing their horses with a heavy hand, heavy aids. It was always a mystery to him how these types could be around horses all their lives and not at some time finally submit their egos and put the horse first. It was really a very simple concept, although not easily put into practice.

"I thought you knew how to ride," he finally said after watching Anne for 10 minutes.

Anne was shocked. Anger surged through her nervous system, her self-conscious frustration a powder keg waiting for a spark.

"Are you kidding me? Of course I know how to ride. It's not my fault that you put me on this untrained trail hack." She was obviously about ready to come unglued.

Nolan knew it was time to pull back and try to calm her down. He needed her for this mission and at this rate she would have Mickey worn to a frazzle within the next hour.

"Well, first thing, you need to completely relax. Your nerves are frightening poor Mickey something fierce."

Anne glowered. "If I relax too much then poor ol' Mickey . . ." she paused her mocking to take a breath. "Poor ol' Mickey will run off and then I'll have real problems."

Nolan shook his head. "Joe chose Mickey for you because he is a follower. You know, the pecking order? Mickey will follow Jasper here almost anywhere. And Jasper will take my lead, as you can see. All you need to do is relax and follow Mickey. Really, it is that simple."

Anne's face showed her complete incredulity. "You want me to let the horse lead me?" she asked with disdain. "So I'm at the end of the pecking order?" The idea went against everything Anne knew about riding. She was the leader, the horse needed a guide. If you let the horse be in charge then you were in real trouble. This is all she knew—her life sum of knowledge in the field. Plus, she didn't at all like the idea of being at the bottom of the totem pole. She had been to the championships; she was one of the few. She had competed on a worldwide stage with the elite. She was a real rider, not a hack, not a cowboy. She was a sought-out trainer with a global reputation. How dare this cowboy hack try to teach her, try to put her last? He obviously had no idea who she was.

"This is not an ego contest," said Nolan. "I mean no disrespect. I am only trying to make it easier for us all. Mickey is a follower; let him do his job. Now relax, why don't you? You've got that horse balled up like a sewing machine. He's a nervous wreck. You need to relax." Nolan's words were direct and getting louder. His masculine energy was shooting out like an arrow and went right though Anne, piercing her hard, protective shell. Anne felt the urgency of his message, and was quite surprised by the power behind it. Still, her ego was puffed up like a strutting peacock, stubborn and proud. She didn't back down.

"You obviously have no idea of my riding credentials, do you? Didn't anybody tell you who I am?" Her face was ferocious; her brow crinkled into a dark tsunami.

Nolan wasn't cowed. This type of bullying might work on some, but he was far from intimidated.

"Oh, believe me, I know who you are," said Nolan with a smirk. "I know all about your career. You almost made it to the top, didn't you? But you couldn't quite get there, huh? You always blamed your horse. You always had an excuse. Then, if not the horse, the trainer. Oh yeah. I know about you and your credentials."

"What are you talking about?" Anne demanded. Mickey was continuing his jigging, almost trotting sideways.

"What am I talking about?" Nolan looked over at her with a clear, soul-piercing stare. "Let's count them. Your prize horse, the mare, what was her name? Oh yeah, Ysabella. You put her out to pasture after the Equestrian Games because she had 'lost her will,' right? And then, the next one, that Hanovarian gelding—Timpson? Yeah, Timpson. He was retired lame. Nothing to do with training. No, just went lame. Right? And then there was the greatest of them all, the one that took you all the way to the championships, Remington. What happened to Remington, Anne? What happened to that one?" Nolan's voice was rising with each account, his indignation and true loathing for this woman were spewing out in a rage that set Anne back.

"Screw you! You stinking redneck hick!" Anne was livid. She exploded, "How do you know that? Who the hell are you? What the hell is this?" Mickey reacted to Anne's anger with an increase in his jig. Anne pulled hard on the reins and the horse came to a nervous stop. Nolan halted Jasper and stood face-to-face with Anne, his eyes were wide, revealing a truth-baring soul. Deep, complex, and roiling. Anne looked away.

"Easy now," he said. "You are getting the horses spooked."

"What's going on here? How do you know that about my horses?" Anne shot back through her teeth. She was seriously thinking about turning around and heading back to fetch Sam to return to Sacramento by nightfall.

"Tammy," said Nolan, calmer now. "Your last trainer before Simon died."

Anne's eyes narrowed. Who was this guy?

"Tammy's my sister," Nolan said.

Anne slumped. Oh, great. He knows all of the dirt. Great.

"I'm leaving," Anne said and turned Mickey around toward the ranch.

Nolan remained calm. "Just like that? Going to run away? Like you did with your career? Just quit?"

Anne stopped and turned back. "Who do you think you are?" She was shrieking now. "You don't know me! You don't know what I went through, why I did what I did!" Actually Nolan did know her and what she went through, but he let her vent. "You presume to lecture me on my riding? Tammy is your sister? That woman lost me the championships. We had a shot at winning, and she—" Anne stammered into silence, she was boiling over. "Is that what this is all about? Is this about Tammy? Some kind of revenge because I fired your sister?"

Nolan smiled slightly. "Are you serious? That was six years ago. Tammy certainly never held it against you. There were plenty more people who needed her talents. She moved on."

"Then why are you bringing that up?" Anne scowled.

"You brought it up," Nolan reminded her. "I am here for one thing, and one thing only. I want to keep Ruud from killing any more of my herd."

Anne's brain took a mental note. Did he just say "my herd?" She remained silent.

"I don't care about your past. I am certainly not here to debate riding skills. I just want to get over that ridge and into the valley, find the horse kill so you can see it for yourself, get some pictures, and get back."

Anne wanted to leave and get home. She knew that would be a job killer for her. She knew Matthew would never forgive her for abandoning this story. It was too close to home for him. If she knew about this beforehand, she would have simply made an excuse and never come. Now she was stuck with this redneck jerk who knew much more about her than she about him. That was unnerving. She didn't like people mucking around in her private affairs. She calculated the options and determined she would have to go on. She needed the story. Plus she cared deeply about horses. Someone was shooting horses? That sense of injustice overrode her desire to jump off the horse and kick this guy in the balls. She knew she was committed; she could get through one day with him, maybe.

Anne let out a long, slow, deep breath. "Okay, let's just get it done. I think you are a jerk, and I don't like you at all. But, being a professional, I can live with that. I work with jerks all the time. Let's just get it done."

"Fine," said Nolan, his feelings not ruffled in the slightest. "The feeling is mutual. But if we are going to get out there and back, you are going to need to let Mickey do the work. He won't make it another hour in that nervous condition."

Anne shook her head, defeated. "Okay, what is it that you want me to do, or not do?"

"Give Mickey the reins, get off his sides, sit back, and enjoy the ride," Nolan instructed.

"Fine!" Anne relented and relaxed. Immediately Mickey's disposition changed and the horse started to calm down.

Nolan turned Jasper and started down the road again. Mickey turned as well and followed Jasper in the same gait and rhythm. Anne shook her head and realized that she was just on a pony ride. All of her skill, talents, and knowledge as a rider tabled and useless. She was simmering inside and would definitely get even—somehow, some way.

Nolan's plan was to move to the southern tip of the ridge, climb over and drop into Ruud's place unnoticed. He knew all too well the real risk of being caught by the men Ruud had on his payroll. Any man that would gun down a wild horse for sport wouldn't think twice about trying his aim on a trespassing—possibly dangerous—human. Nolan was a smart man and had certain advantages that few could understand. He picked up the pace and pushed his horse into a trot. Mickey and Anne followed easily.

Anne struggled against her natural instinct to control the horse. Nolan was right, Mickey was a follower and she found she needed very little input to keep him on track. Of course this grated against her ego. She felt like a passenger when her real desire was to be the driver. She decided to take advantage of this moment and pulled her backpack around to fetch her camera. If she was just sitting around, she might as well get some shots along the way. Her balance was excellent, her seat steady, she had no problem with getting the pack off while riding at a full trot. She pulled her camera out and attempted to look through the viewfinder. Getting the camera was one thing, taking a picture at full trot was a different story. Anne stuffed the camera back and pushed the pack back around. They continued on down the dirt road.

After trotting for a few miles the road suddenly ended. There were remnants of some old shack that had long been blown over; a few dilapidated fence posts showed the marking of some boundary long forgotten. Nolan stopped and looked up at the ridge. At this southern end it was not as steep or as high. Another few miles to the southeast and the ridge gave out altogether, joining back with the desert floor and pointing the way to the creek down at the bottom of the valley. Anne snapped some photos—one of the old shack, and one of Nolan, head up, scanning the ridge for the trail.

"We go this way," Nolan said to Anne as he turned his horse to a small track leading up to the ridge. Anne looked up the hill. Her sour mood changed slightly as she noticed the trail that wound its way up the hill. The sight brought back the memory of her father, long ago, when the two of them would ride for hours up in Grass Valley wandering the trails. The conversation, her admiration for her father, the sweet smell of long grass and pine trees. These memories came glimmering back and filled her chest with a long forgotten feeling of happiness. Anne forgot how much she loved trail riding; it had been so long since she was out enjoying simple pleasures.

The trail was an old game trail that wound its way up and over the descending shoulder of the ridge. As they carefully rode up the narrow track, Anne's spirits rose even more. She actually started to feel better. She looked at the cowboy on the steed ahead of her. His broad shoulders were relaxed, his torso swung lightly with the gait of the walking horse. His chiseled face came into view as he looked from side to side. She watched this man and wondered about him. He seemed to have a secret, something deep inside, some hidden truth. And he knew way too much about her. His masculine energy was admittedly somewhat attractive to her, though she would never consider a relationship with a cowboy. But she wanted to know more.

"So Nolan," she called ahead, "Tammy is really your sister?"

Nolan's back was to her, just ahead a horse length.

"Yes," he said loudly. "She stills lives back east. I see her every now and then."

"I'm afraid she and I didn't part on very friendly terms," said Anne.

Nolan was silent. He could feel her intentions. She was trying to make nice; to reconcile.

"I'm sure you know," Anne continued, "she was a pretty good trainer. I mean …our styles didn't quite match …there were some conflicts there. It was Simon's idea to bring her in."

Nolan nodded his head. "Simon was a good man."

"You knew Simon?" Anne asked, caught off-guard.

"Yeah, I met him when he was doing some training over at Marlboro Hall. He was one of the few who got it."

"Got what?"

"Got that horses aren't machines. That there is a natural dance, a connection that exists between the horse and the rider," Nolan said.

Anne had heard this before. Simon had lectured her endlessly about the need to lighten up, connect, and listen to the horse. She never really got it, not really. She thought she understood, but in the end her technique was to be the master, the horse the servant. It kept her safe, and kept her winning.

"Were you working at Marlboro?" Anne questioned.

"No, Tammy was. I was over at McPhadden's place, bringing up the colts, just for a year or so."

"How come we never met?" asked Anne. "We certainly traveled in the same circles."

"We have met," said Nolan. "I met you, once, at the Carter banquet."

Anne was silent as she struggled to remember. How embarrassing. The Carter banquet was a huge community-wide gathering that took place at the Carter Farms every Christmas season. The house was palatial and stood on 2,000 acres of prime Virginia countryside. She and Simon attended every year for a decade. She had met so many people.

"You don't remember, do you?" Nolan said without resentment.

"Can't say that I do. What year was that?"

"2004."

"Hmm," Anne thought back. "wasn't 2004 the year of that awful fire? Yes, it was. That fire that burned down the main barn at Carters."

"Yes, I remember it well," said Nolan with a sinking tone.

"That's right," continued Anne. "And all of the horses but one got out. Some guy, some hero, came out of nowhere, and saved all the horses."

"All but one," replied Nolan.

"And he was at that party, right?" Anne was searching her memory. "He was being honored by Jackson Carter …that was *you*!"

Nolan was silent. Anne could not see his face. If she could, she would have seen tears welling up in his eyes.

"That was you! You were the hero! I do remember. We talked for a moment before Carter pulled you up on stage. That was you? I'm impressed."

Nolan remained silent. He was thinking back to that horrible night. He got all of them out, he saved all of them, except one; he missed that one. He could still hear and feel the horse screaming as the fire engulfed the stalls of the barn. He could still feel it. His guilt and sorrow about that night was still with him. He certainly didn't feel like a hero. Yes, he saved the majority of the horses but missed that one, that very important one.

Anne noticed his silence. Was he just another silent type? She couldn't see his face, couldn't fathom his reaction. She could see his back, his tapered shoulders rising and falling slightly with each step of the horse.

"That was you ...right?" she asked directly.

Nolan took a deep breath and pushed the memories of his failure back down to the recesses of his mind. He needed to focus on this mission.

"Yes, that was me," he said.

"Well, then I do remember meeting you. Hmm, small world."

Anne was enjoying this puzzle, this piecing together of the past.

"If I recall, you left the area right after that," she stated.

"Yeah, it was time to move on. I went to Montana and worked with the Cheney Ranch operations; was there for five years," Nolan said.

"And Tammy? Where is she now?"

"Oh, she is still at Marlboro, working with the colts."

Just then the trail crested the ridge and came up on a long, flat, grassy spot that overlooked the southern end of the valley. The morning breeze was gusting up the slope behind them as the rising sun warmed the air. A bright blue sky showed no sign of weather, just another perfect clear day on the Nevada range. The two riders came up to the crest and stopped side by side. Anne was not quite getting the hang of being purely a passenger and she once again had Mickey a bit nervous. She relaxed and Mickey settled down.

"Listen," she said to Nolan as they came to a stop. "Sorry about my meltdown back there." Anne was not one to apologize and the words came out stiff and brittle. Nolan could sense her willingness to get along, fighting her natural-born stubbornness.

"It was uncalled for," she continued. "I …a …it's just been awhile since I have been on a horse …and I'm a bit nervous …I guess. Anyway …sorry."

Nolan looked at her. The new day sun cast a soft glow on her face. The breezy wind had her hair twisting around her forehead. Her eyes were earnest and sincere. There he saw a simple beauty, an honest smile, and a glimpse of friendship.

"Okay," he said. "Apology accepted." There was a silent agreement that settled between them; an understanding. The tension dropped and the horses settled even more. Jasper arched over and took a swipe at the green grass just below his feet. The two riders sat atop their horses studying the landscape below.

To the far right and miles down in the valley floor was Ruud's cattle operation: a series of building, barns and equipment sheds. The facilities were gleaming in the morning sunlight. To the far left was a flat horizon as the desert floor rose up and disappeared in the east. Straight ahead was a large valley filled with an assortment of scrub oak, sage brush, creosote bush, and farther away, down by the creek, were tamarisk, cottonwood, and juniper.

"Well," said Anne, as she looked at the vast expanse before them. "Where are we going to look first?" Nolan was eyeing the valley before them. Anne had no idea that he knew this place intimately.

"Well, the herd likes to stay over there along that short bluff line." He was pointing ahead and to the left. "Down there, closer to the water. But lately, the cattle have been running that part of the range so they have moved closer to the middle part over there." He was pointing out the lay of the land. "There is a run between that low swale and the creek. It's about a mile long. I think we should start there. If we don't find anything, then I am sure the herd would be across the creek up in that stand of rocks." Now he pointed to a rock-line outcrop several miles away, on the other side of the valley before them.

"Let me get a shot of this," Anne said as she pulled out her camera and snapped a few frames. "Ready when you are," she said professionally.

CHAPTER SIX

Samantha stood on the bottom wooden rail of the fence and watched in fascination as Rosie worked the horse in the arena. Sam was fascinated by the fact that the horse, named Vandi, wore no halter, had no lunge line, and was free to move about as he wanted. Rosie held a long stick with a short rope attached at the end and was encouraging Vandi along in low soothing tones that rang across the quiet of the morning. The sight of this "at liberty" work was mesmerizing to Samantha. She had never been around cowboys before. She had always existed in the world of English riding, where the way you looked was equally, if not more, important than the way you rode your horse.

The yellow mist had descended upon her mind. It was something that had been with her as far back as she could remember. It always came down on her when she was around the horses. She had named it the yellow mist because it seemed to swirl around the back of her head cradling her brain like two large misty hands, and it was yellow. Not a brilliant solid yellow, not crayon yellow. It was misty, shimmering, sometimes thick, sometimes wispy, but it had a yellow sheen. Yes, it was definitely yellow. It never frightened her, at least not anymore. It wasn't menacing. It was just something she noticed whenever she was around horses.

The yellow mist could tell her things …things about horses. She didn't know how, but she could tell what the horses were thinking, or feeling rather. Actually she couldn't tell if they were thoughts or feelings, she just could sense certain nuances from the horses that were around her. The horse in the arena in front of her was calm, happy, and secure, but his rear left hoof was causing him a little pain. How did she know

know this? Those communications were so natural to her now; so automatic. She had accepted this connection as part of being alive. Like the effortlessly beating heart, we don't ask why it keeps beating, it just does.

Samantha was happy that her mother was gone for the day. Her mother was becoming a problem, a controlling force of unreasonable requests. This unreasonable part of her mother was getting more and more apparent each day. It was very apparent in the way she was trying to train Sam for the Olympic Team. Sam was excited when her mother first proposed the idea and got caught up in the heady vainglory of imagining herself in the ring with the best horse in the world, taking first place. She didn't think like that anymore.

What changed? It was the yellow mist, her innate understanding of what horses were feeling, thinking, and experiencing. She could tell her schooling horses were mostly frightened and nervous. She could see her own horse was lonely and resentful for it. Of course these horse emotions were not the same as human emotions, but Sam didn't know how to interpret them other than through her human experience. She knew they were different, slower maybe, not as self-concerned as human emotions, but emotions just the same.

Sam felt this the first time she mounted a horse. Of course, with her parents' occupations, Sam had been on a horse since before she could remember. But the first time she consciously mounted her horse, the first time she took charge, the first time she had will, that is when she noticed it. Something slightly different in her perception, something ever so slight. It took years before she would name it the yellow mist. She ignored it really. For years it was no concern to the mind of a young, growing girl. Preoccupied with school and friends and horses, she didn't bother with the feeling, until one day about 18 months ago.

The first time she took notice of her special gift she was alone in the barn at her mother's farm. It was late at night. She had taken up a habit of sneaking out of the house and giving the horses a midnight snack, maybe an apple, maybe a carrot, a few flakes of hay. The horses were always on very strict diets dictated by her mother. These clandestine trips were Sam's way of mounting a small rebellion, plus making friends with the horses at the same time. It was their little secret, these midnight visits.

She was alone in the barn. There was a small nightlight that kept the gloom at a minimum and allowed her to move freely around without turning on the main lights. She had entered the barn and the yellow mist descended upon her mind as usual. She didn't really notice, as she was completely accustomed to it by now. The horses were nickering, and she felt a great joy. They were also getting used to these midnight visits and looked forward to their favorite human handing them a treat. She went from stall to stall handing out carrots she had taken from the house. Each horse gratefully accepted the forbidden snacks until she got to the horse named William Tell.

Peering into his stall Sam saw the horse near the back in the corner. His head was low and he looked like he was sleeping. The yellow mist jumped and swirled, still Sam took no notice. She was trying to coax William Tell to the front of his stall.

"Come on, silly," she said in a low voice. "Come and get your carrot."

The horse didn't move.

"William," she taunted in a sing-song voice, waving the carrot out into the stall.

Suddenly and with a start she heard a voice. Quickly she turned around to see who was there, her eyes wide with the fear of being caught, knowing her mother would be furious. But she was alone. Completely alone. Maybe just a bird, she thought.

She turned back to William Tell. The horse was now alert and watching her from the corner of the stall. Again she heard a voice, a muffled voice. She turned again to look down the barn alley but she knew she was alone. The voice continued. It sounded like it was under water, very remote. She listened intently. The sounds she heard amidst the midnight silence were the other horses crunching their carrots in a soft, steady cadence. There was a little breeze scraping some outside tree against the side of the barn. There was a humming noise coming from the nightlight. And there was a voice. But the voice—it was coming from within her—she was hearing it in her head. That was when she first took real notice of what would later be called the yellow mist.

Suddenly, the mist grew, enveloping her entire inner vision and, for a moment, a slight tick of time, it shimmered and exploded into a glimmering firework just in front of her eyes. She felt like she would be swallowed up by it, like she was losing herself. She was confused and frightened. That's when she heard it, a very clear voice coming out of the mist, rising up from her very self.

"Help me," she heard it loud and clear. It was William Tell. She looked at the horse in astonishment and saw a bright red glowing light emanating from his gut area. The light pulsating like a dying ember. She dropped the carrot from her hand and ran out of the barn unsure of what to do. She crept back into the house and went to her room, locked the door, turned on the light, and crawled into bed holding tight to her favorite doll. It was hours before she could will herself to close her eyes. She wanted nothing more than to go into her mother's room and crawl into bed with her, but that was out of the question. She was scared half to death and would have to deal with it on her own. Falling into a troubled sleep she dreamed of the yellow mist chasing her through dark hallways.

The next morning there was a buzz in the house. The barn manager was talking loudly on the house phone. Sam's mother was sitting at the table with a horrid look on her face. Something was wrong. Samantha came down and sat at the table.

"William Tell died last night," Anne told her daughter in that abrupt fashion that Sam had grown used to.

A vein of terror raced up Samantha's spine. "What? How?"

"We don't know, honey. I suspect a twisted gut, but the vet is on his way." Anne noticed the look on her daughter's face. "Are you okay, Sam? You look horrible."

Sam burst out in tears. She didn't know what to do. She wanted to tell her mother what had happened, but she didn't feel safe. She got up and ran from the table heading back to her bedroom.

"Sam!" her mother called out after her. Anne shook her head. She didn't think Sam was that attached to William Tell. After she dealt with the vet, she would go and try to comfort her daughter. First things first.

That was almost two years ago when Samantha was 10 years old. Over the ensuing months, Samantha had grown to trust the yellow mist. It no longer scared her. She had found no one to talk to about it and it remained a curiosity to her. Something that was just there, something she liked to test, to challenge.

"Samantha!" Rosie called out from the middle of the ring. "Come out here and give me a hand."

Samantha smiled and squatted through the fence, running out to where Rosie stood. Vandi stopped and faced the two. Samantha could tell he was curious and not frightened.

"You've lunged a horse before, right?" Rosie asked with a twinkle in her eye.

"You bet," said Sam. "But we use a rope."

Rosie laughed, "Well, sometimes I do too, but today we're working at liberty, without a rope."

Samantha liked this woman. She could see in her something wise, trustworthy, and authentic.

"Okay," said Sam. "But how does it work?"

Rosie smiled, "We use the horse's natural communication and instincts, and this stick to communicate and to apply pressure from a distance." She handed the stick to Samantha. It was about four feet long with a three-foot rope attached to the end. Sam took the stick and looked at it with curiosity. Holding it upright she looked at the rope and gave it a quick flick. Vandi's ears perked up. Sam smiled.

"Cool," said Sam. "But first let me check something." She handed the stick back to Rosie and slowly walked toward Vandi. Rosie watched the girl approach the horse confidently, say hello, and then walk to the back of the horse and lift up his rear left hoof to inspect it.

"There you are," she said gently, and Rosie watched as the girl picked out a small stone that had wedged itself between the shoe and the sole.

"No more pain," Samantha said to Vandi.

"What is it, dear?" Rosie called out.

"Oh, just a stone. No big deal," replied Sam.

Samantha let the foot down and patted the old horse on the hind quarters. As she walked back to center ring where Rosie stood, Vandi followed her at a distance. Rosie looked at the girl curiously. She noticed the horse had already attached.

"How did you know there was a stone in that hoof?" she asked.

"I could just tell," said Sam, a bit nervously. She had never talked about her gift to anyone and, astonishingly, no one had ever noticed before.

"Hmmm, well great. Let's get started." Rosie didn't press it. She knew much more than Sam could have ever guessed—about her gift, about the yellow mist, and about what it meant.

"Here, take the stick." She handed the stick back to Sam.

"Now, what we are doing here is trying to gain Vandi's trust. In order to do that, he has to feel safe, and in order to feel safe he needs a strong leader. You have to be the strong leader."

Sam frowned. She understood leadership as being forced and heavy handed. That was no way to get a horse to trust you. She was confused. Rosie picked up immediately on the girl's confusion.

"Don't worry, honey. We never force or hurt horses here …never."

Sam wondered how Rosie knew what she was thinking.

Rosie continued. "You know, horses naturally live in herds and in the herd there are leaders and followers. All we are trying to do here is get Vandi to understand that you are the leader. That's all. So the first thing you have to do is act like a leader. Not a human leader—you have to act like a horse leader."

Sam's spirits lifted a bit. She understood this. She knew what horses were thinking and feeling. She could measure their reactions to what stimulated them.

"Okay," she said. "What do I do?"

"Well, one of the things horse leaders do is to push the herd along. They lead from behind. So what I want you to do is make the horse move. Just walk behind him and wave your stick to get him to move. Then follow him and keep him moving. This will tell him that you are the leader."

Sam understood immediately, but something else happened when she went to engage the horse on this level. The yellow mist started to undulate, slowing and softly bouncing as Sam looked at Vandi. Vandi's ears perked up and the horse trotted up and stopped right in front of Sam. His head dropped and Sam wrapped her arms around his head.

"Oh, you are a good horsey," she cooed, as she stroked the top of his head.

Rosie stood there completely amazed. She had seen this before, a very long time ago.

Laughing out loud she proclaimed, "Well, I guess we can skip this part of the lesson."

Out on the range the sun was rising fast and the mid-morning was growing hot. Last night's moisture on the tall range grass was rapidly rising up, giving the air a mugginess that made any slight breeze a welcome friend. Anne pulled out her large-billed ball cap and slid it onto her head. She and Nolan had ridden down off the ridge and had made their way across a long, flat, open field. They were now traveling down a series of deep swales that crisscrossed the valley floor, all leading downward to the river bottom. Nolan knew the way. He didn't stop once. He kept moving forward, first left, and then another left, and then right. Anne could not tell exactly which direction they were going. Down in the swales the sun got lost in the shadows. It was a maze of gigantic proportions and Anne was a bit suspicious about Nolan's great confidence in his directions. The signs of cattle were everywhere. Large swaths of trampled and eaten grass dotted with cow pies were a constant reminder that this land was overrun with cattle.

After about an hour of this wandering, the two came across a small creek burbling at the bottom of a large swale that opened up a bit more of the sky. Nolan stopped. Anne and Mickey drew up beside him.

"Here we go," said Nolan. Then he dismounted, walked a few feet ahead, and bent to the ground studying the earth for clues. Anne followed him and swung her leg over the saddle, hitting the ground with a light thud. She noticed a pain sweeping up from her inner thighs into her lower back.

"Wow, I am out of shape," she thought to herself. She wouldn't let on to Nolan; not one bit.

Walking over to where the cowboy was hunched on the ground, Anne finally noticed what he was looking at—hoof prints, made by horses, lots of them.

"They were here for the water," said Nolan, looking up and away down the swale. "They went that way …about two days ago."

Anne was amused. "Didn't I see this in a movie?" she quipped.

Nolan looked at her, deadpan. "Let's get going. I think I know where they are," he said. "We should find the kill site somewhere between here and there."

A shiver went down Anne's spine. The thought of coming upon dead horses, especially out here, gave her a creepy realization of exactly what they were here for. She took out her camera and clicked off about 10 pictures of the swale, the creek, the hoof prints, and a couple of Nolan—great American tracker hot on the trail.

The two mounted up and Nolan noticed Anne wincing a bit.

"Butt hurt?" he asked nonchalantly.

Anne was disheartened. She always kept the upper hand in her relationships. To be saddle-sore already felt like a defeat, an embarrassment.

"No!" She lied while holding in her pain. "I'm fine. Let's go."

Nolan looked at her and smiled, turned his horse, and started down the swale following a small trail next to the creek. The water was flowing at a medium pace, obviously coming from some unknown spring up on Angel Ridge that was now behind them.

As they progressed down the swale, the air grew thick and still. Small gnats flew in great clouds, hovering above the creek. Here, the wide swale narrowed a bit and the water picked up speed. The hooves of the horse herd that ran this way had all but completely ripped up the grasses next to the trail. They moved in and out of the water, flattening out the creek banks and splashing mud over the tall grasses that grew up the steep bank on the far side. Anne tried to imagine the sight of these great horses running en masse down this small ravine; the sound of the pounding hooves, the heavy breathing, the flowing manes. If she could just get a picture of that, it would really be something.

Nolan kept the pace at a medium trot. Anne could sense his tension and wondered what lay ahead. It wasn't long before the true horror of their mission would be laid out bare before them. As they came around a bend, they noticed a new track entering the swale from the right. Nolan stopped to observe. It was an ATV—a four-wheeler. The narrow distance between the tire marks, and the width of the tires was distinctive.

"These tire tracks came after the horses passed here," Nolan pointed out. "They were chasing the herd on an ATV."

"Hunting from an ATV?" Anne asked with surprise.

"I don't think so," said Nolan. "They were most likely chasing the herd into some ambush. There may be a corral down the way or some other trap. The tracks are still a couple days old. They look like they were laid down the same day."

Anne's heart sank. Was she ready for this?

Nolan saw the look on her face. "This is going to be ugly," he said. "Are you okay?"

Anne wasn't one to wallow in self-pity. She girded her resolve; with fierce determination she was going on. Whatever lay ahead needed to be brought to the world. She was the one to do it.

"The reality of this is shocking," she said. "I'm okay. Let's go see what happened."

Nolan nodded his head and turned Jasper back to the trail and trotted off. Mickey followed and the tension grew.

The trail opened up into a small bowl-shaped area where two swales merged. The ravine coming in from the right was wide and flat and it was obvious that some kind of vehicle had been using the route to gain access to the creek water. The road that was there was a track of deep sand that had recently been churned up. As they rode into the area, Anne could feel a heaviness in the air; some foreboding. They were immediately hit with a stale, terrible smell of rotting flesh that was lingering in the stillness. Mickey and Jasper became nervous, nickering with some perception of unknown danger. It took Anne's mind a few moments to understand the picture that she saw before her.

Nothing looked out of place. There was the creek, the sound of water streaming in the creek bed. There was the dirt road coming into it from the right. There were signs of some commotion, as the earth was turned up, scratched away under tires and horse hooves, bare patches of earth where the vegetation had been torn away. Nothing particularly out of place, but that smell. It grew heavier as they walked into the bowl.

Anne looked down at one of the bare patches. She saw something curious. Horsehair. Great mats of horsehair covering the dirt. It looked like a horse wallow but the hair was stretched out into a trail. That's when her mind focused on the reality of what she was seeing.

"Oh, my God!" Anne gasped and held her hand to her mouth. A

wave of nausea swept through her gut.

Nolan was just ahead, silent, brooding, and stoic. He had already discerned the horror that had befallen his herd at this place. It was then that Anne noticed the flies, and the sound of the buzzing that the creek noise had been masking.

Below Mickey's legs was a patch of earth that had been colored black; the stain was matted with horsehair. As Mickey stepped down, a swarm of flies exploded from the stain. Mickey spooked and jumped hard to the left. Anne's riding experience paid off and somehow she stayed on, but the horse had a mind of its own. Rearing up, Mickey snorted and gave out a great mournful cry, his front legs pawing at the air. He came down hard, throwing Anne forward. She moved her head to the side just in time to avoid bashing her face on the back of Mickey's head. But now she was too far forward and in a very vulnerable position. Mickey ran backward, and with a small buck threw Anne over his shoulders and into the middle of the black, fly-covered stain. The flies swarmed up again and buzzed furiously around Anne's face and hair. She was on her hands and knees with her face inches above the ground when she realized what that black stain was. Blood, a large thick patch of dried horse blood, congealed on the ground, mixed with earth and horsehair. The flies reconfigured onto the bloodstain, the smell wafted up strong and hard, and Anne wretched, emptying her stomach onto the blood-soaked earth. Her entire nervous system was overloaded by the reality of her surroundings. Unable to control her nausea, she stood upright, turned away, and collapsed again to her knees, vomiting uncontrollably.

Nolan and Jasper were a few paces away. Mickey trotted over and stood nervously by Jasper's side. Nolan had tears in his eyes as he counted the bloody patches. Seven in all he figured. Seven horses were gunned down. Killed, right here, just two days ago. He figured the ATV tracks were laid down by the chaser, chasing the herd along the creek and into this bowl where men from above took their shots with ease. The road into the bowl served them well, as they could take the carcasses out and dispose of them with little notice. Nolan looked at the tracks from the remaining horses; they continued on down the creek. He knew that way led to another creek and to a complex series of ravines and small ridges. Depending upon which way the horses turned, they would either be at the river bottom or up in the safety of the ravines. He hoped for the ravines as the herd could be safe in there, at least for a while.

Nolan looked over at Anne. She was kneeling in the dirt, panting, mouth open and drool pouring to the ground.

"You okay?" he called out. He moved closer to her and threw down his canteen. It landed in front of her with a thud in a puff of dry dust.

Without saying anything, Anne wiped her face off with her sleeve and reached for the canteen. Her hair was a spider's nest; her backpack drooped heavily to one side as one strap had come undone. Her hands and arms were covered with blood-stained dirt matted with horsehair. The rest of her was covered in the fine grey dust that permeated the region. She removed the lid and took a swig, swished her mouth and spit out the water. She took another big gulp and swallowed. She was still panting as she closed the canteen and threw it on the ground in front of her. She removed her backpack and threw it alongside the canteen. Her shock and disgust were blooming rapidly into anger.

"I swear," she said between pants. "If I ever come across those bastards responsible for this, I will be scratching out eyes."

She rose to her knees. "Who does this? What kind of animal does this?" Her voice was getting louder. Nolan sat in compassion and watched her deal with her pain.

Anne got to her feet and staggered back a few steps. She had clearly taken a huge blow from the reality that surrounded her. She looked around at the bloodstains.

She was yelling now. "What kind of reprobate shit pile of a human being would do this?" She swung her hands around the bowl. "I don't understand …Who does this?" She looked up at Nolan who was silently pursing his lips. She noticed the tear streaks across his dust covered cheeks.

"This is not over!" she declared in a rage. She wagged a grime-covered finger at Nolan. "Oh, no! This is not over. I'm just getting started. Wait till I'm done with these bastards. They don't have a chance. This will be a national story with far-reaching consequences, trust me! Oh, they will be sorry they ever crossed me! Just you wait."

Her rant continued on as she walked into the creek and washed the filth from her hands, arms, and face. She continued to make vows of revenge, shout her disbelief and blindly rage. Nolan sat quietly and watched her. He felt a deep, profound sorrow for her having to see this. No one should ever see this. No one should suffer this kind of damage to the soul.

Samantha and Rosie were having a great time in the arena. Vandi was completely at ease with Samantha and was following her lead with no resistance at all. Rosie was completely amazed at the innate talent and intuition of this young girl. The two stood side by side as Rosie gave Samantha directions on what to do next. Samantha was happy to be with someone who understood the gentle nature of horses and didn't want to rule by force or coercion. The girl was radiant.

In her mind the yellow mist had changed somewhat. Samantha noticed it; a subtle difference. More focused, more concentrated, more honest. She could hold her stick out to the left and Vandi would respond immediately. To the right, and Vandi would turn and move at once; there was already a link between them. She could feel it, she could sense it, and somehow she knew that Vandi could too. She could see Vandi, actually see the horse in her mind. There seemed to her a clear voice connecting them. Not an audible voice, but silent words that passed through the space that separated them.

Slowly, as the lesson progressed, Sam realized the yellow mist was moving. It moved down her body, spreading from her head through her neck and settling around her heart, her chest, her rib cage. Sam felt a surge of elation as her awareness expanded around the whole arena. At that moment time slowed down. Sam watched the horse in front of her click down into a slow-motion dance, each moment separate, distinctive, and precious. Each second filled itself with an eternity of sensation and awareness and in that eternity she could tell exactly where each foot would fall, how each shoulder would move, and every flick of the tail. She smiled. There was no fear, only love for the horse in front of her. It was then she saw it; a yellow thread stretching out from her heart, moving toward the horse, a shimmering yellow, golden thread. She could sense this and suddenly as it reached over to the horse there was a small click, a jolt, a new sensation.

"Vandi, my sweet friend," she said.

"I am here," said the horse. "At your service."

The language was as close to words as thoughts come, but still not like spoken words. There was graciousness in the horse's communications that Sam had never experienced—ancient wisdom, long years of silent suffering, completely at ease with itself, completely connected to the earth, completely connected with the herd. Sam sensed that she was not just speaking with one horse but all of the horses, the herd, the earth horse, the horse spirit.

Sam heard the words "At your service. I am at your service!" She sensed the thread dancing between them, vibrating. In her mind she envisioned Vandi in a dignified trot with head high and tail straight up, big and proud. She wasn't surprised to see the horse collect himself and follow her direction. She was watching him going to the straight side of the arena; he was showing off for her.

Of course, Rosie was watching all of this as well. Although she could not see the yellow mist, or the golden thread, Rosie knew far more about this than almost anybody …almost. She was watching the girl's face and could see her inward focus. She was watching the horse and how he responded to this young girl that he had never seen before. Oh, what a joy! Oh, what a marvel! Rosie had a feeling about this girl the first time they had met. She was glad to know she could still count on her intuition, although this was much bigger than she even imagined.

"Ask him to shorten his stride into piaffe," Rosie said very quietly.

Sam heard the words and communicated the idea to Vandi. Vandi was happy to show his moves. His big, proud, collected trot slowed in stride, slower, slower, until he was barely moving forward at all. Rosie was smiling.

"Now ask him to circle right," she said in a whisper.

Sam was right there. She thought the words and Vandi started to the right.

Rosie giggled. Sam giggled. All three of these earthbound creatures were connected and just playing, dancing, living in the moment.

"Sam?" said Rosie.

Sam looked up at her new friend, "Yeah?"

"Look at your stick."

Sam looked down and noticed that the stick was resting on the ground. She was holding one end but the other was pointed down.

Rosie smiled at the girl. "You don't need that old stick, do you?" Sam looked back out at the horse still in the piaffe.

"No, I guess not," she said with a sense of utter joy and wonder.

"What else can he do?" asked Rosie in a low calm voice. She was completely at ease with this girl's ability, like she had seen it before.

Sam didn't think twice. She trusted Rosie like no one before. There was an ease just being with her. Sam moved the horse out of piaffe and into a full, extended trot. Vandi was moving, big and impressive, in his two-beat gait across the arena. The yellow thread danced and vibrated, shimmering in Sam's mind. At the corner, she asked for the canter and Vandi transitioned flawlessly, naturally into the three-beat gait, halfway across the arena, a flying change, then another, then another. Rosie was engrossed in the moment; there was nothing else except this girl and this horse and an overwhelming sense of pride and joy. Sam was just as engrossed, feeling more alive than she ever had, playing with the gift that was given to her, like a symphony conductor, exploring the mind of the horse, the nuance, and feeling his joy. The moment was a crescendo, cascading into higher and higher energy. The yellow mist was as big as Samantha had ever seen it; the moment was an eternal bliss as big and wide as the universe itself.

Suddenly, the whole thing came crashing down. Sam saw a huge black shadow fall heavy and quick between her and Vandi. The shock sent her falling backwards. The yellow thread was broken into shards that splayed across her inner vision and she heard a great, deep, booming, dark sound. The abruptness of the separation also rang through Vandi's inner core. He jumped and bucked and kicked wildly, letting out a long sour neighing cry.

Rosie rushed to the girl's side. She took hold of her arm and lifted her gently. Her eyes were wide with fear and surprise. The girl's face was white, pale, and glistening with cold sweat.

"Oh, Sam! Sam! Are you all right?" There was an immediate urgency in Rosie's voice.

Sam burst into tears. She was frightened beyond anything she had ever felt.

"What's happening?" she cried. "What's happening?"

Rosie wrapped her arms around the girl and held her tightly. "It's okay, Sam. It's okay. I'm here with you. You are going to be okay."

She was comforting the girl as best she could, inside she was praying for light to return, to surround them, to protect them. Something bad had happened and Sam was in a very vulnerable place. Rosie should have known this; she should have protected the girl. She was careless and caught up in the moment. She would have to be more careful from now on.

"Oh, baby girl, I'm so sorry. It's going to be okay," she whispered in the girl's ear.

Across the ridge and out in the valley, Nolan and Anne were listening to a sound coming up the swale. Small and muffled, rapidly popping, the sound was unmistakable—gunfire.

"That sounds like several rifles," said Nolan warily.

"What do we do now?" asked Anne. She was cleaned up, had completely photographed the scene, and was back on her horse.

"The best thing to do would be to follow that road. I'm guessing it will lead us to the next kill site," Nolan surmised. "They will want to dispose of the dead animals to cover their tracks as much as they can and they will need to get a large truck in there for that."

"Yeah, but won't they see us?" asked Anne.

"If they do, it will surely be a fight."

Anne thought for a moment. "I need to get a photo of the truck. That will seal the deal. We should risk the road."

"Too dangerous. These guys are playing for keeps," said Nolan.

"What are they going to do? Shoot me?" Anne said naively.

Nolan looked at her. The look on his face was enough to convince Anne that, indeed, if they were caught they would probably be killed. The stakes were too high.

Anne's eyes widened. "Really? Holy shit!"

"Welcome to the wild, wild west," said Nolan with a smirk. He was silent for a moment. "Okay, there are two objectives here. First, stop these guys from killing any more horses. Second, get a photograph that will be good enough to convince a jury of their crimes. One thing leads to another; we must get to the next kill site. The safest way is to follow the creek, down the swale."

"Okay," said Anne, not too convinced. "You have a pistol, right?"

"Yes," said Nolan, patting the holster on his hip.

"Let's hope we don't need it."

The two galloped full throttle into the ravine leaving the bowl behind. The creek was narrow and deep and it was running faster here. The trail was wide enough for two horses abreast. They were about twelve feet below ground level and could not be seen by anyone for miles around.

After riding for a mile or so, the ravine was intersected by another. Nolan stopped Jasper and climbed down for a look at the ground. He was looking at the hoof prints from the herd.

"The herd followed the creek. Let's keep going that way," he said, then looked up. "First let me climb up top and see if I can spot anything."

Anne dismounted as well. Her aching backside was getting worse, but she had too many other things to worry about just now. She took the reins from Nolan and led the horses over to the creek for a drink and a quick munch of sweet grass. Nolan scrambled up the steep embankment to get a better look at their position. The rocks and gravel chattered down the side of the hill as he pushed his way up through the dust. As Anne watched him climbing up the hill, she realized her ill feelings toward him had all but vanished. Things had changed after the incident at the kill site. Few men had seen her in so awkward and vulnerable a condition; yet it hadn't seemed to faze Nolan. And she had to trust him now—she had no choice. She watched him disappear over the hilltop.

Up on top, Nolan hunched behind some large sagebrush. He was situated on a small rise that put him slightly above the surrounding land, giving him a very good perch to take in the view. He heard no more gunfire since before they started riding again. Scanning the horizon, he looked for any signs of Ruud's men. It was midday; the sun was hot in the cloudless sky, beating down from directly overhead. He pulled his canteen around and opened the lid for a drink. With a stab of anxiety, he noticed the dirty bloodstains left by Anne's small hands. He brushed off the dirt and blood and took a drink. She had such delicate hands.

"Focus, man. Focus," he chastised himself. For a horse rider her hands were small and delicate with almost perfect skin. Her brusque demeanor, her foul mouth, her constant need to be in control irritated him endlessly. But maybe they could at least be friends after all this was over. Until then he needed to keep his head in the game. There was a very real danger of not having any future at all, let alone one in which he and Anne could be friends. He didn't want to scare Anne with the truth, but he couldn't turn back now. The herd needed his help more than ever. He was not going to let them down. The world depended on it.

Nolan continued his surveillance. He needed to find the herd. He could sense their presence somewhere up ahead a few miles. He had a connection, his own "yellow mist," although he didn't call it that. He could feel the herd, the angst and confusion, the fear. The herd was definitely being pursued at this very moment, but where?

A small pop rang out, coming from his far right. He swung around and far off saw the glint of light reflecting off the windshield of a large flatbed truck. The truck was moving slowly across the range, the dust from the dirt road billowing behind. It was coming up from the river bottom onto the plain and was now in full view. It was headed toward the bowl. A sense of dread came over Nolan. Simultaneously, he heard the faint buzz coming from his left, far away, down the creek toward the herd. It was the sound of an ATV, followed by more gunfire popping. His blood ran cold. About a mile down the creek he could see dust billowing up from the ravine, moving toward them. Ruud's men were doing it again. They were running the herd towards the bowl to another kill.

He looked down at Anne casually tying her backpack to her saddle. Down the creek, the billowing dust raised by 150 stampeding wild horses would soon be upon her. With lightning speed he skidded down the hill, the loose soil breaking free as he slid barely under control.

"Mount up! NOW!" He was screaming with an urgency that jarred Anne's already fragile nerves. She looked up at him sliding down the hill, screaming at her to get on her horse. She couldn't comprehend. She just stood there in a daze.

"Mount up! STAMPEDE!" he shouted again.

"Stampede?" Anne's mind barely registered what he was saying. It was then that she noticed a strange vibration beneath her feet. The two horses suddenly became agitated and pulled on the reins. She clenched them tightly as she began to register the danger they were in. Nolan was at the bottom now, running full speed in her direction.

"Get on your horse! Now!" he yelled.

Anne finally understood. She quickly went to put her foot in the stirrup, but her foot missed and plopped to the ground. Her leg was stiff and incompliant; that's when she noticed the pain.

"Come on!" Nolan was 20 feet away, running straight for her. The vibration was getting stronger by the second. From the corner of her eye she noticed the creek water was rippling, shaking.

She tried for the stirrup again, but her stiff leg ached as she forced it up. Her foot slid into the stirrup but at that angle her disabled thigh didn't have the power to push her body up to the saddle. She hopped a couple of times and tried to push up to the horse. The fourth time she made it. Standing sideways with one foot in the stirrup, she leaned forward and swung her leg over the horse. The pain was blinding. Her aching torso, buttocks, and upper legs were stiffened to the point of almost being locked up.

Nolan, on the other hand, was in top shape. With one quick jump he was up and over Jasper's back and in the saddle. He grabbed the reins and was ready to take off.

"We gotta move!" he yelled. "Now!" The urgency in his voice was frightening. The ground was shaking more violently now and suddenly, several hundred yards down the ravine, Anne saw the earth moving. The danger now very real and present; she completely understood. The herd was stampeding up the ravine directly toward them. They had 30 seconds maximum to get out of the way or be swept up and run over by the wild horses. The noise was deafening.

Both Jasper and Mickey were startled and ready to bolt. Anne seated herself and Mickey ran backward a few steps. Anne was ready for it this time, and despite her stiff and weakened muscles, was firmly atop his back. The wild horses were nearing, the dust and dirt flying up from beneath their stomping hooves.

"Come on!" yelled Nolan, as he turned Jasper toward the intersecting ravine. It was the only way to safety— a quick shelter from the raging stampede. The horses were nearer now, the sound of their labored breathing audible over the thundering earth. Mickey spun around. Anne kicked hard, but the horse was paralyzed, unresponsive. He reared up; Anne hung on. The herd was seconds away now; an angry tidal wave of pounding hooves, flying manes, and massive bodies.

Suddenly, Anne felt Nolan's strong hand wrap around the back of her shirt and vest. With a forceful jerk, she was pulled off her mount and into Nolan's lap. Jasper exploded into a full gallop heading directly into the side ravine. Just as Jasper's tail disappeared into the crevice, the stampeding herd swallowed up the ground. Mickey was overcome. He toppled over and rolled into the creek. Scrambling to stand again, he was swept into the running horses. The pounding of the thundering legs, the horse screams, and the water being splashed out of its bed— all came together in a terrifying tornado that raced by with surprising speed. In seconds the herd had passed and the noise subsided. Then, like an afterthought, an ATV screamed by full speed, its tires flinging up the newly overturned ground in a great brown and grey rooster tail. Its rider, dressed in black with a grey ball cap, was too busy to notice Nolan watching from within the side ravine.

It was all over in seconds. Anne was lying across Nolan's lap. Jasper was tramping nervously. Nolan sat solid, steady, and alert. He still had one hand holding the back of Anne's vest, his fist tightly clenching the soiled fabric.

"Okay, let me down," Anne said with a slight edge.

Nolan let loose his grip on Anne's collar as she slid off the horse and onto the ground. Her legs were shaking so badly she was forced to hold onto the saddle for stability. Her breathing was heavy and she felt sick. The air was thick with dust and the hot sun was pounding on the back of her head. She wasn't about to let Nolan see her break down again so she forced her nausea aside, and willed her natural fear into the back of her mind. Fixating instead on her flaring anger, she focused on the men that were chasing those horses.

"We need to move," she said. "We need to get down there to the bowl before it's too late." Nolan looked down at her. She was a complete mess, but there was something that struck him, an inner strength, all but hidden beneath her disheveled exterior.

"Are you alright?" he asked.

Anne looked up at him. "You're asking me if I'm alright?" I'm damn lucky to be alive, I'd say. But that doesn't matter right now. Right now we have to get back to the bowl and see if we can stop the next slaughter. We have to move!"

Nolan knew the horses were still okay. Something had stayed the slaughter. He wasn't sure what it was, but he knew they had some extra time. He wanted to be very careful. The stakes were high and Ruud's men were playing for keeps.

"Get on," Nolan said. "We'll have to get out of this ravine. We aren't safe down here by the creek. We'll have to risk being spotted; keep your eyes open."

Anne climbed up onto the back of the horse. Her entire body now ached with stabbing pains from her thighs up to her shoulders, but she wasn't going to complain. Not in front of this cowboy. She slipped her hands around his waist as Nolan turned Jasper around and moved down toward the creek, then turned right and headed back toward the bowl. There was an easy bank just ahead where they could climb out of the swale and come in from the top.

CHAPTER SEVEN

The two-way radio crackled in Richard Striker's hands. He was listening to a voice on the other end describing something that gave him heartburn, or worse. The signal was weak and he was having trouble understanding what he was hearing. He held the small device to his face and pressed the button on the side.

"Say again?" His voice was gruff and growled with authority.

The small speaker crackled again and a thin voice came forth from between the static.

"We have a ...situation. You should come out here ...now." Crackle, crackle.

Striker was perturbed. "Can you describe your ...situation?" he enunciated slowly into the radio.

"We have visitors," said the speaker. Crackle, crackle.

That's what he thought he heard the first time. This particular operation called for complete discretion on the radio or else he would have asked for details.

"On my way," he said. "Keep everything intact until I get there."

He was already in his truck that was parked outside the small office he kept at Ruud's ranch. He threw the radio onto the passenger seat, turned the key and gunned the engine, heading for the dirt road that would take him out to Tanner Creek, where his operation was underway.

His truck bumped along the uneven dirt track. In a few weeks the graders would be out and smooth out these back roads but until then the ruts and tracks made over the winter months were like waiting obstacles testing even the most experienced drivers. And Striker was experienced. He had been out on this range thousands of times. He knew every back road, every swale and hill, every creek and spring, almost down to the blades of grass. For the last 15 years he had roamed these hills tending to the business of raising cattle. He was Ruud's man on the ground. He was the head honcho, the big cheese, and he was tasked with getting the horses off the land, a distasteful but necessary task. He was managing the horse removal operation from the safe distance of the main office. He really had no stomach for killing horses, but now he would have to go out and get directly involved. Visitors—this could be disastrous. Killing wild horses was a federal crime. He would have to do whatever it took to protect the ranch and Senator Ruud from scandal. A great billow of dust rose up from the dry earth as he moved as quickly as he could towards Tanner Creek.

Nolan and Anne were out of the swale, riding tandem on Jasper, moving up the creek toward the bowl. Nolan had no idea what they might find but he knew there was no killing going on. He had a deep connection with the herd. Horses were intuitive creatures and when they were in their natural environment, living within a herd, they were as one. The spirit of the herd was connected deeply to men like Nolan. He could sense their whereabouts, their fear, or their peace. Nolan knew.

For now he was glad that something had stopped the slaughter, but he knew it wouldn't last. They had to get close enough to get a look at what was going on. This was the only thing he could think of. After that, he was fresh out of ideas.

Anne was quiet, sitting behind him. He could feel her body pressed against his back. He could feel her energy. She was in pain and she was very angry. He knew the anger would sustain her for a while, but when it wore off she would need something else to keep her going.

"Anne?" he whispered.

"Yeah?" her voice came from behind his head.

"I don't know what we are going to find up here. This could go bad pretty quick."

Anne was silent. She was thinking about Samantha.

"Look," Nolan said, "maybe you should get off here and let me go up and take a look. You didn't sign up for this. I don't want anything bad to happen to you."

His voice was sincere and genuine. Anne appreciated his honesty. She was aching and could use a rest, but the thought of him leaving her alone was frightening. She could sense the danger. She knew that these men, whoever they were, would have great motivation to protect themselves. She understood the risk of getting discovered and caught.

"Maybe you're right," she said. "Let me stay back with Jasper and you go in and take a look. Then we can go from there. I am not sure what we can do at this point. Mickey ran off with my camera ..." She stopped mid-sentence. The thought came to her like a bolt of electricity.

"Shit!" she hissed. "Mickey is with the herd. Those guys have my camera and all of my stuff; they know we're here!" Suddenly she felt completely exposed, sitting out on the range in plain sight. The scrub oak and sage gave some protection, but they were exposed.

Nolan had already figured Mickey was discovered. He didn't know what to do about it. They should probably turn back and try to get some authority involved, but he was afraid by the time anyone got out here the damage would be done and the evidence destroyed. He couldn't leave now. He had to save this herd—this special herd of those that remembered. He couldn't risk leaving them alone. He stopped Jasper aside a large creosote bush.

"Get down," he told Anne. Anne slid off the back of the horse, her legs burning as she touched the ground. Nolan dismounted and handed Anne the reins.

"Okay, the bowl is just over that rise there," he signaled with a shake of his head. "Let me sneak over and take a peek and see what's going on. You stay here and if anything should happen—"

"Like what?" Anne interrupted, her voice plainly agitated.

"If anything should happen," Nolan continued, "you take Jasper and get back to Angel Ridge. You know the way, right?"

"What do you think might happen, Nolan?" Anne asked directly.

"I don't know," said Nolan. "These guys are killing horses. That's a federal crime. Now that they know someone has discovered them, they may get desperate."

"Well, then let's get out of here. Come on, let's go," said Anne.

"I can't," Nolan stated flatly.

"You can't or you won't?" Anne asked.

"I can't. It is that simple. There is too much at stake here."

Anne didn't understand. "Is it worth getting killed over? These horses?"

"I wish I could explain it all to you," Nolan protested. "If we get out of here alive, I will try to help you understand. But right now we don't have time. Just know that this is something that I must do. I don't have a choice. I cannot allow those horses to die; I just can't."

Anne saw desperation in Nolan's eyes. It was oddly disarming. She was speechless.

Finally, she said, "Okay, do what you must. I will stay here and wait. If something happens to you, I will go for help."

"Okay," said Nolan. "Do you know the way back?"

"Yes," said Anne convincingly. "That way." She pointed north to where the top of Angel Ridge could barely be seen over the plain.

"Good," said Nolan. "Now wait here. I'll be back in a few minutes. I want to see what is going on, how many men there are, that kind of thing."

"Just your average reconnaissance," Anne smiled wearily.

Nolan looked into her eyes and saw Anne's barriers dropping. She was starting to let him in. As he turned to leave, she grabbed his arm. "Please be careful," she said almost tenderly. "Come back."

With that Nolan turned and moved quickly toward the direction of the bowl.

Back at Angel Ridge, Samantha was sitting with Rosie and Joe in the main house. Sam had a worried look on her face and inside she felt a great weight of black heaviness. She never felt that before, she had no experience to match it to. It was something that hit her hard and fast, something scary, something evil. Rosie looked at the girl with sad eyes. She felt responsible.

Joe sat back and sank deep into himself. In a deep meditation he plumbed the depths of the otherworld, the world where Sam had connected with the horse Vandi. He was still and silent while his breath rattled and swooshed. Sam sat and watched him, not really knowing what else to do. He would breathe in very deep and fast, drawing the air in through his nose, causing the mucus to rattle loudly inside his sinus cavities. Then he would hold his breath for a second and slowly release the breath through his vocal chords making sounds, sometimes groaning, sometimes shrill. He had been doing this for about 10 minutes when he finally connected to Sam.

He saw the yellow mist; he saw the magnificent colors twisting around in a helix strand of golden shimmering light crystals. He recognized the patterns immediately. He now knew Sam's secret. This would have to be handled very delicately. In his mind's eye, Joe could see the strand connected at the girl's heart, the other end stretched out toward the distance, fading into infinity. Joe understood, but it was troubling to his probing mind. Although he remained completely at peace, he knew instinctively that he should follow the strand and see what was connected to the other end.

With another deep rattling intake of breath, Joe's lungs expanded into his giant barrel chest. His eyes closed, his head tilted slightly back. Rosie looked at Sam and winked, trying to comfort the girl. Inside the mind, Joe swiftly followed the golden-yellow strand of light. In here, in this place, the light was real, it was tangible. In the outer world these were all merely ideas and ideals. But in the deep expansive matrix of the soul, this was as real as it gets. Joe knew how to navigate this world. He knew many things that would never be told.

As the yellow strand continued on, Joe sped up. His imagination guided the way; he was as free as his mind in this place. Only his own self-limitations could slow him down. Only the strongest of minds with years of practice could move in this world, the mystic otherworld of the horse angels. Joe followed the strand and sensed he was near the end. He was very far away. It was a cold and dark part of the universe. He felt strange and alone. Again, Joe remained completely at peace, detached from the harsh emotions that surrounded this place he found himself in.

At that moment Joe saw the end of the strand, wrapped around a large amorphous cloud of darkness. The end of the strand had split into several smaller strands and was connected into this silent mass of heavy darkness. Joe looked on. It appeared to him slowly …what the strands were connected to. He looked into the darkness, into the blacker hole and saw the outline of seven forms. He couldn't tell at first what they were, but in his heart he knew they were horses. Then clearly the forms came into view. Seven dead horses stuck together in a dark massive ball. Splinters of the yellow strand were connected to all seven horses. In his mind's eye and using his imagination, Joe reached out and took hold of the yellow strand just before where it split into seven and gave it a quick yank. Immediately, in a flash, he was back with Samantha.

Samantha felt it. A shock of energy shot through the middle of her body just below her neck. There was a quickly growing warmth that rose, flashed, and subsided. Sam shuddered uncontrollably; she looked over at Joe and he opened his eyes. Sam suddenly felt better; the heavy darkness lifted from her soul and she felt lighter. A sense of peace came over her. Joe smiled his big goofy grin. Sam smiled too, barely. She was utterly confused about what just happened.

Rosie noticed the difference right away.

"Oh, thank God," she whispered. "Joe what happened?"

Joe was looking at Sam. "Do you feel better?" he asked gently.

"Yes," Sam said quietly, suddenly was missing her mother terribly.

"Sam, I have a few things to tell you," said Joe as he watched for the girl's reaction.

Richard Striker was nearing the bowl. Because of the spring road conditions, it took him almost 22 minutes to get to the site. On the way, he instructed Raymond Bulling, his right-hand man, to find the "visitors" as fast as possible. They had to talk in code because they had no idea who else might be listening in on their open-band radios. Soon Striker would be able to get details in person.

Bulling eyed the situation at the bowl carefully. The herd was trapped and huddled together at the far end. Several cowboys stood guard at strategic points keeping the herd together. The steep bank at the back of the bowl made escape impossible, although several horses tried and failed. A large flatbed truck along with two cowboys blocked the entrance of the swale where the creek waters flowed into the bowl. An ATV and three guards blocked the ravine where the creek flowed out of the bowl. Bulling and two more sat on another truck at the road access. They had the herd surrounded and would have been finished with the grisly job by now had not the stray horse shown up; the stray horse with the saddle.

The herd—around 50 horses in all—was restless, frantic, and wide-eyed. They ran in small circles, breathing hard, stamping the ground, glistening with lather. Raymond Bulling had Mickey tied to the bumper of his truck and was going through Anne's backpack which was found tied to the saddle. He already sent three of his men back up the creek to look for tracks and any signs of where the rider of this stray horse was. They had to find out what was going on before they could continue their operation.

"What's this?" said Bulling, as he pulled out Anne's digital camera. After studying it for a few seconds, he flipped on the power and pushed the view button. The small screen on the back of the camera blinked to life. Using the scroll keys, Bulling was privy to everything Anne and Nolan had seen. The blood stains, the piles of matted horsehair, the obvious signs of struggle shown by the hoof prints, the tire tracks of the getaway vehicles. There was nothing that would hold up in a court of law, but it was damning just the same.

Bulling looked up and scanned the horizon wondering who might be out there watching. He clicked off the camera and emptied out the rest of the bag, obviously belonging to a woman—hair band, lip gloss, hair brush, and a few articles of clothing. Bulling was puzzled.

"Seems we may have one of those crazy horse protector ladies on our hands," he said out loud. The two men that were with him looked on, more out of boredom than curiosity.

That's when Striker pulled up. His green Ford truck slid to a stop just in front of Bulling. A thick cloud of fine dust pushed its way forward and covered the men standing there. Striker jumped out of his truck and immediately interrogated Bulling, getting briefed, almost military style. He quickly learned that the operation was on track. They had found the herd down the creek by the grove of cottonwoods. Soon after, they positioned the men in the bowl as planned and ran most of the horses up the creek with gunfire and the ATV. Everything was going according to plan, but when the herd entered the bowl, there was a horse in their midst, this horse with the saddle. No one saw anybody, or any sign of trespassers. Bulling said he sent three men out looking for signs but so far nothing had turned up. Then Bulling handed Striker the camera.

"I found this on the horse," he said.

Striker took the camera and looked at it. He wasn't as tech savvy as Bulling. "Do you know how to work this?" he asked in his gruff and condescending tone.

Bulling looked at him, an insubordinate look in his eyes. "Of course I do." He took the camera from Striker's hands and turned it on. He pushed the right buttons and handed it back to his boss. "Push those arrows to go through the pictures," he said in a monotone.

Striker did as he was instructed and as he scrolled through the pictures his blood ran cold. He knew that whoever this person was, they knew what had happened here a few days ago. If this story ever got out, he would be the one taking the fall even though his orders came directly from the senator's office. There was no way the good ol' senator was going to ever fess up about knowing anything regarding the killing of wild horses at his ranch. No, Striker was on the hook and he knew what would happen if anyone on the outside ever found out what was going on out here. A wave of panic ran through his body. He turned away from Bulling and took a deep breath. He had to maintain control. He had to get on top of this situation no matter what. No matter who he had to squash in the process.

"Okay," said Striker as he turned to face Bulling. "Get those guys on the radio! I want a report now! Have they found anything?" He stalked over to the ATV and shooed away the cowboy sitting on it. He held up his radio and yelled across to Bulling.

"Give me the word when it comes in, I'm going down to take a look myself." He got on the ATV and fired it up. With a flick of his wrist he disappeared into the ravine.

Bulling's radio crackled, a voice came booming out from the speaker, "We haven't found anything yet," the voice said.

Bulling held the radio up to his face, "Well, you better look busy cause the boss is on his way. Over." He set the radio down and picked up the camera, switched it on, and went through the pictures again, one by one.

Anne sat on a flat rock holding Jasper by the reins. The hot sun beat down even though she was semi-shaded next to a large sage bush.

There was an eerie silence in the air and her nerves were on end. Straining to listen for any clue, the land seemed to pulsate with silence; not even the bugs were out. Then she heard some low rumbling in the far-off distance. Time was moving very slowly. She resisted the urge to follow Nolan although she would have felt much safer with him. He had been gone for about 15 minutes and she was expecting him back any moment.

Through the silence she thought she heard something. It started faintly, but soon grew into an all-too-recognizable, low-pitched whining buzz—an ATV. She heard it clearly now. Coming from below, about 100 yards in front of her and deep in the swale, an ATV was moving slowly down the creek.

"They're looking for us," she thought with a horrid sense of vulnerability. She wanted desperately to be invisible. Standing up from her rock she pulled Jasper further into the sage bushes, trying to get out of sight. The branches and tough needles of the large shrub scratched and poked her exposed arms. She grimaced and backed her way into the middle of a large bushy stand. The horse followed, but she still didn't feel safe …and with good reason. Plain to see and completely noticeable in the otherwise unbroken earth, Jasper's hoof prints would lead anybody looking directly to her.

"Shit!" she said out loud. She looked through the bushes and over the horizon for any signs of Nolan. There was no one. It had been 15 minutes by now, at least. She listened hard again and heard the ATV sounding a bit farther away.

Down in the swale, Striker was slowly moving through the creek bed looking for anything that would help him find the woman who rode the stray horse. The three men who went before him were nowhere to be found. He was watching the ripped-up earth where the herd ran through. There were two sets of tracks: one leading up the creek from two days earlier, and the fresh set coming down the creek laid down about an hour ago.

He kept the ATV moving at a slow, steady speed. Suddenly his radio crackled.

"I think we found something." The voice was clear and the signal strong.

"Go ahead," said Striker into the handheld.

"I see a set of tracks leading off from the main stampede line. It looks like one horse, shod …not part of the herd." Striker's spirits rose slightly.

"Where are you?" he asked.

The radio crackled again, "At a cross ravine about a mile down the creek." Striker twisted the accelerator and zoomed up to speed, the sound echoing off the walls of the ravine and up into the surrounding area.

Anne froze when she heard the noise. The ATV was on the move. They found something. They found the hoof prints. Her spine quivered as she crouched low into the brush. Her aching thighs made it hard to slouch down, but her fear overrode the pain. Jasper was standing next to her as big as a road sign. She stood up. This was ridiculous! She wasn't going to be able to hide, not with this horse standing next to her and the trail leading right up from the swale.

"Shit!" she said again out loud. Her mind was whirling with panic and fear. She was consumed with the thought that any minute an army of cowboys would be coming up the hill with guns blazing. She waited. The sounds of the ATV faded into the silence.

Striker pulled the ATV up to where his men were waiting. The creek was running faster here and the trail was narrow. On the left, a cross ravine opened up where a small trickle of water came out and joined the main creek. He knew this place. This ravine was inaccessible from the top due to its steep sides. It ended about a quarter mile around a bend where a small spring generally ran until about mid-June. Striker jumped off the ATV and walked into the ravine. Sure enough, a horse with shoes had been there recently.

"That's it," he said. "Now the question is, was this the horse we found? Or are there two of them?"

"No one's gonna be out here alone," said one of the cowboys. "Can't see no footprints either …no one got off this horse."

Striker shook his head in disagreement. "What do you call those?"

he said as he pointed to Anne's footprints. Sure, they were hard to spot in the trampled dirt, but they were there to the trained eye. "Looks like a woman's prints …small …short stride." The others looked on, amazed they could now see the boot prints where before they couldn't.

Striker turned and followed the horse tracks out of the ravine back to the creek. Now he could clearly see the tracks. A walking horse moved through after the herd. It was clear to see from this angle.

Striker smiled. "Bingo!" he said. "Follow me!" he commanded the three men. He moved quickly to the ATV, fired it up, and drove away, following the hoof prints. The men followed as best as they could on foot.

Anne stood motionless surrounded by the sagebrush. She couldn't decide what to do. She could try to find Nolan and risk blowing his cover. She could stay where she was and risk being caught herself. Or she could get on the horse and try to get away. The last thought stuck in her mind, but she knew she couldn't take Nolan's horse and leave Nolan out here alone. She heard the ATV again, buzzing with furry. She knew it was just a matter of time until someone came over the hill and spotted her. Without really thinking about it, she led Jasper out to the clearing. She slipped her fingers under the saddlebag and released it into her hands. With a swift smack and a yelp she sent Jasper running off toward Angel Ridge. It was enough of a scare that the horse kept running up and over the hill until he was safely out of site. This might throw the men off the trail for a while until she could find Nolan. She snatched a fallen branch and covered her footprints as she fell back into the bush, just as she heard the ATV coming over the hill at full speed following Jasper's trail. Anne sank as low as she could into the brush, which was dense enough to give good cover. The ATV came booming up and stopped right in front of her. She could see the tires of the vehicle as the dust came floating up and over them. She couldn't see the man on the ATV.

Striker squinted at the ground, trying to read the prints. There had obviously been a horse here, but something wasn't quite right. Clearly the horse had gone over the hill. He gunned the engine and sped away following the prints. Just feet away, Anne let out her breath as she wriggled out from under the bush.

She stood and looked up the hill to where the ATV disappeared. She had to find Nolan. He needed to know they had been found out. Grabbing the saddlebag, she hoisted it over her shoulder and looked to where Nolan had gone. There was still no sign of him. Not wanting to leave any more tracks, Anne leaped up on a nearby rock and surveyed the land for a way out, a way that would not involve walking through the sand.

At that very moment, she realized her mistake. A large chunk of the rock right in front of her left foot exploded into shards. A millisecond later she heard the sound of a gunshot coming from the far left. Anne's heart leapt to her throat, then a surreal time shift as her mind whirled in an attempt to surmise what was happening.

"Hold it right there, lady!" a voice yelled. Anne heard the words but they came to her mind in a slow-motion garble of disconnected syllables. She turned toward the sound and saw three men running up the trail, one with a rifle. Suddenly she shifted into full panic mode and her instinct to run took over. She jumped off the rock and hit the ground hard. Her weakened thighs were too flimsy to hold the full weight of her body and she collapsed to the ground. Jumping up, she ran toward the swale; Nolan would protect her. Mindlessly, she dropped the saddlebag as her legs pumped hard in the deep sand. The men were yelling at her, but she couldn't waste the time to listen. She jumped up on another rock to get better traction. Again, just below her foot a bullet exploded on the rock sending stinging shards into her leg. The sound of the shot was much closer now as the men were gaining on her. She leapt across the low rock formation running blindly in her panic toward the swale, the ground rising before her in a steady incline. Her breath was hard and labored; her mind was swimming with panic and fear. In this surreal state of mind she saw herself as a wild animal running for its life.

An exposed root brought Anne's escape to an abrupt halt. The root snagged her right foot, catching her arch, bringing her to an immediate stop, and breaking two of her toes in the process. She fell forward with a thud, where her cheekbone found the hard surface of a fist-sized rock. She bounced once and came to rest, unconscious. The dust puffed up and around her. The predators had won the chase. The prey would be eaten for dinner.

Nolan lay on the ground, eyes closed and motionless. He was partially covered by a small wall of tamarisk that grew on the edge of the swale. Down below, the herd was restless, stamping, and still turning in circles. Nolan saw what he needed to see. He knew there was nothing he could physically do to overcome these men and free the herd. So he lay down and closed his eyes. He could feel the panic of the animals that were below him in the bowl. The panic overwhelmed his nervous system as his mind swirled with fear and desperation. He went completely limp as he relaxed his body, the uneven dirt and rocks pressing uncomfortably into his back.

He let his mind settle, calm, and find its center. Slowly he drew in a deep breath and let it out in a great whoosh. He drew in another and held it slightly before exhaling purposefully, full of intention. In his mind's eye he found what he was seeking. A yellow misty light came into view. He let it linger and grow; stronger with each inhale, more focused with each exhale. This was a place he was both familiar and comfortable with. The sheer panic of the herd was making it hard for him to control and focus. Nolan struggled to ignore the panic, to let it pass over him like a cloud in the sky. Soon the yellow mist in his mind covered his inner eye and was bright as day. He whispered his intention and watched the yellow light bounce and start in motion. A growing strand of this mystical golden glow was calling him away from his physical form. It was guiding his thoughts now, with an intention of its own. Through the darkness of his interior world, Nolan followed the strand. Gently it took him along, over and under invisible obstacles.

After some time he found what he was seeking—the bulky bay stallion mustang that watched over this herd. Cloud Runner was waiting for Nolan. Cloud Runner knew his man-friend would come, one way or another, to keep the bond, to keep the promise, Xu's promise. Cloud Runner was waiting. Nolan found the horse to be in dire spirits, agitated and upset. The two, man and horse, conversed in the secret language of the soul. They exchanged their regrets, reestablished their intentions, and formed a plan to free the horses that would otherwise soon be slaughtered. Somehow the herd split in two and Cloud Runner led only half of his mares and young colts into safety. The other half were pushed up the creek; they went the wrong way. Without some miraculous intervention, they would all soon be dead.

Time was short and the dreadful circumstance called for bold action. Nolan pledged his life, for all it was worth, to help his friend. Cloud Runner knew it might come to that. Many humans, through the ages, traded their lives so horses could live. He never understood why; the horse lived in a world where all but a few men were cruel, dumb-minded creatures with no awareness. Cloud Runner was grateful to know this man named Nolan.

Faintly, remotely, in another world far away, Nolan heard a muffled popping sound. It came across the distance as if it was carried on a string, strung between two cans. The sound was gunfire. It had the timbre of newspaper slapping on grass. Two shots came from nearby his physical form. Nolan knew it was beyond his control. He stayed with Cloud Runner for some time establishing the details of a rescue plan. This was Nolan's first responsibility, his most important task. He could not fail now. The two spirits, man and horse, danced and twirled in a cosmic connection few would ever know. It was settled. Now was the time. Nolan wanted to linger; this was as blissful a state as he would ever know, but time wouldn't permit it. Slowly, he found his way back from Cloud Runner, back to his own physical form that lay motionless on the ground above the bowl.

Nolan opened his eyes. Each time he contacted the horse spirit he was surprised by the amount of energy it sucked from his body. He lay still for a few minutes while his senses slowly came back online. After awhile he struggled to sit up. First up on one elbow, then a weak push up to full sitting position. He lugged his body off the ground, staying low to avoid being seen. He crawled over to the edge of the bowl and looked down to see the trapped horses. His heart seemed to catch in his throat.

Across the bowl, two men were putting Anne into the cab of a green truck. She seemed drugged or unconscious, as her limbs hung limply and her head lolled to one side. Nolan's eyes widened as he grasped the situation.

"They have Anne." The thought flooded into his sluggish mind and stung his heart. He shook his head to clear the cobwebs. "They have Anne." The thought came through again. His adrenal gland kicked on and a surge of clarity rushed over his vision. "They have Anne!" He stood up without fear, and in righteous indignation he shouted to the men.

"Hey!" his voice echoed through the bowl. "Hey! What do you think you're doing? Put her down! Now!"

All eyes turned up to see the man on the hill yelling down at Striker. Most were in complete disbelief. Striker was standing beside his truck stuffing the limp body of Anne Harper onto the passenger seat. He looked up at Nolan, his eyes narrow and grim.

"Take him out," he hissed. The men standing around him raised their rifles and opened fire. It wasn't but a few seconds when all of the men in the bowl joined in. The loud bangs of exploding rounds drowned out the sound of Striker slamming the truck doors. He ran around to the driver's position and with a turn of the key the engine roared to life.

Up on the hill the first few rounds went singing by Nolan's head. The next one caught him on the shoulder and with a violent, and surprisingly fierce jolt, Nolan was knocked off his feet and onto his back. This one probably spared his life for the moment as the barrage of gunfire converged on his position with the ferocity of an attacking lion. Nolan lay stiffly on the ground. There was no pain, just a dull, numb feeling as he rolled over and covered his head with his hands. The brush above his head popped, crackled, and exploded into shards and splinters, as greenery, leaves and pieces of wood showered down upon his rigid body. Suddenly the shooting stopped and Nolan could hear a man's voice echoing up from the bowl.

"Hold yer fire, dammit!" Nolan's heart was racing and he was breathing hard. He looked down to see a bright red bloodstain blossoming rapidly on his shirt just over his right shoulder.

"Shit!" Nolan said aloud. His mind immediately went to Anne. They had taken her. She was in serious trouble. Reaching over with his left hand, Nolan applied direct pressure to the wound. That's when he felt the pain, a bone-deep, searing pain that made him shake uncontrollably. His adrenaline was peaking; he winced, but lay still, listening.

"Roger! Jack! Pico! Git up there and find him!" The voice coming up from the bowl was strangely clear and audible. Fear welled up in Nolan's chest. He turned around and looked at his position. A tall wall of tamarisk was the only hope of avoiding detection. He twisted painfully and pushed himself into the bushes. His hand was soaking with blood now. Nolan pushed harder on the wound. He had to stop the bleeding, the pain could wait. His right arm hung limp, but his fingers still worked. Slowly and painfully, he pulled his pistol from the holster and held it in his right hand, contemplating what use it would be if he couldn't raise his arm. He lay on the ground, breathing hard, waiting for the inevitable confrontation with the men who were coming to kill him.

In the green pickup, Striker drove as fast as he could over the bumps and ruts. The truck rattled, banged, and jumped. Anne lay collapsed and still unconscious against the locked passenger door, her head bouncing every time the truck hit another obstacle. One side of her face was swollen, her eye blackened. A stream of dried blood held some matted hair against her cheekbone. She was covered in dust and dirt with small twigs stuck in her hair. Striker raced down the dirt road hoping she wouldn't wake up before he made it back to the ranch complex.

Roger and Pico went first, Jack followed closely behind—three grizzled farm hands doing what they were told. Roger was sure they killed the man. Pico was sure he was still alive and was waiting for them. Jack just followed along obeying orders, not too thrilled to be part of this operation. The hill where they say Nolan was at the back of the bowl above the horses. It was too steep to climb directly out of the bowl, plus it was blocked by the herd. The horses were now so agitated by the gunfire it would be dangerous to get too close. The three men crossed the bowl and disappeared into the ravine following the creek. To get to the top they had to circle around through the creek bed and up a lesser incline.

Up on top, Nolan was lying beneath the tamarisk, holding his shoulder wound with one hand and his pistol in the other. His breathing had slowed and he was starting to calm down. Still, pain wrenched his entire body with even the slightest movement of his arm. He waited. Knowing that someone was coming for him kept his fear alive. He listened intently but heard nothing. The silence was ringing in his ears.

Soon enough Roger and Pico crested the steep hill and climbed up and out of the ravine. Jack was behind moving at a slower pace. The two men started to their left, following the brim of the ravine toward the bowl. Keeping a wary eye out for the stranger that was lying up ahead, they moved silently, cautiously, but with deadly intention. The bowl was just ahead; so far they could see nothing but a great wall of tamarisk rising high above the rim of the ravine.

Nolan lay in his lair, his shoulder bleeding badly. The pain was constant, clear, and intense. He wondered how long he could wait like this. He listened again, straining against the silence. He desperately wanted a sign of movement, something to give him a clue to what was happening out there, just out of sight. Still nothing. His fear grew as he struggled to maintain his composure.

Jack came up out of the ravine and followed Roger and Pico. He lost sight of them behind the wall of tamarisk thicket that stood between him and the bowl. He clearly saw their footprints though and moved along as silently as he could. In front of him about 100 yards and well behind the thicket, Roger and Pico pushed ahead nearing their target. Both had their pistols drawn. They moved with stealth, silently approaching their prey.

It was Pico who heard the first signs of movement. He paused and silently signaled Roger. Roger shrugged his shoulders as if to say he heard nothing. Again Pico heard a soft noise. He looked over at Roger who still detected nothing. Pico frowned, something was moving. He could hear it. He waved at Roger to continue forward.

Behind them Jack was standing outside the thicket. He had a wide view of the surrounding land. He also could hear something moving. He looked to the right and saw a cloud of dust rising up from the horizon. His face twisted in confusion. The cloud seemed to be moving towards him. It was growing and the sound coming from it was a low, rumbling, rolling thunder. Jack thought it might be a truck coming up the road. But he knew there were no roads over on this side of Tanner Creek. He stood motionless watching the cloud approach, but as he finally recognized the sound, it was too late. Over the small rise just before him came a rumbling rampage. In front was Cloud Runner, mane flying, head high, flaring nostrils, eyes proud and wide. Behind him were nearly 100 trampling mares and colts all running at full speed straight for this unfortunate man. Before Jack could raise his pistol and fire off a shot, the herd ran over the top of him, crushing him without mercy into the desert floor.

Inside the thicket, Pico was now running full speed toward the bowl. He left Roger behind and was concerned only with his own survival. The sound of a stampeding herd of mustangs was one he knew full well, and even though it was strange indeed for these animals to be running through this part of the ranch, he wasn't stopping to find out why. As he neared the bowl another surprise caught him; a shot rang out and a bullet knocked him back to a dead stop. Nolan was under the tamarisk, his pistol barrel smoking. Within seconds the herd came up to the edge of the bowl. All of the horses, led by Cloud Runner, flew over the rim, onto the steep-sided ravine, plunging down into the bowl. Nolan watched with wide-eyed amazement as the herd went crashing by, just yards from where he lay safely under the tamarisk bushes.

In the bowl the scene was not so safe. Bulling was standing on the far side next to his truck. Mickey, reins tied to the bumper, grew agitated and reared up violently. With a quick pop of snapping leather, the bridle broke and the horse bolted off. Bulling saw Mickey break free while hearing the rolling thunder of the running herd. Sensing some unusual danger, he was climbing into his pickup as he saw Cloud Runner and the herd flood over the rim and into the bowl like a tsunami washing down the hill and sweeping up to the opposite side. Bulling could not believe his eyes. He never saw an aggressive herd of horses.

Horses are prey animals. They run away; they do not attack. Bulling watched with a strange morbid fascination as the herd came over the rim roaring down the steep embankment. A great cloud of billowing dust was kicked up into quickly towering angry twisted swirls. The dry earth rumbled and shook with a random cadence of tearing hooves and trampling terror. In the bowl, the horses that were trapped by the men exploded into a fray of bucking and rearing. Their fear suddenly converted to rage as Cloud Runner and the others galloped down the hill mixing with them at the bottom. The dust cloud that preceded the raging herd made it difficult to see just how many horses there were, but Bulling, feeling safe in the cab of his truck, thought it to be about 200 head.

The other men in the bowl were completely taken by surprise and shock. As the mass of animals stormed into the bowl, the men's fate was clear. Some turned and tried to scramble up the steep embankments, but the loose, dry soil kept them from getting to safety. Some made a run for the flatbed truck parked across the creek, blocking access to the north swale and certain safety. Others stood frozen with fear and confusion. A few managed to squeeze off a couple of rounds before they were overwhelmed and swallowed up by the terrible cloud of dusty anger, trampled to death one by one into the dry unforgiving earth.

Bulling watched all of this from the front seat of his truck. With an uncontrollable rush of adrenaline, he pushed himself far back into his seat as the mass of raging animals swooped down into the bowl and moved quickly toward his truck. Eyeing Anne's camera he picked up the unit with the intention of getting a few pictures of this unbelievable spectacle. He fumbled with the controls but in his anxiety dropped the camera as the horses ran up. Within seconds, the herd was in front of him moving at full speed. Several of the horses ran up onto the hood and over the top of the cab. The truck racked violently. The noise was deafening. Bulling flattened himself across the seat, instinctively covering his head. The front windshield exploded inward, shattering under the weight of one or more hooves as the safety glass particles sprayed across the interior. The dust puffed into the cab like a ruptured vacuum. The cab was immediately filled with a thick choking dust as the noise of the herd amplified into an even louder roar. Bulling lay on the seat, arms over his head screaming out in utter terror.

Then it was over. The herd ran up the road and out of the bowl; the thundering sound diminishing as fast as it had appeared. Out in the bowl the scene was ghastly. All of the men lay dead, nine in total. Crushed into the dry broken earth, heads smashed open, guts splayed, limbs broken, it was a scene of complete devastation. Bulling lifted his head and slowly sat upright. Through the front of his truck, where the windshield used to be, he took in the death scene slowly unveiling as the cloud of dust parted and started to settle.

Two horses lay on their sides, breathing hard. Some of the bullets had found their marks. The bodies of his crew were scattered across the bowl here and there, most of them the color of dust mixed with the new red of fresh blood. It was suddenly eerily quiet.

Bulling opened the door of his truck and stepped out into the bowl.

CHAPTER EIGHT

Samantha, Rosie, and Joe sat at one end of the large cluttered kitchen table. Through the window they could look out across the ranch. The afternoon sun carried itself over the house and long shadows were gathering in the backyard. The day was growing old. One short day was all it took to change Samantha forever. Never before had she felt this close to truth, this close to her own true nature. As she listened to Joe tell her about the yellow mist and what it meant, it was like someone had opened the shutters in a dark room. Suddenly she understood. Suddenly the light of truth was pouring in, chasing away her doubts and finally letting her see clearly that which was only murky darkness moments before. She was as a butterfly, finally crawling from the cocoon, a changed person.

As she listened to Joe tell her about the real truth behind the legends of Xu, she heard the story not as a narrative, but as an autobiography. Deep within her psyche she sensed a clear, white light—small but intense. It was a strong sense, a feeling she had missed ever since her father died, a feeling of being home. In her mind's eye she could see the yellow mist, swirling softly, resting, at ease. Joe's deep, soft monotone voice resonated within the mist and she listened. She understood and could feel the truth in his words.

"Samantha," Joe was saying, "we are getting close to losing this bond forever. This herd, the one out there, is the last large group of those that remember. They came here because of Nolan. They came because they knew we would help them, we could help them. I think that is why you came here too."

Rosie was watching the child intently.

"Sometimes our hidden intentions can be a strong guide," she said to Sam. "Sometimes it leads us without us really knowing."

Sam looked at the woman, Rosie's clear eyes were bright with love and her tenderness was showing through. Sam understood.

"I came here for a reason," Sam said reflectively. "The yellow mist led me here. To help the horses. To save the herd."

Joe looked at Rosie with wide eyes. "This girl is much more in tune than I would have guessed," he said. "This gives me a great reason for hope." Rosie nodded her agreement.

"I am not sure what I can do," said Sam. "I mean …what can I do?"

"Most of the time we can't see the road ahead of us," replied Joe. "We just have to put ourselves on the path and see where it leads. I am pretty dang sure that you came here for something."

Sam sat still, reflecting on this new truth she was discovering.

"When I was little," she said, "I used to have a dream. I remember it several times. In the dream there was a large herd of horses. A herd so large that it stretched out into the distance. I would be up on a little hill so I could see the whole herd and they were all looking at me. There seemed to be a leader that was close to me and the leader-horse would ask me questions, but when I tried to speak only music would come out of my mouth, not words. And when I sang, or whatever, the entire horse herd would move to the music, to the tones. They would be dancing; it was really beautiful." Sam looked up. "I think I know what that dream means now."

Joe and Rosie were astonished at this girl. They looked at each other with knowing eyes.

"Okay, Sam, you look like you are feeling better," said Joe.

"Yes, I guess I am," Sam smiled. "Thank you for everything."

At that moment, Sam suddenly thought of her mother. She sensed something—down deep she had an anxious feeling. It was like a call for help. It didn't frighten her, but it was something real, deep, and far away.

"Do you think my mom is okay?" she asked.

Joe sensed the change in the girl. Pausing for a moment, he took a check of his own intuition. "That is a good question," he said after a few seconds. "Let me see what I can find." With that Joe closed his eyes, took a deep breath, and drifted away.

Anne was unconscious in Striker's truck. Internally she was having a strange dream. A very small man was sitting up on a rock looking down. He was laughing and his joy radiated throughout the space around him. Bright colorful flowers backed by green velvet grass were dancing within the joy. Behind the man a bright blue sky pulsated with life and energy. As she watched, the man began to chant. As the words came out of his mouth, the man's happy visage became dour and his body shifted into a strange shape. His neck elongated, his ears moved up his head as the shape of his skull pulled out into the shape of …of a horse. He was now a horse. The horse-man looked down at her and said, "Wake up!" Suddenly the whole scene rotated as if a pinwheel was set in motion. The colors faded into black and the pinwheel turned to a whirlpool sucking everything into its black gaping maw. There was a long tunnel of swirling mass, a loud pop and Anne opened her eyes.

At first Anne was confused. She was in a truck, bouncing along a dirt road. She looked over; a man she didn't know was at the wheel concentrating wholly on the road. Just as quickly as her memory returned, a tidal wave of fear swept over her body. In a purely adrenaline-fueled move, and with the quickness of a cat, she drew her feet up, leaned back against the door and kicked the man in the head with both feet. The force caught Striker across the lower jaw, smashing his head into the driver's side window. The angle of the blow twisted his neck against the bottom of his skull breaking his C2 vertebra and severing his spinal cord. His body reflexively tightened up causing the steering wheel of the truck to lurch hard to the left. The vehicle spun violently crosswise, and caught its right front tire at the edge of the road. It flipped over, rolled once and came to rest amidst the dry puff of a dusty cloud.

Nolan stood on the edge of the bowl, pistol in hand, looking down at the grisly scene below. The earth under his feet was shredded and turned over by the hundreds of hooves that passed here just minutes ago. The air was silent and still. The path of the stampede clearly marked the direction of the torrent down the steep hill, into the bowl, up and out onto the road. On the other side of the bowl, and sitting directly in the earth-worn path, was a brown pickup truck, windshield blown out and hood crinkled. Next to the truck stood a single man.

Nolan raised his pistol and took aim. He desperately wanted to kill this man, this thief, this nightmare of a human, this horse killer. With no thought of consequence, with no pity, Nolan squeezed his trigger finger, then again, and again. The three shots split the quiet, sending the deadly projectiles sailing toward their target. On the ground by the truck, Bulling heard the sound of his fate. Before he could react, the three slugs found their targets. The first hit the front tire sending a billowing hiss into the air, the next struck the ground just before him and threw up a small dust cloud. The third slug whizzed over his head. He heard the chilling sound as the bullet struck the back part of the pickup and ricocheted into the desert.

Bulling instinctively dove for cover and rolled under the pickup. He was a small man and had no trouble getting to safety.

He screamed out in panic, "Don't shoot! Don't shoot!"

Nolan's adrenaline was pumping. His heart pounded. The wound on his shoulder was shooting knives of pain up and down his arm. Ignoring the pain, he jumped onto the slope in front of him and in one gliding movement slid down the deep, loosened dirt. In a flash he was at the bottom. Pistol raised, he ran toward the truck. He had the man trapped. It would be over soon.

Bulling saw Nolan running towards him and was confused. The gunfire came from the top of the hill. This man was running through the bowl. Bulling immediately thought there must be more than one man gunning for him. He rolled again to the other side of the truck and scrambled to his feet, keeping low for cover. Looking around, he searched for a retreat. There was nothing but wide-open spaces. No safety in running.

"Shit!" he cursed aloud. He turned and looked at the quickly approaching man. "Hey! Wait a minute!" he called out. "Let's talk this out!" He was desperately jabbering, looking towards the top of the hill searching for the other man. Nolan did not respond and was closing in.

"Hold your fire!" Bulling yelled. "Let's talk ...can we talk?" Bulling was terrified. He peeked up over the driver's door through the demolished cab of the truck and saw Nolan 50 yards out and coming fast. Bulling eyed the contents of the cab searching for a weapon. His eyes locked onto a pistol that was lying on the floorboard near the passenger door. Urgently, Bulling pulled open the door and crawled into the truck; it wasn't seconds until he had the pistol in his quivering hand.

"I've got a gun!" he shouted. "I've got a gun!" He needed some time, just a little time to think, but his brain was paralyzed with fear. It was now or never. He raised the gun up and tried to get a look at the approaching threat. As his head pushed up over the dashboard, a shot rang out. The bullet caught his hand, knocking the pistol from his grip. Bulling pulled his hand to his chest and gripped it closely. In horror, he noticed one of his fingers, detached, lying on the seat with blood spattered in a neat symmetrical line across the back of the cab. Screaming in agony, he looked for his pistol. At that moment the passenger door was yanked open and Nolan stood above him, pistol drawn.

Nolan reached in and grabbed the man's collar. His anger seethed, pushing the pain of his injured shoulder even further away. With one move, Nolan pulled Bulling from the truck and onto the ground. Bulling was balled up, holding tightly to his deformed, bleeding hand. He hit the ground hard and started screaming.

"Shut up!" Nolan demanded, and kicked the man square in the head.

"Stop, stop, stop!" Bulling pleaded. "Please …don't kill me …let's talk …let's talk this out." In pathetic desperation, Bulling resorted to the only survival tactic he knew.

Nolan stood solid and quiet above the man, his finger firmly on the trigger, his deadly aim trained at the man's head.

"Okay," he said between his teeth. "Let's talk. Who are you?"

Bulling saw a tiny light of hope bloom into the middle of his fear.

"My name is Ray …Ray Bulling." His voice quivered with adrenaline. "I work at this ranch, the cattle ranch. I …I manage the crew …"

"You work for Ruud?" Nolan asked with obvious contempt.

Bulling didn't want to play into this man's anger, "No, no, no …I work for Striker, Rick Striker …he's the one I work for. I manage the crew …"

"You're a horse killer," said Nolan.

"Now hold on. No, I didn't kill nothin'. I just follow orders ...I just manage the crew. I haven't killed anything." Bulling was rambling. He was trying anything to deflect this man's anger, anything to get through the next few minutes alive.

"Where's Anne?" Nolan asked, increasingly agitated.

"Who?"

Nolan kicked the man's bleeding hand. Bulling let out a bloody scream.

"Argh!" he screamed. "Stop! Please ..." Bulling was desperate.

"Where's the woman?" Nolan interrupted Bulling's pathetic bid to survive.

Bulling's mind was still clouded with fear and pain. He struggled to get his brain working.

"Uh, oh! Striker. She's with Striker. She was hurt; he was taking her to get help ...medical help."

Nolan knew he was lying. He looked down on this pitiful sight, but had no mercy. Seven horses were dead; two were lying in the bowl near death. The loss could not be put into words. No one but a select few would ever know why.

"So, Mr. Horse Killer, why are you so intent on killing my herd?"

Bulling heard the words "my herd" and his blood ran colder still. He had to deflect this guy's anger, somehow.

"Look, it's Ruud who's running this show," he said between panting breaths. "He's got some kind of vendetta against the wild horses. I don't know why. But Ruud gave the orders to get rid of these animals. We were just doing what we were told. No one wanted to, really. We are hired hands trying to make a living."

Nolan paused and considered the pathetic man that lay on the ground before him. "Yeah, I've heard that one before," said Nolan. Just then one of the horses lying wounded in the bowl let out a mournful cry. Nolan turned his head instinctively towards the heart-wrenching noise. Bulling saw his chance. Quick as a snake he pounced, catching Nolan around his lower torso, pushing him to the ground.

A fight to the death is a curious thing. It is probably the only time in a man's life where the stakes are so high, the outcome so immediate as to focus his purpose singularly, intensely, on one thing only—to survive. This focus of intention bends the will into an uncompassionate and uncompromising force, directing the body without regard to injury, pain, or weakness. Without distraction and in the complete alignment of the will to survive, the two men entered the death match; each one bringing the entirety of his wit, strength, and experience. Game on.

Nolan fell back as Bulling reached up and pushed Nolan's gun hand up and over his head. The pistol went off in Nolan's hand as the two hit the ground with grunts and a puff of dust. Bulling was on top. The blood from his hand slathered a red smear up Nolan's arm as Bulling reached wildly for the pistol. Being taller, Nolan was able to hold the gun just out of reach while he shoved his free hand into Bulling's face, clawing at the eyes. Bulling responded with a couple of hard blows to the side of Nolan's head. Nolan persisted. Bulling grabbed Nolan's hand and wrenched it from his face, careful to keep Nolan's gun hand pinned down and useless. The two rolled over while Nolan brought his knee up hard into his opponent's gut. Bulling furiously held onto Nolan's gun hand while he again leveled two strong blows to Nolan's head. Enraged, Nolan yanked his gun hand away and brought the pistol sharp and hard against Bulling's face. Shards of teeth erupted with a splash of blood. Bulling didn't notice. With immediate surprising force, he swiped at Nolan's gun hand knocking the gun free from Nolan's grip; it landed just out of reach. Bulling grabbed Nolan's shirt and pulled him close. The two rolled over again and Bulling broke free. He lunged for the gun while Nolan picked up a rock and bullseyed Bulling right in the back of the head. Bulling fell onto his stomach, writhing on the ground, one hand grasping at the back of his head. The other hand reached out and took hold of the gun. Nolan leaped on top of the man, pinning Bulling's gun hand to the ground. Nolan attempted to use his free fist on the back of Bulling's head, but his shoulder wound minimized the force he could administer. Bulling rolled again, knocking Nolan to the side. One more roll and Bulling brought the pistol up, aimed at Nolan's chest.

"Ha!" Bulling gloated as Nolan's eyes widened with the sense of certain death.

Bulling pulled the trigger twice.

The gun clicked. Empty.

Nolan sprung up and over, landing his full force on top of Bulling. With a super surge of adrenaline-soaked anger, loathing, and disgust, Nolan landed a series of hard blows that left Bulling stunned and helpless. In the last feat of death-match savagery, Nolan picked up a large rock and smashed it down into Bulling's face. The force crushed his nose and cheekbones, pushing them back into the sinus cavity spewing forth a geyser of blood. Bulling went limp and Nolan rolled off and lay on the ground panting.

After regaining strength, Nolan got to his feet. He was shaking with fear and adrenaline as he bent over to pick up his pistol. Pausing for a moment, he tried to recount the shots he fired. He was sure there was one more round. Feeling very lucky he reached into his pocket to retrieve his extra clip. He slid it into the pistol and placed the gun back into his holster.

Down the road toward Ruud's cattle operation, Anne climbed from the wreckage of Striker's truck. The doors were jammed shut and she was forced to climb through the passenger window. Aside from her broken toes and aching jaw, she came through the wreck largely unscathed. Striker was dead, twisted up in an odd configuration between the driver's side door and the steering wheel. The contents of the truck were strewn about the cab helter skelter. Anne pulled herself through the window and lowered slowly to the ground. Her senses were on high alert as she limped up to the road to assess the situation. The land was open and bare, leaving her vulnerable. The sun was fading into the west; it would be dark soon. She looked back down the road toward Angel Ridge. Her thoughts immediately went to Nolan. She had a very bad feeling about his situation—afraid that he was dead. Suddenly a sense of sorrow overwhelmed her for having treated him so rudely. It brought back an old and ugly feeling. The same feeling she had after Simon died. She treated Simon so badly just before his accident. It was one of those lifelong regrets that could never heal. Feeling utterly alone she wished that Nolan was here by her side. He would know what to do.

Racing through her mind was a mental cacophony of disjointed thoughts and mounting fears. She knew if she went back toward the bowl the men there would catch her for sure. And she couldn't stay on the road; they would most likely be coming this way soon. Limping back to the truck, she took a quick inventory of the available resources inside. She grabbed a quart-sized bottle of water, a flashlight, and the ball cap from Striker's head. She headed into the desert bound for Angel Ridge. She would make a wide circle around the bowl and avoid that certain doom.

Nolan stood in the bowl near the dead body of his enemy. He knew his first order of business was to tend to the two horses that were downed in the bowl, then to go find Anne. He couldn't leave these precious animals to suffer. His anger and rage turned to agony as he looked into the bowl at the two horses that lay dying in the waning sun. A deep, profound pain welled up in his soul at the sight. He walked up to the first horse as tears began to fall from his eyes. The medium-sized buckskin mare was on her side panting hard; her eyes wide open, the whites showing. She had two bullet holes in her loins, blood streamed out. Nolan, forgetting all of his own pain, knelt down beside the frightened creature, his hand pushed up onto her shoulder as he closed his eyes.

The yellow mist twisted angrily around the man and the horse. Nolan reached in with his mind to offer what little comfort he could to the dying animal. He saw into this creature's mind and in turn the horse saw him. They greeted each other in the melancholy truth that the horse's life was at its end. Each knew what was to come. In a flash of compassion, Nolan saw the horse—its life, its family, its given name. The horse knew what Nolan did for the herd and expressed its thankfulness. Nolan was crying; the horse was offering its gratitude. After a long hesitant pause, Nolan stood up, pointed the pistol and fired off a single round, mercifully ending the mare's suffering. The recoil of the pistol, the sharp crack of the ordnance, and the last movement of the horse pierced his soul. He stood over the dead horse, shaking with grief. The yellow mist vibrated for a moment and then was gone.

Now the tears were streaming down Nolan's face. In a grim determination to do the right thing, he walked up to the second horse. His breaking heart took another blow as he looked down and recognized the horse in front of him—Cloud Runner.

"Oh no!" Nolan's voice cracked, as his knees buckled and he fell to the ground next to this once-magnificent steed. "Oh, no!" he said again. "Why? ...why this? Why you?" His heart shattered as his face went pale white, his mind giving way to clouds of despair. Sobbing uncontrollably, Nolan laid his head on the stallion's shoulder. The yellow mist grew up calmly, like a soft glowing light.

Out of the yellow mist, a voice of ancient wisdom and compassion came calling.

"Nolan, do not despair."

Nolan heard and recognized the strangely comforting voice.

"Cloud Runner," he replied. "How can I not? This is the worst thing that could happen."

Cloud Runner's voice was clear, strong and proud. His words were not verbal, but carried by the yellow mist in the ancient bond of Xu.

"We knew the risks. We knew what must be done. Many were saved today ...because of you."

Nolan shook his head. "I will save you," he said. Nolan got to his feet and came to the other side of Cloud Runner. Desperately he sought out the gunshot wound to assess the damage. A bullet entered Cloud Runner's chest between his shoulders. Red blood pumped from the wound. Nolan reached down and applied pressure; it did not stop the flow. Blood squirted through Nolan's fingers and dripped to the pool forming on the ground. He knew that the bullet must have pierced the heart; the grim reality of certain death settled in on his anguished mind.

"Nolan," came the voice again. "It is too late for me. Your task lies with the rest of the herd. I am finished here."

Nolan wracked his mind for a solution; there must be some way to help this majestic horse live.

"But there is so much more to do," Nolan's voice was wrought with desperation. "We have so much more."

"Those things will be done without me," said Cloud Runner, his voice becoming noticeably weaker.

Nolan sat silently, caressing the stallion's magnificent head. The last few minutes of Cloud Runner's life were at hand. Nolan did not know how to say goodbye to his friend. The circle of life was closing quickly. Death was nearby as Nolan tried his best to comfort the dying king.

"Nolan, you have done every human thing possible for the sake of our ancient bond. You have been a true friend and ally. For the first time in hundreds of years, you have shown the honor of men. You have taken on the mantel of responsibility and leadership. You have truly loved us, helped us, and honored us. For that I commend you. It has been a long time, my friend. Now you must take the final step and move to the next stage in what it means to be a horse angel. A true man."

"What do you mean?" asked Nolan.

"I am going to show you something," said Cloud Runner. "Do not fear."

Nolan immediately felt a shock through the yellow mist. The mist swirled slowly at first then began to twist, increasing its speed. Soon it was a violent torrent. Nolan released his grip on the horse and fell back onto the ground, his body convulsing. In his mind he was being drawn into a vortex, falling backward into a deep, swirling, yellow hole. Again he heard the voice of his friend.

"Fear not," Cloud Runner called to him.

Suddenly the yellow mist enveloped Nolan, the torrent quit and he was in the middle of a bubble. Another moment and the bubble collapsed onto Nolan and another great shock convulsed through his body. Then there was a second light starting in the middle of Nolan's chest. A different light. At first he could not discern it; the experience shook his mind. After a few seconds it was clear, the yellow mist was changing colors, first a brilliant green followed by a deep sky blue. The vision unfolded like an oriental fan spreading out across Nolan's inner mind in a brilliant blue hue. The yellow mist was all but gone as this new marvel was revealed to Nolan's heart and soul. The blue color wasn't a mist, it was a solid form, a great blue fan-shaped form directly in front of Nolan's inner eye. As he watched, Nolan began to see an intense hallucination—images coming through the fan, images telling the story, the history of horse and man.

In a flash of consciousness, Nolan saw the entire history unfold before his eyes. The reality of these images was both stunning and confusing. He saw Xu, releasing the first horse from his certain doom. He saw the gradual development of the partnership, the first riders. He witnessed the first culture to use the horse as transportation. The bond between man and animal was new and joyful. Then came images of the spread of this knowledge and the loss of Xu's bond. The new men used their horses as machines, careless in tending and care. But the horses remembered and again the bond was renewed.

Nolan watched as the horse and rider developed new trade routes bringing prosperity and new ideas to regions once isolated by great distances. The knowledge of the value of horsepower spread slowly but certainly from the Steppes into Asia Minor and Eastward across China.

In the south, Nolan watched as the ancient Greeks took in the horse and nourished the relationship. Xenophon, the great General, was writing his treatise of equine training, care, and discipline. The great relationship was alive and the ancient horse angels carried the spirit of Xu's promise, feeding it forward to following generations.

Nolan saw the development of bit and bridle, saddle and yoke, the chariot, the carriage, and the plow. As the knowledge spread and as the promise of Xu with it, mankind was lifted from the drudgery of hunter/gatherer existence into the efficiencies of farming, all this on the back of a horse.

The Romans developed the horse for transportation, sport, battle, and barter. This spread the knowledge into early Europe, across Africa and the Middle East. In the Far East the terrible Genghis Kahn took the horse in as a true partner in his building of the Mongol empire. Sparing no man who abused a horse, Genghis powered his armies on the backs of these magnificent creatures.

Nolan watched this history unfold as a great blue lotus flower, each petal another story of horse and man. He saw the horse in the early development of Europe, the expansion across the Atlantic and the horses brought to the Americas. He watched as the United States, harnessing the partnership with horses, developed and expanded westward. Then came the rise of the industrial revolution where horse and machine labored side by side in creating the greatest expansion of prosperity the world had ever known.

In a great kaleidoscope of vision and ideas, Nolan saw the roll the horse played in logging, farming, mining, road building, transportation, war, peace, sport, art, and culture. In those few moments Nolan saw the veritable rise of Western Civilization bloom like a flower, in all its glory and prosperity all in league with this great animal, the horse. He knew without the horse, all of this progress would not have come to be. Suddenly Nolan had a profound understanding of why Xu's promise was so important, so necessary, and why man owed the horse such a deep debt of gratitude.

This vision ended in a perfect blue flower cast across Nolan's mind. He saw the entire history of the rise of man aided by the horse. He felt each emotion, in every epoch and age since Xu made the first bond. The thrill of this experience never left Nolan. Cloud Runner gave him the next level of understanding, the truth behind horse and man. It only strengthened Nolan's understanding of the deep debt each man owes to the horse.

Nolan opened his eyes. He was exhilarated, his senses heightened. He sat and looked at Cloud Runner. The horse was dead. Nolan crawled over to the great horse and laid his head on his shoulder. Nolan was no longer distraught about Cloud Runner's passing. His perspective was forever changed. He knew the endless thread of life was just moving forward, to the next one in line.

"Rest in peace, brother," Nolan whispered. He patted the horse gently and got to his feet. The blue flower in his inner vision remained, even with his eyes wide open he could sense the vision. His awareness was expanded, his consciousness enhanced. He could feel the entire herd somewhere out on the plain. They were okay. His mind next turned to Anne. Enhanced by the blue flower, his intuition told him Anne was free and safe …for the moment. Then another thing popped into his mind—Mickey, the horse Anne had been riding, was over the hill, waiting for someone to come. Nolan called to the horse asking it to come to him, to come back. Shortly, Mickey appeared on the horizon, saddle on his back. Nolan smiled. Maybe things *will* work out for the better, he thought.

It was about this time when a rider-less Jasper ran into the barn at Angel Ridge. The horse was lathered with fear and exhaustion. The startled workers sent out the word. Soon the whole ranch was in an agitated state wondering about Nolan's and Anne's fate. Rosie did her best to comfort Samantha as Joe worked out a plan to go in to Ruud's ranch and find the two. In his heart Joe could sense that things were okay, but his mind wouldn't let go of the fear that something terrible happened. He struggled to find a balance.

Nolan caught Mickey and after making a quick repair to the broken bridle, mounted up and went after Anne. He left the scene at the bowl as it lay. There was nothing more he could do here. He hated leaving Cloud Runner and the other horse for the scavengers, but he had no choice. There were at least 10 men lying dead plus a few vehicles. He knew someone would be out looking for these missing assets. It was just a matter of time. But now he had to find Anne and assure her safety.

Riding up and out of the bowl he came onto the relatively flat plain. The sun was kissing the horizon; it would be dark within the hour. Asking Mickey to gallop, he moved quickly down the road, all the while keeping his eyes open for anything that might turn to trouble. Nolan mulled over the events of the day. When he and Anne set out earlier that morning, he knew there would be trouble but had no idea it would degrade into this mess. He blamed himself for getting Anne caught up in the drama. He felt responsible for her safety and committed himself to stop at nothing to bring her back alive. The vision of her soft face was reeling within the blue flower. This new vision was powerful and had a grasp of Nolan's mind. He saw her face, her brunette locks falling around her cheeks, her health and vitality, her toned body. The entirety of what made up Anne Harper filled his vision and moved his heart. Yes, she could be difficult, prideful, isolated, and angry, but Nolan could see all of those undesirable traits as a symptom of her one, real, deep-seated attribute—her pain.

Nolan now saw Anne's pain as her defining characteristic. She kept it hidden in some deep part of her soul but the effects were immediate and clear in the way she treated herself, her daughter and those around her. He didn't know the whole story of her life but he could see that it was Simon's death that held her sway. His new intuition gave him a deep insight into Anne's heart. His empathy stretched across the years and in one dark and dismal moment, he got a glimpse of what she went through, what she was still going through. A vision flashed in his mind. It was the scene of Simon's accident, the loud crack, the horse struggling, the shredding hooves, the cries of the spectators. He knew that her tortured soul was suffering from an inner loop of blame and frustration. He also knew that it was Anne herself who kept it alive.

A deep sense of sadness rolled through his core as he plumbed the depths of this new understanding. Nolan wanted to hold her and to comfort her.

It was the pain in his shoulder that brought him back to his immediate situation. The rhythm of the horse was exacerbating the discomfort of his gunshot wound. The bleeding stopped and he had some mobility in his arm, but the pain was racking. He had to move forward. He couldn't let this setback stop him from finding Anne. He pushed the pain back down and focused on the task before him.

Out in the desert Anne was getting desperate, feeling alone and tormented by the thoughts of impending doom. She constructed the worst-case scenario and was playing the tape over and over in her mind. Her imagined reality was far worse than the truth, but as despair fell over her already-weakened resolve, she was convinced that her version of reality was the only thing that mattered. She trudged through the deep sand with the fatigue of the day's events dragging her spirits down.

She was sure that Nolan had been killed. Curiously, this made her very sad. She had little regard for the cowboy when they set out earlier that day, but now she was missing him terribly. She had to admit she admired his gentle nature, self-control, tremendous empathy, and his deep connection with horses. He wasn't a pushover. He was decisive with a masculinity that was compelling. But whatever remote chance there was for a possible romance, her sense of reality reminded her that he may not have survived the slaughter which she barely escaped. She bit her lip and held back her tears. She had to survive; no time for a breakdown.

In the distance Angel Ridge was looming brilliantly, lit by the last of the sun's rays. Soon it would be dark and she could continue with little chance of being spotted. She felt vulnerable, alone, and hollow. There was no telling where all this would lead, but she was anxious to contact her boss back in Sacramento and give him the full scoop on what Ruud was up to. Of course it was all hearsay with no evidence to show, but she would get back to the ranch, regroup, and think of something.

Nolan had ridden several miles down the road. He was feeling lightheaded but sheer determination kept him going. The land was eerily quiet as the sun disappeared over the far mountain range. Dusk was gathering. The sounds of Mickey's gait clomped along in a two-beat rhythm. Following the tire tracks laid down into the dusty road, he saw where the vehicle had veered suddenly to the left and then to the right. There was a violent, deep scar in the road's shoulder and beyond he could see Striker's truck. Nolan slowed Mickey and walked the horse over to the smashed pickup. He could barely bring himself to look inside for fear of finding Anne's dead body. Nolan stopped, and with a great deal of pain, dismounted, hobbled to the truck and looked inside. Anne was nowhere. Striker's oddly twisted body lay jammed between the driver's door and the steering wheel, his lifeless face contorted and grey. The flies already started the process of nature's recycling. Looking around the cab, Nolan found the hand-held radio and stuffed it into his pocket, hoping to get some idea of what the enemy was up to when they decided to start communicating again.

Closely scouring the ground, he saw Anne's footprints leading off into the desert. By the lopsided indentations he could tell she was limping. She was undoubtedly hurt, but not badly enough to stop her from heading back to the ranch. He mounted up and trotted off into the desert following her trail. He had to keep moving; time was running out. Once darkness fell, he would lose the trail.

Out here in the desert where the sand was deep, Anne's footprints were easy to follow. A few ragged sagebrush were scattered here and there, but mainly it was wide-open spaces. Anne trudged almost due west; he knew she was headed back to the ranch. Feeling safely alone, he called out in a long droning yell.

"Anne! …it's Nolan." The force of his voice carried off over the land, the effort sending a searing pain through his shoulder. Again he called.

Ahead, Anne was desperately trying to gauge her position. The sun had gone down and she was sure she was destined to spend the night out in the open. When she heard the noise come rolling up from behind her, she froze, gripped in fear. Instinctively she crouched down listening intently. Again she heard the call. It was not immediately familiar to her, but she thought she heard her name. She stood up and peered off into the gathering dusk. She could discern no movement. Again the call came. She heard the man's voice a bit clearer and her heart lifted. Was it Nolan? Could it be? She stood silently, hoping. Again the voice called across the dead-quiet desert floor. She heard it clearly this time.

Her mind reeled a bit trying to make sense of it. She looked intently back down the sloping landscape and could finally see a man and horse riding up. Mistrust seized her and she crouched down again. She had no place to run and she sensed danger. She scanned the ground for a weapon, but found nothing of use. Again she heard his call. Standing once more, she stared down at the rider. In this light she could see few details but the voice was clear and comforting. It was Nolan. Her mind played over the scene—it was Nolan.

"Nolan!" she screamed out. Her emotions were right at the surface as tears started pouring out. "Nolan! Over here!" She was waving her arms almost hysterically.

Nolan heard Anne's call but looking ahead could see nothing. He pushed Mickey into a gallop and the two moved up the hill with intense urgency. Anne jumped excitedly and waved her arms. When Nolan finally did see her, his heart swelled up; he couldn't help but feel absolute gratitude for finding her. Even Mickey seemed excited to see her again.

Nolan rode up to her and quickly dismounted. They rushed toward each other and in full embrace Anne broke down completely. All of her fear, anger, and trauma came pouring out. She sobbed uncontrollably as Nolan held her close. The pain in his shoulder made him wince, but he was so happy to see this woman that he ignored the pain as Anne let it all go, wrapped tightly, securely in his arms. She cried for a good three minutes, saying nothing as Nolan reassured her.

"It's okay Anne. You're okay." Nolan repeated.

Anne tried to speak. Her voice was halting and thin as she clung to Nolan's chest.

"I thought you were dead," she said. "Oh my God, I thought they killed you."

"Well, they tried," Nolan replied gently. "So glad I found you,

Anne. So glad you're alright."

Anne continued to cry, unashamed, feeling safer than she had for years. Inexplicably, she felt at home with this man. She was overcome with a sense of security. Nolan, too, felt a strange and unexpected connection to this woman who had bolted into his life that morning.

"Oh, dear God," she whimpered. "Thank you …thank you for coming after me. Oh, Nolan …thank you." Anne broke off into more sobs.

"I would have never left you out here alone. No way. I'm just glad I found you," said Nolan.

Slowly Anne quieted. She brought her hand down to wipe her tears away and was shocked to find blood smeared across her palm. Immediately her attention focused on Nolan.

"What's this? You're bleeding!" Anne pulled back and looked into Nolan's face. Her eyes scanned his body and she saw the gunshot wound. Her protector instincts kicked in.

"Nolan, what happened? You were shot? Oh, my God, you're hurt!"

Nolan's face registered his pain. Anne insisted he sit while she took her flashlight and inspected the wound. Dusk had fallen and the light was dimming.

Nolan submitted and lowered himself to the ground. The adrenaline that kept him going was tapering off now that he found Anne was safe. The pain in his shoulder was an icy, throbbing pulse. Anne helped him off with his vest and gently unbuttoned his blue cotton shirt. She pulled open his shirt revealing his muscular chest, toned by the constant effort of life on the ranch. Nolan watched her face as she intently and carefully peeled back the shirt to reveal his wounded shoulder. She was close enough that he could smell the musky scent of the day's drama in her hair as it brushed against his face.

Anne chatted nervously as she worked, recounting what happened after he left her on the bluff—about how she woke up in the truck and kicked Striker in the head. Nolan sat silently watching this brave and determined woman fuss over him. With her flashlight in hand she inspected the wound, gently touching his skin as she assessed the damage. The bullet entered just below the collarbone and lodged somewhere in his shoulder. The entry wound was a small dark hole.

"We need to get you to a doctor," she said sympathetically. "How far is it to the ranch from here?"

Nolan looked around toward Angel Ridge, surveying their position. "It will take about an hour or two from here depending on what it takes to get across Tanner Creek."

Anne pulled Nolan's shirt back around his shoulder and buttoned the front. "Well, let's rest up a bit and then we'll get you back so we can get that wound taken care of." Her voice was kind and reassuring, quite unlike the woman he started the day with.

The hand-held radio in his pocket crackled, making them both jump. The voice was weak and small but clear.

"Striker, you still out there? Come back now." It was typical CB radio chatter. "Striker, this is base, come in."

Nolan pulled the radio out and held it up. He and Anne looked at each other with grim faces.

"They'll come after us," Nolan said, gritting his teeth against the pain.

"Yeah, but not tonight."

The two stayed put for almost an hour before they considered getting on the horse and making their way back to Angel Ridge. Nolan had a hard time getting into the saddle with his arm in the temporary sling that Anne had fashioned for him. Anne climbed up on the back of the horse and slipped her arms around Nolan's waist. She pressed up against his back and rested her head on his shoulder.

They rode in silence for a long while, the horse picking its way through the sage. Darkness fell over the land and the stars hung overhead like crystal. Far off they could see the headlights of cars moving slowly down the highway. Here and there were scattered lights of ranch houses and barns dotting the range.

"What happened to Jasper?" Nolan finally broke the silence.

Anne thought for a second. It seemed like such a long while ago she had forgotten about the horse.

"I had to let him loose. I chased him away to throw those guys off my trail."

"Did it work?"

"Yeah, but there were others I didn't see. One guy was on the ATV and the others were behind him on foot. I lost the ATV guy but the others saw me when I was coming to look for you."

Her words were soft. There was no fear or anger, just a slow reminiscing.

"Do you think he will make it back to the ranch?"

Nolan nodded his head. "Yeah, Jasper knows the way home. I just hope no one comes out looking for us when he shows up at the ranch without a rider."

Anne reflected on the impact of the horse returning to the ranch riderless. She knew it would traumatize Samantha.

"How long before we get there?" Anne asked quietly, her head rising and falling on Nolan's shoulder with the gait of the horse.

"Probably a couple hours. We could make a beeline and cut some time but we'll need to be careful to hide our tracks. I am sure they will have dogs tracking us."

"How will you do that?"

"I've still got a few tricks left. The creek will help, and there are some rocky stretches up toward the west end of the ridge." Anne was in the relaxed state of aftershock. The adrenaline surge of the afternoon had left her body exhausted and numb. She tightened her grasp around Nolan's waist.

"Nolan?"

"Yeah?"

"Why are you doing this? Why the big deal about this herd? Why is it worth all this?"

Nolan considered the question. He did want to tell Anne about the true nature of these horses, the truth about Xu's promise. He wanted to tell her everything and share with her the passion co-existing with his fate as the carrier of the blue flower.

"I am not sure you would believe me if I told you."

Anne wrinkled her brow. "What is that supposed to mean?"

"Well, it's kind of an unbelievable story."

"Try me."

Nolan didn't know where to start. There were few who knew the realities of his experience. There was so much that could be misunder-

142

stood or misconstrued. It was a secret world that he shared with only a select group of knowing individuals. He had never spoken about it to anyone outside his close-knit circle. He wanted terribly to bring Anne into this world, but his intuition told him it could be dangerous and could actually drive them apart. But he couldn't keep it back. He had to tell her, to share this passion with her.

"I have a gift," he said.

The words caught Anne off guard. "A gift?"

"Well, it's kind of like that. Sometimes it seems more like a curse."

Anne was silent. She tightened her grip on Nolan's waist, her head resting on the back of his shoulder. The cool air was starting to penetrate her clothing.

"You know that story Joe told us last night? The story of Xu?"

Anne widened her eyes in sarcasm. "Yes," she said slowly.

"Well, to say it bluntly, that story is true. There exists a promise between horse and man, a sacred bond that has been passed down through the years. And I know it sounds crazy, and maybe it is crazy, but I am one of the keepers of that promise."

Anne didn't quite know what to say. It didn't feel right to launch a critique of his claim.

"Umm …okay," she said.

Nolan sensed her loosely veiled skepticism and it made him falter. This was the reason he never spoke of his calling, his gift, or his special abilities. But there was something about this woman that made him move past this initial barrier. He wanted to tell her everything.

"I know this makes no sense to the rational mind," he continued. "So let that part go. But …basically …I can talk to horses. I know what they are thinking and feeling, and what motivates them."

"So you are a horse whisperer?"

"Well, it's a bit more than that."

"How do you mean?"

"A horse whisperer knows the instincts of horses. They can relate to horses on that level. It's an action-reaction thing. They can speak the horse's language, so to speak. And that's all well and good. That's a special skill, a great skill, one that I have too. But I have been given a gift that takes me to the next level."

"You are a horse angel."

Nolan bristled at the words. He didn't like being called an angel.

"You must have heard that from Rosie," he said. "She likes to call me that."

"Yeah, well, I think that did come from Rosie. But really, what does it mean?"

"Umm," Nolan hesitated, "we call it the yellow mist."

Now Anne was engaged. "Yellow mist?"

Nolan could feel Anne's soul stirring. There was a slight twist in her energy.

"This kind of borders on mystical," said Nolan, paying attention to her reaction. "Well, maybe it runs over the borders and goes right to the heart of the mystics. I don't know. Anyway, we call it the yellow mist because that's how it is seen. It looks like a misty yellow light that connects me to the horse. Through that light, that mist, I can directly communicate with the horse."

Anne didn't believe a word of it. But her subdued condition made her open to anything.

"You mean …a conversation?"

"Yes."

"You converse with horses …" Anne said with an inflection that was more of a statement than a question.

"Well, only certain horses."

Anne was silent waiting for more.

"You see, only certain horses share the gift; only certain horses see the yellow mist and connect with it. Those are the horses I can communicate with. It is quite astounding. The mist lets me probe the minds of all horses, but there are only a few that can talk back, so to speak. The ones that can talk back? They are very special, very rare."

Anne was listening intently now. "Yeah?"

"Well, this herd is one of the few wild herds left that has the gift, that remembers."

"They remember? Remember what?"

"Xu's promise. They remember the oath that was declared way back when. They remember their allegiance to humans, their debt and our debt to them, their gratitude, their partnership. They remember the ancient bonds that bind us together."

Anne rolled her eyes and smiled. "It sounds like an old Indian legend."

Nolan smiled. He always thought it amusing when people dismissed ancient truths as legends or myths. As if a myth was some made-up story with no basis in reality.

"It is an old legend for sure," he said, slightly condescending. "But the fact is, this herd needs to be preserved at any cost. They possess that thread that weaves back through time, back through the ages to the true connection between man and horse. If we can cultivate this herd, we can bring back that knowledge and spread it to all horses, all humans. This is why I care so much about this herd. This is why I am here."

The conviction in Nolan's voice stirred Anne's imagination. She had long been consumed by her own singular goal of getting Sam to the Olympics. Now that goal seemed shallow and empty. Compared to what this man was doing, she saw her dream as selfish and completely self-centered. The thought tortured her. Her inner vision seemed to unfold and expand across the ages of history. She saw the thread of existence between man and horse weaving its way through the centuries. With it came the insight of the overwhelming number of interactions that occurred between the two species—all of the hope, inspiration, partnership and love, as well as the countless episodes of despair, disappointments, abuse, and abandonment. This vision unfurled across her mind like an intricately embroidered tapestry of red, blue, purple, green, yellow, orange, and brown with goldenrod brocade and silver-tasseled fringe. The vision rushed into her mind so unexpectedly that she let out a long, audible sigh. Nolan could feel the torrent of images rushing through her soul. He felt her energy twist again, spin upward, then slowly, softly descend. Unsure of what just happened, Anne tightened her grip on Nolan and pushed ever tighter against his back. She looked out at the vastness of the desert, the cloud of stars overhead, and suddenly felt very small and insignificant.

Anne felt herself drifting away. Nolan's voice came to her and settled her back into the moment.

"There is another thing you need to know, Anne."

"Umm …okay, what's that?" she said, not really wanting to hear anything else.

"Samantha," Nolan continued, "She has the gift, too."

Anne's mind refused the information. "What do you mean?"

"Samantha …she sees the yellow mist …that's what I mean."

Nolan could sense Anne's disbelief and was curious as to where this would lead.

"What? Samantha? Why do you say that? How do you know that?"

"I just know. It comes with the territory."

Anne tried to process the information.

"Sam? How would she learn to do that?"

"You don't learn—it's a gift. It shows up and there it is. The key is to develop it, nurture it, and train her to use it wisely."

Anne submitted to her feelings. Somewhere deep down inside of her a call came up to just accept what was happening with no fight, no pushback, no competition. This attitude was completely new to her, but somehow she knew she must go with it.

"I don't know what to say," she said, as her mind went searching for the meaning behind what Nolan had told her. The two rode on in silence.

Close to midnight, Anne and Nolan finally arrived at the Angel Ridge ranch house. About the same time, county sheriff Daniel Parker's bedside phone woke him from his sleep. The call was from a hysterical man at Senator Ruud's cattle ranch.

CHAPTER NINE

The morning was bright, the air cool. Seven police cars gathered at the edge of the bowl by Tanner Creek. Sheriff Daniel Parker surveyed the scene as he leaned back on the front grill of his Crown Victoria highway cruiser. Parker was a tall man with jet black hair and unsympathetic coal-black eyes. Next to him, sipping coffee from a Thermos lid, was Deputy Sergeant Chris Miller who was slightly shorter than Parker, and sported a military crew cut and dusty brown mustache. The two men were obviously perplexed by what lay before them.

"Did you call your uncle?" Miller asked.

"Yeah, I put a call in to his office," said the sheriff. "Only talked to that mealy-mouthed assistant of his. God, I hate that guy."

Miller nodded his agreement.

"I don't know what the hell happened out here," continued the sheriff, "But when word of this gets out ..." His voice trailed off as if the thought was too terrible to say out loud.

Miller sipped his coffee watching his fellow officers out in the bowl taking photographs and bagging the dead bodies.

"Well, it's obvious that a mess of horses came through here, but I've never seen horses do this kind of thing." He was looking over at Bulling's smashed truck. Bulling's body lay next to the truck, covered by a sheet.

The sheriff shook his head as if to clear the cobwebs.

"The way I see it is we have two murders, Striker and Bulling. We have two dead mustangs, shot and killed, a federal crime. And the rest of these boys, well, seem to be the result of a farm accident."

"Yeah? But who, and why?" asked Miller.

"I don't know, but when Uncle Harry calls, I better have some answers," said the sheriff. "There's an election coming up and he don't need no trouble like this."

Just then one of the officers came to report.

"Whadya find?" asked the sheriff.

"A camera, sir. Found it in the cab of Bulling's truck. We dusted it and pulled the prints off. You will want to see these pictures."

Sheriff Parker took the camera and flicked it on and viewed the pictures one at a time. After a few minutes he looked up toward Angel Ridge. "Some of these photos are looking down from Angel Ridge."

"Lemme see," said Miller, taking the camera. He nodded in agreement. "Looks like someone from the rescue farm was down here looking for trouble."

"Would appear so," said the sheriff. "Looks like they found what they were looking for, too." He looked at the officer, "Get copies of those pictures to me ASAP. Make sure they're eight by twelves. Me and Miller are gonna make a run up to the Angel Ridge Ranch and pay a visit to Joe. That ol' Indian probably is behind this some way or another."

"Will do," said the officer, taking the camera. "You want me to have the bodies delivered to county?"

"Hell, no!" said the sheriff. "We need to keep a lid on this thing for a while longer. Load 'em down in the main hay barn; tow the vehicles there, too. I'll be back in a couple hours. Get this cleaned up and I'll meet you back at the barn around noon. And tell the men to keep their mouths shut. Clear?"

"Yes, sir." said the officer as he turned and walked away.

Miller looked at Parker. The sheriff saw his stare.

"What?" Parker asked in a huff.

Miller raised his eyebrows and said, "We're not going be able to keep this under wraps. Too many men involved; too many dead."

"I know," said the sheriff. "I just want some time to do a little damage control. We need to put together a story and act fast. This news will go national if we're not careful. And that will be the last thing my uncle will want. Jesus, we need to keep in front of this mess or it will roll over us fast and hard."

The sheriff took one last look at the carnage in the bowl and motioned to Miller to get in the car. They loaded up and proceeded down the road.

Ten minutes later they were driving up to Striker's crashed truck. Two police units were at the scene going over the wreckage. Striker's body was bagged and lying in front of the vehicle. Sheriff Parker pulled to a stop where he and Miller got out.

"Find anything useful?" the sheriff asked.

The leader of the unit nodded his head. "Yeah, there's a trail leading off up the hill, someone on foot and a horse."

Parker looked at the prints left in the deep sand.

"No shit," he muttered.

The leader continued, "I had Smalley follow it up a ways and it seems to be headed off towards the Angel Ridge outfit."

Miller looked at Sheriff Parker with raised eyes. "Okay," he said to the leader, "I want you to get the dogs out here. Follow that trail to its end. Find out exactly where it goes. Take a camera and document the entire trail. This could lead us right to the ones who did all this. Take that body to the ranch and keep quiet until we get back. And make sure nobody talks about this. Got it? The sheriff and me will be back in a couple hours for a full report."

"Got it, Sergeant. We're on it."

Parker and Miller climbed back into the cruiser and headed off down the road, kicking up a billowing cloud of dust. Inside the car Sheriff Parker's phone rang. He looked at the incoming number displayed on his phone.

"Oh, shit!" he said as he pushed the button and held the phone to his face.

"Sheriff Parker speaking," he said professionally.

The voice on the other end was male, authoritative, with a tone of condescension. "Sheriff Parker, stand by for Senator Ruud."

Parker said nothing. He held the phone, staring out the windshield, one hand on the wheel. It was but a few seconds when the senator's voice came on.

"Good morning, Daniel," Ruud said. His thin weak voice belied the power he held as a leading member in the United States Senate.

"Hello, Uncle Harry," replied Parker, sounding a bit thin himself, although for different reasons.

Ruud continued. "What is happening at my ranch, Daniel? I can't seem to get a straight story. Are you boys on top of this thing?"

"I am out here right now," answered Parker. "It looks like a double homicide, and a bunch of your men killed in what appears to be," he paused, "a stampede."

"A stampede," said Ruud, almost reflectively. "Tell me, Daniel, were there any horses down?"

This caught Parker off guard. "Well yes, Harry, two horses were found... shot. Why do you ask?"

"Because about an hour ago my office received a call from a certain television station in Sacramento asking about details on an incident that happened on my ranch. An incident that included the killing of wild horses."

Parker's blood ran cold. He looked at Miller who was intently listening to the conversation.

Ruud continued, "It seems our old pals over at Angel Ridge are connected to this in a very real and intimate way."

"That's funny you should say that. I am on my way over there right now. We found a camera with some photos that were taken from up on the south side of the ridge, plus tracks leading from the scene up to their operation. This could be the chance we've been waiting for."

There was a silence on the phone.

"Harry? You still there?" quizzed Parker.

"Yes," came the reply. "I am thinking. Listen, be careful moving forward. We need to assure this story is managed ...managed carefully. If that old bat Rosie is involved, as it would appear, we need to play this right. We just may have a chance to finally settle this once and for all."

Parker understood what the senator was saying. The long running feud between the Ruud family and the Clark family was almost legendary in this part of the country. Parker, being the son of Senator Ruud's only sister, knew the score on a personal level. This could be good.

"Okay, Uncle Harry. I'll handle it on this end. I'll keep you posted."

"Thank you, Daniel. I know you will."

Sheriff Parker ended the call and looked over at Miller.

"Set up some check points. I want to cover all the roads leading out of here. These perps may be long gone but we are definitely in a manhunt scenario."

Miller was on the phone coordinating with the various departments. He talked while they rode all the way to the cattle house where the dirt road ended and the pavement began. Now they could make some speed. Parker gunned the cruiser and soon they were approaching the highway. Up ahead, near the entrance to the ranch, Parker saw a couple of vans parked near the main gate. As he got closer he couldn't believe his eyes. One van was emblazoned with the KTVX Sacramento logo. The other was a vehicle from a local Reno station. As Parker drew closer, he saw the news scramble as camera men, producers, and reporters hurried into position for the shot of the police cruiser coming out of Senator Ruud's cattle ranch.

"How did these guys get tipped off?" Miller said in exasperation.

"Rosie Whitehorse," said Parker with distain. "Her brother runs the Sacramento station. There is no doubt that Angel Ridge is into this thing up to their necks."

"Whatcha gonna do?"

"I'm gonna stop by and see what they know."

As the police car drew closer to the highway the two news crews formed a gauntlet at the entrance to the ranch. Parker pulled up to cameras and microphones. He came to a slow stop and rolled down his window.

"Hello, folks," he said in a cold professional police operations tone. "Can I help you with something?" He could hear the whirl of the cameras.

"Good morning, sheriff. I understand there was some sort of incident during the night involving wild horses on Senator Ruud's ranch. Care to comment on it?"

It was one of the reporters from KRNV out of Reno. Parker met him several times over the years but didn't know where his loyalties lie.

"Yes, we are investigating a farm accident. But that is all I can tell you at this time."

"A farm accident? What is the nature of the matter?"

"I am sorry. Until I know more I cannot comment."

"Does it involve wild horses?"

"No, it does not," replied the sheriff.

"Was anybody killed?"

"Like I said, I can't speak about the investigation until I get all the facts."

"Where are you off to now?"

"Official business. Now, you will have to excuse me."

The sheriff rolled up his window and pulled slowly out onto the highway. He pressed down hard on the accelerator and in a moment was flying down the road toward Angel Ridge.

Rosie, Joe, Samantha, Anne, and Nolan were all in a small room at the far end of the bunkhouses set up for the crew's living quarters. Anne and Nolan arrived just past midnight in dreadful shape. The rest of the night was a flurry of medical attention, questions, strategy sessions, and tears. The showdown was coming and each of them knew it. The main question was how to deal with the onslaught Ruud would unleash in order to protect himself from scandal. The other equally nagging topic was how to save the wild horse herd from additional and certain attacks. Anne placed a call to her boss Matthew and requested a TV crew, immediately. The sheer number of men who were killed on Ruud's ranch would surely capture a national audience. She also informed him about the missing camera. The night ended around 3:30 a.m. when sleep could be delayed no longer. Daylight came too soon, but with renewed vigor the five gathered to discuss the next move.

"The TV crew should be at Ruud's right now," said Anne. "They'll shake it up over there and perhaps stop the slaughter of the herd for at least a few days."

"It may help temporarily, but we can't take that chance," said Joe. "We need to get that herd off the land and into safety."

"The only way is to get them up here," said Rosie.

"It will be difficult without Cloud Runner," replied Nolan. "He was our link to the herd. I haven't found another yet."

Joe looked at Nolan. Anne noticed the two men and the look that passed between them. They knew something more than they were saying. Her reporter's intuition signaled something deeper going on.

She looked at Nolan. "What, Nolan?"

Nolan said nothing. He was lying back on a leather couch propped up by a pillow, his arm hung in a sling. Anne was on a chair with her foot up on an old blue ottoman, her foot encased in a black Velcro splint, her purple swollen toes jutting from the end.

"Whatever we do, we will have to act fast," said Joe. "I fear our window of opportunity will be short."

Rosie sat with Joe at a small table against the far wall. She was fidgeting with a linen napkin. "Look, we have to get the herd off of Ruud's land. If we can move them across the CF Ranch and to the BLM on the other side of Stratford then they won't be hunted. They will be safe. That's the only way."

"Rosie's right," said Joe. "If we can get the herd up to the BLM opposite Stratford, at least they will be protected from Ruud's exterminators."

Samantha was at her mother's side sharing the chair. "But why aren't they there now? Why are the horses living down there where they aren't safe?"

Again Joe looked at Nolan. Nolan looked at the floor and muttered, "That's my fault."

Anne furrowed her brow. "How could that be your fault?"

"Oh, it's nobody's fault," Rosie blurted out changing the subject. "We're all agreed then to get the herd up to the Stratford BLM as quickly as possible. Yes?"

Anne continued to look at Nolan with curiosity. Nolan refused to return the glance. Anne could tell there was some deeper subject not being discussed. Rosie, Joe, and Nolan were hiding something, something to do with the horse herd. Her curiosity bubbled up, but she decided not to press the subject. She would wait until the right time.

The phone on the table next to Joe rang. Rosie jumped. Joe picked up the receiver. "Joe here."

The tension in the room stretched a bit tighter as they all watched Joe's face, his eyes narrowing as he listened to the caller.

"Okay, I'll be right there," he said before hanging up.

He looked at Rosie, then Nolan. "The sheriff's here."

"Sheriff Parker?" Rosie asked, her voice rising in disbelief.

"Appears so."

"Damned asshole." The words slipped out before Rosie could catch herself. She looked over at Samantha with a sheepish expression. "Sorry, Sam, I shouldn't curse."

"Who is he?" asked Anne.

Rosie looked angry. "He's Ruud's nephew, handpicked to run the county. He has been nothing but a pain in our side ever since he was sworn into office. A real nasty man."

"What does he want?"

"He wants to talk to me," said Joe as he stood up. "You all stay here and I'll go talk to him. Please, stay inside. I'll be back as soon as I can."

Rosie stood up, but Joe protested. "Oh, no; you stay here. We don't need you and Parker going at it right now. Just stay put."

Rosie uncharacteristically obeyed and sat back down. She had a frown stretching to her chin.

"I'll be back soon," said Joe, as he opened the door and stepped out into the daylight. The others watched him go, feeling a sense of dread as they heard Joe's truck engine start and the vehicle pulling away.

"They must have found the bodies," said Anne to Rosie.

"And no telling what else," she replied.

Joe pulled up to the house and parked next to the police cruiser that was waiting in the parking lot. Inside the cruiser he could see two men. He immediately recognized both of them. Through the years he lived at Angel Ridge, Joe came to know all of the folks living around the area. Parker was no exception. Joe knew him as a petty man who craved authority and demanded respect, and one who had no affinity for truth or honor. In short, Parker was an entitled nephew of a senator who would throw his weight around just for his own amusement. Although Joe despised the man as much as Rosie did, he had the ability to remain completely detached. Joe's true emotions would never be known. He stepped from his truck and walked over to the police cruiser.

Parker and Miller came out of the car with an air of pseudo authority.

"Well, hello, Sheriff." Joe offered his hand.

The sheriff reached out and officiously shook Joe's hand. The look in the sheriff's eye belied his feigned smile.

"What can I do for you?"

"Joe, there was some trouble over at my uncle's ranch yesterday." The sheriff was looking for any kind of reaction. Joe's poker face showed nothing.

"What kind of trouble, Sheriff?"

"It appears to be a double homicide."

Joe raised his eyebrows. "Oh dear. What happened?"

The sheriff looked deep into Joe's eyes, trying to read his mind.

"We are not quite sure, but it looks like two of the ranch hands stumbled onto someone out messing with the mustangs. We found two horses shot and two of our men dead at the scene."

"Oh, my God!" Joe was visibly shaken. "That's horrible."

"There was a trail—foot prints, human and horse—leading up to your ranch. I wondered if anyone around here saw anything related to that."

Joe remained unreadable.

"So there's a couple of killers on the loose? And they came through here? Well, I haven't heard anything unusual. What time did this all happen?"

"Yesterday afternoon," said the sheriff.

"I had better get everybody together and spread the word. This sounds dangerous." Joe was playing his part perfectly.

"I'm going to have some men come up here and have a look around. That's not a problem is it, Joe?"

"Of course not. Whatever you need, Sheriff."

"Meanwhile, you folks keep your eyes peeled. These guys are definitely armed and dangerous. My men will be here soon. Call me if you see anything before then, yeah?"

"Yeah.!"

The sheriff and Miller turned to get into their car. As Parker opened his door, he motioned to Anne's car parked nearby. "Hey, Joe, you got visitors? I noticed the California plates."

Joe blinked. "Uh, yes, a lady up from Sacramento, looking for a horse to adopt."

The sheriff paused and gazed into Joe's coal black eyes. "Okay," said Parker. "Let me know if you hear anything."

Parker and Miller got into the cruiser and a minute later they were gone.

In Sacramento, at the KTVX headquarters, Matthew Clark was leaning over a man sitting at a computer. The two were staring at the screen. Matthew held a logbook filled with hand-written cross-references, names and numbers. The names were those of his staff. The numbers were serial numbers of production equipment issued to each name on the list. Cameras, recorders, microphones, even cables were all recorded and cross-referenced to the person to whom they were issued. Of course, this log was notoriously rife with incorrect information. As the comings and goings of reporters at the station happened at near-lightning speed, the list was never quite complete or up to date. Equipment was shuffled between crews; emergencies stopped the administrative functions of recording who had what equipment. It was the classic example of the second law of thermodynamics where all systems are subject to entropy. Things break down.

"Is that it?" Matthew pointed at the screen.

"No, that's Thom's video pack."

"Is there any way to sort by serial number?"

"Maybe, let me try ..."

The man at the computer typed some commands on the keyboard. He grabbed the mouse and clicked here and there.

"Okay, I think that will work. Let's see what we get."

The screen blinked and a new list popped up.

"Here it is."

Matthew ran his hand through his hair. "Okay, now we are getting somewhere. Sort through that list for any Canon product numbers."

The man clicked a few more buttons and the screen responded with a rather long list of numbers.

"We are looking for the EOS-1D." The man was scrolling through the list.

156

"Oh," he said, "is this it?"

Matthew looked at the screen then opened the logbook and looked at the page. A wave of frustration overtook him and he threw the logbook into a nearby trashcan.

"Damn, useless piece of crap."

"You said EOS-1D, right?"

"Yeah, that's what Anne told me."

"Well, here is a list of all 1Ds we purchased about four months ago."

"Oh, good. Four months ago?" Matthew bent over and pulled the logbook from the can. He opened it and flipped back a few pages.

"Here it is. June 17th ...let's see ..." He went through the list. "Okay! Here it is. Seven cameras—one checked out to Anne Harper on the 17th, serial number 003466578."

The man repeated the numbers as he typed them into the screen. After hitting the return key, he sat back as both men focused on the results.

"Yes!" Matthew cheered as the screen presented the information he was looking for. Just then the door to the small room opened and a woman walked in holding a CD.

"Here's the software you asked for, Mr. Clark."

Matthew took the CD from her hand. He thanked her as she turned and left the room, closing the door behind her. He handed the disk to the man and asked him to load it in the computer. The man took the disk and put it into the multimedia drive.

"Okay, so what does this do?"

"The new Canons can be accessed remotely, over the Internet. This is the software that lets us do that. We need to find that camera and download the photos."

"What happened? Did Anne lose her camera?"

"I think it was stolen," Matthew said unconvincingly.

"Hmm, okay; this will take a few minutes to load. I'm going to get a coffee. You want something?"

Matthew looked nervous. "No thanks. I'll wait here and make sure this goes smoothly."

The man got up and left the room. Matthew watched the screen as the progress bar slowly worked its way across the screen.

Sheriff Parker and Sergeant Miller pulled up to the main building at Ruud's cattle ranch. They didn't stopped to speak with the press who remained outside the main gate. Exiting the police cruiser, they entered the corrugated tin-sided building. Inside was a main office area with several adjacent smaller rooms. A series of old surplus desks sat at one side of the room. On the other was a bookcase and a table surrounded by chairs. The whole room seemed to be covered under a layer of thick yellow dust. The place was empty except for a few ranch hands who were basically waiting to be told what to do. In one of the smaller rooms was an officer with Anne's camera. Miller walked in to check the progress.

"Got my pictures yet?" he demanded.

The younger officer was one of Parker's nephews, the middle son of the sheriff's oldest sister. His name was Stanson Bentley; everyone called him Stan.

"Almost," said Stan nervously.

Stan had the camera connected to a laptop that was connected to an inkjet printer. Stan was downloading the pictures when Parker walked in. The sheriff grumbled and left the room walking out into the main area.

Miller was at the table with a phone to his ear. As Parker approached, Miller hung up.

"The K-9 crew will be here any minute. Mobile command is rolling and the county is sending down two ambulance details. Everything is on schedule."

Parker nodded his understanding and sat down across from Miller. He looked over at one of the ranch hands.

"You got any coffee in here?"

"Yes sir, in the back there," replied the old cowboy pointing to the hallway.

"Would you mind getting me and my partner a coupla cups?" The question came out more like an order. The cowboy looked at the sheriff and decided it would be best to do what he was told.

"Sure 'nuf." The cowboy rose from his chair and wandered off toward the coffee pot.

Parker looked at Miller. "We need a plan for the press. I really don't want pictures of a bunch of dead cowboys being toted off this ranch in body bags. We need to give 'em something to chew on."

Miller nodded. "Let's let one of the ambulances through. That'll give them the photos they want. Then we'll call a press conference down at the station. That'll give us some time to clean up this mess before we let 'em come in and film the crime scene."

Parker thought for a long minute. "Okay, that's a start. We need to coordinate this pretty close to keep the lid on. Those bastards from Sacramento aren't going to go away easily."

Parker stopped as the thought came crashing into his conscious mind. He sat staring at the table with a crinkle on his brow.

"What is it?" asked Miller.

"Sacramento," said Parker. "There was a car from California at Angel Ridge."

"Yes," confirmed Miller, "a maroon BMW X5."

"That was no coincidence. Something tells me we should have looked closer at that vehicle."

"5FMB334," said Miller robotically.

Parker looked at Miller in disbelief. "You mean to tell me you got the plate number?"

"I keep telling you I have a photographic memory. One day you will remember."

Parker didn't like to be upstaged, but Miller was one of the few he would let get away with it.

"Run it and let's see who really *is* up there."

Miller picked up the phone and punched in a number. Parker got up and went to see the progress on the photos.

Stan was at the desk furiously punching buttons on his computer. Something was wrong and Parker picked up on it immediately.

"What's going on?" he demanded.

"Look!" Stan pointed to the camera. The back screen had changed to blue and there was a yellow line across the top. The line was shrinking rapidly. Parker didn't understand.

"What? What are we looking at?"

"The pictures—they're being erased."

Parker reached over the young man, pushed him aside and grabbed the camera. He yanked out the cords as he stood upright. Frantically, he found the power switch and flipped it off. Nothing happened. The yellow line was three quarters gone. He turned the camera over and flipped a tab opening the cover to the SD card. Pushing the release, the card popped up. Parker grabbed the card and pulled it from the camera. The screen went black with a flashing red warning.

"What the hell?" Parker looked at the camera. "How many pictures did you get off of here?"

"All of 'em," said Stan. "I was printing them out when the camera seemed to reset automatically."

Parker thought for a moment. Then he handed the camera back to Stan.

"Research this camera. I want to know all of the features on this thing. I want to know what this thing can do. And I want to know NOW!"

Stan turned and launched his web browser, typing in the model number.

Matthew Clark stood above the computer. He was frowning.

"What happened?"

"We lost the connection."

"Can you get it back?"

"I'll certainly try."

"How many pictures did you get?"

"We got all the pictures, no worries. It was the erase function that got stopped."

Matthew stood silent.

"The connection is lost. Not sure why."

"Well, okay," said Matthew. "Get me copies of those photos right away. Thanks for your help."

"No problem, Mr. Clark. Glad to be of help." The man reached over and plugged a blank CD into the media drive. "I'll have those photos for you in just a minute. Hang tight."

The 40-foot mobile command and communications unit pulled up to the complex at Ruud's ranch. A puff of dust kicked up as the large vehicle came to a stop and its airbrakes hissed their final release. Built by LDV and fitted to the Blue Bird chassis, this machine was top-of-its-class in terms of size, technology, and operation. The jet-black finish was offset by the county's golden emblem and the words Nye County Sheriff's Department painted three feet high on each side. Inside was the latest surveillance and communications gear, courtesy of Uncle Harold who made sure his nephew had all the law enforcement toys one could ever want. The mobile command vehicle had rarely been used in actual law enforcement, but it did come in handy for weekend training exercises held out by Diamond Lake when the fishing was good.

Immediately upon arrival, the crew of the MCU busied themselves with setting up the vehicle to operate as the main center for coordinating the investigation and manhunt. Parker watched the men work. Two slide-outs hummed into position. An awning was deployed for the external operations center. The skyline satellite was calibrated; several communications antennas were positioned; even high-energy floodlights were deployed in case the team had to work through the night. Within 15 minutes the mobile command unit was deployed and operational.

Parker climbed aboard. At the front of the unit behind the driver's seat were four workstations lining each wall. Each station was equipped with a laptop, two monitors, a radio com, a telephone, and a grey swivel desk chair. Two officers were at their stations making electronic connections to the outside world. Just beyond this cabin was a galley, toilet, and several large storage cupboards. Farther back in the bus was a small conference table surrounded by swivel chairs. The walls in this cabin were lined with monitors. A large LED clock hung on the back wall underneath a 60-inch flat screen.

Parker took a seat at one of the workstations and picked up a headset. The K-9 unit was on its way out to Striker's truck. The dogs would be on the trail within 30 minutes. Additional men were being brought in to mount an extensive manhunt. The bodies of the dead ranch hands were being loaded on a flatbed ranch truck and would be brought to the main complex. The forensic team was gathering evidence, which would easily take a few more hours. Highway checkpoints were set up to the north and south as well as the eastbound dirt road. The area was locked down. Parker turned his attention to Angel Ridge.

"Vanders," Parker said turning to one of the men at the workstation, "I want a thorough search of Angel Ridge ASAP. I'll call the judge for a warrant, but we need to move fast. Get some men up there. Tell 'em not to discuss the details of this situation. There is one, possibly two, fugitives considered to be armed and dangerous."

"Yessir, on it."

Miller stepped up into the command unit and sat down next to the sheriff. He slipped a paper onto the desk.

"Here is the info on that X5. It belongs to Anne Harper. She lives on a horse farm outside of Sacramento."

Parker looked at the paper. "Well, that seems to add up."

"Except for one thing."

"What's that?

"She is an investigative reporter for KTVX."

Parker's blood ran cold.

Nolan woke up from a dreamless sleep. The sun illuminated the light cotton curtains pulled across the window. The room was empty and quiet. Slowly he maneuvered his body to the sitting position, struggling against the stiffness in his shoulder. He had to stop and let the pain subside, then he stood up. Putting on his clothes was another matter entirely, but he managed through the ordeal, opened the door and stepped out into the sunlight. Joe was sitting on the porch looking into the clear blue sky.

"How ya feeling, Nolan?"

Nolan was blinking in the sunlight. The cool air felt good on his face.

"I'm feeling lucky to be alive. Where's Anne?"

"She's taking a shower. Getting ready to leave."

"Leave?" Nolan was surprised. "She's going back? Now?"

"I think she's had enough. She's really shaken up."

Nolan's heart sank. "This is all my fault. I should have known better; those guys over there at Ruud's are animals."

"You didn't know. None of us did," reassured Joe.

"I should have."

Joe didn't move. He had his face toward the sun soaking up the rays. To Nolan he seemed unusually calm.

"I want to talk to Anne before she goes," said Nolan. "What's her plan?"

"Not sure, but Rosie probably knows. To tell you the truth I have a feeling that Anne won't be going anywhere for a couple of days."

"Why's that?"

"Because Sheriff Parker is organizing a manhunt. There are checkpoints on all the highways, and he knows Anne is here."

Nolan looked at the old Indian. The man's black hair was glimmering in the sunlight; his braids almost twinkled. He was leaning back on his hands, eyes closed, head up. The serenity was palpable.

"How do you know all this?"

"If you must know, I have a friend on the inside."

"One of the cops?" Nolan was shocked.

"Someone called in Anne's plates, the sheriff noticed her car up at the house. Must have got suspicious. I told him she was up here looking at horses, but it won't be long 'til they figure out she is with the news station."

"What else?"

"Sheriff is organizing a manhunt for two armed and dangerous murderers."

Nolan's face twisted into a frown. He pondered the implications of what his friend just said. He slowly lowered himself down to the edge of the porch and sat next to Joe.

"Murder," Nolan said softly, reflectively.

"Yeah, they are going to try to turn this thing around and place the blame squarely on you and Anne. Of course they don't know it's you and Anne they are looking for. Anyway, she's nervous and wants to get out of here as soon as she can."

"Where is she? I need to talk to her."

Joe opened his eyes and looked at Nolan.

"Let me call up to the house and ask Rosie. But you need to stay here. Parker and his men will be at the gate any minute. I want to keep you hidden for now."

"This is bullshit," said Nolan.

"Yes, it is, old friend. For now I want you to go to the clinic. There is a basement in that building that Parker will never find. Stay there 'til I come. It may be several hours but we need to keep you out of sight for now."

"I'm not going to hide away. How's anyone gonna know I was out there when all that happened?"

"Just do as I ask. Please, this is for the sake of the ranch, as well as you and Anne."

Nolan didn't like the thought of running away and hiding. It went against his entire moral fiber. But he knew Joe. He trusted Joe and wouldn't let him down.

"I'll head down to the clinic, but I want to talk to Anne before she leaves."

"Let me handle that," said Joe. "You had better go. They're coming."

Nolan was frowning. He looked down at Joe who still seemed annoyingly calm. Without saying another word he turned down the hill and headed toward the clinic. It was about 300 yards down past the bunkhouses. As he stood at the doorway, he looked back up the hill toward the house and saw the first of the officers coming down the hill. No one noticed him slip into the clinic.

Inside was Dennis Carter, one of the veterinarians, who seemed to be ready for him. Dennis waved Nolan into the back of the building and through a doorway. Behind a curious movable wall there was a stairway leading down to a well-lit basement cellar. Nolan looked at Dennis who said nothing but nudged Nolan onto the stairway. Before Nolan was at the bottom, Dennis closed the hinged wall. On the outside, the wall was fitted with coat hooks where a number of aprons and white lab coats were hung. It was completely camouflaged.

Nolan moved into the cellar. It was a large room with two tables and several chairs, a cot on one side, and a toilet and sink on the other. In the corner was a small refrigerator next to a water cooler. There was also a bookshelf with a dozen books stacked neatly in rows. Nolan never was told about this safe room. He wondered what it was built for.

He sat down at one of the tables and tried to think.

Joe sauntered up the hill toward the house and met the officer in charge of the search. His name was Jared Parker. He was 27 and directly related to the sheriff. Joe found him to be cold and unfriendly. He asked Joe about the layout of the ranch—how many buildings there were, how many people were on the ranch, if they had any visitors on site.

"As a matter of fact, we do. We have two visitors," Joe offered.

"We have a mother and her daughter up from Sacramento looking at horses."

The younger Parker gave Joe an icy stare. "Where are they?" he asked in an overly demanding tone.

"They're up at the main house. Poor woman was trying out one of the stallions and was thrown off. Broke her foot and banged up her face." Joe gave the man a distraught look.

"Are your people aware there are two killers on the loose?"

"Yes, officer, we have taken precautions. But we can't shut down the operation; life must go on."

Young Officer Parker didn't like this old Indian. There was something too accommodating about him.

"I have orders to search the entire ranch, out-buildings and all. Is that going to be a problem?"

"A problem? Of course not. You let me know if you need anything, officer."

The officer gave one more stony look then turned his back to Joe, signaling his men to gather around. The large group swarmed around the younger Parker as he gave each team quick instructions. With a yell the teams dispersed, each in a different direction.

At the main house, Anne and Samantha had their belongings packed. Samantha watched the whirlwind happenings over the last couple of hours with curiosity and dread. The focus of attention was, understandably, on Anne and Nolan. Sam was on the periphery of the action, and as the story unfolded, it seemed to her like some kind of movie drama. The yellow mist was a persistent companion, a calming force that kept her somewhat detached from the real pain of the chaotic situation.

As Anne stood in the living room next to her luggage, she thought about Nolan. Something in her heart wanted to go and say goodbye; to thank him for not abandoning her out in the desert. After all, he did come after her. He was chivalrous and brave and she owed him the courtesy of a farewell. But that feeling was overruled by her sense of practicality. She couldn't deny she was angry about what happened, and it was his fault. There was nothing to say. The feelings that passed between them were nothing but false infatuation. They had nothing in common—he was a hardened cowboy, she was an urbanite used to finer things. She resisted the urge to seek him out. She and Sam would leave this place and forget the nightmare, return to their home and settle back to the routine. That was how it would be. That was what she was thinking just before young Officer Parker and his men came barging through the front door.

Officer Parker entered the room first. The sight of Anne stopped him with a double take. Her left eye was swollen, black and blue and yellow contrasting starkly with her pallid, sallow face. She stood half hunched over with a crutch under one arm. Her right foot was bound with a walking cast and her pant leg was pushed up over the top of the black plastic-and-Lycra boot. Parker noticed other scratches and bruises on her hands and arms. The woman's general demeanor showed anger, frustration, and abuse. Parker saw this characteristic in women that were victims of domestic abuse. In this part of the county there were endless cases of women bearing the brunt of their husband's or boyfriend's frustrations. Parker got to witness it over and over again. In most of the cases, the women had a look about them, a particular intention, a motivation. It was the desire to flee, to get away. Parker looked at the luggage on the floor next to the woman and his instincts immediately told him that this woman was a big piece of the puzzle. Yes, she was his first person of interest.

Parker moved into the room with his men and took stock of the situation. In front of him was the beat-up woman, a girl who looked to be her daughter, Rosie Whitehorse, who he knew all too well, and some ranch hand who he saw around town. After a perfunctory greeting, Parker turned his attention to Anne.

"What happened to you?" he asked in an accusatory tone.

"She was thrown off one of our new stallions," Rosie said, pushing herself between Anne and the younger Parker.

Parker bristled; he never liked Rosie Whitehorse. She was the enemy and a troublemaker.

"Rosie, if you don't mind, I will talk to this woman directly. Please stand aside."

Rosie backed down and Anne fixed her gaze onto the policeman.

"That must have been quite a spill," said Parker.

Anne said nothing, her anger was boiling up and she knew where this was going.

"I need your name."

"My name is Anne Harper."

The cop looked at Samantha. The girl had nothing readable in her eyes; she looked detached, far away.

"And you?"

"I'm Samantha." She took hold of her mother's hand. "I'm her daughter."

"Okay," Parker continued. "My name is Deputy Parker. We are investigating the murders of two men at the High Star. Ms. Harper, I need to ask you some questions."

When the officer said the word murder, Anne's pulse quickened. A shiver of injustice careened down her spine. Her eyes narrowed. If this man only knew the truth of the matter but truth didn't matter here. Parker had an agenda and Anne knew it. She would have to play this cool or risk being swept up into the long-standing feud between the Clarks and the Ruuds. She knew Parker was here to even the score, but her anger was fueling her desire to unload on this guy, to tell him to go to hell, to accuse his masters of crimes beyond the scope of his puny mock investigation. She took a deep breath.

"Will this take long? I am just leaving, and, as you can see, I am not feeling well."

"Where were you yesterday?"

Anne knew better than to lie to a police office in the midst of a so-called murder investigation. She would have to play word games, keep it very general.

"Here, at Angel Ridge."

"Were you here all day?"

"Well, I was out riding for part of the day."

"Alone?"

"No, who rides alone? That would be reckless."

"Who were you with?"

"One of the trainers."

"Can I get a name?"

Anne looked over at Rosie who had a defiant look on her face.

"She was with Nolan Powell," said Rosie.

Parker didn't look at Rosie. He kept his attention on Anne. The tension in the room was growing.

"Is that right, Ms. Harper?"

"Yes, Nolan was helping me choose a horse."

"You are here to choose a horse?"

"I am here investigating the horses, yes."

"Where do you live?"

"I am from the Sacramento area."

"So that is your X5 out in the driveway?"

"Yes, it is."

Parker paused and stared into Anne's eyes. She didn't flinch, but returned the stare with equal intensity. Parker could tell he was getting to her.

"Ms. Harper, did you ride out to the High Star Ranch yesterday?"

"Well, we rode for a couple hours. I am not familiar with the boundaries."

"So, you don't know if you were on High Star's property?"

"I guess we could have been there. Like I said, I don't know where the boundaries are."

"Ms. Harper, two men were killed out at the ranch yesterday. Did you see or hear anything related to that incident?"

Anne thought for a moment; she didn't want to lie. She really wasn't witness to any murders; she was unconscious and came to in Striker's truck. In her mind Striker died behind the wheel during the crash.

"No, nothing at all," she said confidently.

Parker sensed she was hiding something.

"How did you sustain those injuries?"

Rosie interrupted again, "Like I told you, she was thrown off the horse."

Parker ignored the old woman and kept his eyes fixed on Anne waiting for an answer.

"That's right; I fell."

"Can you tell me how it happened?"

"Oh, I don't know. One minute I was up, the next I was down. It happened pretty quick."

Parker nodded his head. "Okay, I must ask you to delay your departure until we finish our search of the property. I have orders to lock down the area while we conduct our investigation."

Anne was fuming inside. She told herself to keep cool.

"What? You can't keep me here!"

"Well, I can if I have to. Right now I am asking for your cooperation. Two men were killed and those responsible are still at large. Let us do our work and in a couple hours you can leave. Right now I am asking you to stick around. Is that going to be a problem?"

"Fine," Anne snapped back. "How will I know when it is safe to leave?"

"I will personally let you know. This shouldn't take too long."

He turned to Rosie. "Mind if I look around?"

Rosie did mind, but knew better than to provoke this man. He was the enemy and he had all the power in his grasp to make life very difficult. It was best to play along.

"No, feel free. If you need my help, let me know."

"I do need one thing," said Parker. "I need to talk to Nolan Powell."

Rosie shrugged her shoulders. "Well, you missed him, he left last night for Reno. He had to run some errands in town."

"Do you know where he is staying up there?"

"No. Sorry, I do not."

Parker shrugged, "When is he due back?"

"In a couple of days."

"Can you describe him for me?"

Rosie gave a general description of Nolan, leaving out anything specific. Parker took down the information while his men searched each room in the house.

Meanwhile, Anne and Samantha took a seat in the living room. Sam sat quietly at her mother's side, looking like she was in a daydream. Anne's anxiety was peaking. She sat on the couch, her stomach churning. What to do? She wanted nothing more than to get in her car and leave. Her wrath focused on the young Officer Parker and his arrogant treatment of her. Couldn't he see that she was in pain? Her mind wandered into the memories from the night before. Nolan left her on her own. He abandoned her on the bluff; that's when the whole situation turned. She broke her foot and bashed her face. She was kidnapped and being taken to God knows where. Her fears rehashed a scenario of being held in a dark room with strangers abusing her with all hope fading into a nightmare of torture and a slow death. Her daughter would have suffered most. Anne's mind swirled with fear and hopelessness. Rosie's voice drew her back to reality.

"Anne? Are you alright?" asked Rosie, who sat across from her.

Anne snapped out of her frightful daydream.

"No, I am not alright. This is complete bullshit. If these people want to keep me here they should arrest me for something. I need to get out of here. I need to go home."

"Try to relax dear," said Rosie tenderly. "Take a deep breath."

"Bullshit," Anne whispered. "I just want to get out of here, get far away and never think of this again."

Parker came into the room once more and gave Anne a hardened glare. Having finished their search of the house, his men followed him to the foyer.

"I'll let you know when it's okay to leave," he said before he and his troops stomped out the front door.

"I'll be right here waiting," Anne replied sarcastically. "You just let me know."

The door shut and the room was quiet. Sam looked at her mother with confusion.

"Mom, the horses need you."

"The horses?" Anne's words sounded harsh. "That wild bunch of animals? They are on their own. It's you and me Sam; we need to take care of ourselves. This is not my fight; this is not worth the risk of losing you forever."

These words did not make any sense to Sam. Over the years she had known her mom to be a fighter, someone who never backed down, even when she was clearly wrong. Anne was a fierce competitor with a fire for the chase. Something wasn't right.

"But what about Nolan?" asked Samantha in a curious tone.

The name of Nolan sent Anne even further toward a blind rage. "Nolan? He almost got me killed. I am lucky to be alive. Nolan? Bah! He's just another man who will turn his back and leave me to survive on my own." Anne was clearly not thinking rationally, her anger was red and flaring.

"Oh, honey," said Rosie, "Nolan didn't leave you on your own. He came after you. He did the right thing by you; you even said so last night."

Anne turned to Rosie with daggers in her eyes. Rosie's face didn't change; rather she had an air of pure compassion, pure love, and pure heart. Anne saw in her a deep understanding and knowing. Rosie's powerful, innate soul revealed a truth too deep for words. Her face displayed a reality that mirrored back to Anne the long years of pain and depression since Simon's death. She saw in Rosie's eyes the eternal depth and breadth of her own pain, her own ridiculous suffering. It was too much. Anne burst into tears.

Covering her face in shame, Anne sobbed uncontrollably. All of the trauma, stress, and chaos burst up into her mind and shivered through her body. Accompanied by loud moans, her pent-up anger and loneliness came rushing forth in waves of convulsions and tears. Sam, typically affected by her mother's emotions, felt the yellow mist quickly swirl up, providing an unnatural calm and detachment from the terrible emotions spilling out around her. She looked at Rosie who had her eyes closed chanting some inaudible prayer. Sam took a deep breath and waited for her mother's tears to exhaust themselves. Anne continued to bawl for five minutes.

Nolan sat in the basement safe room unsuccessfully trying to contact the herd. The blue flower was radiant in his mind and filled his vision with a source of beauty and wonder. But try as he might, there was no horse on the other end that could respond even a little. He patiently searched the landscape of his inner vision. But in his heart another vision kept intruding on his consciousness. It was Anne.

Nolan never met a woman as strong and as brave as Anne Harper.

His first impression of her had not been good. But, as is often the case, first impressions mostly reflect our own self-imposed misgivings. Anne was just such a case. What he interpreted as pride and condescension was her competitive nature, her striving to conquer. He didn't see that trait as particularly negative or as anything more than Anne's attempt to conquer her own inner demons. Not too far below the surface of this imposing woman was a caring heart that was courageous yet kind.

And then there was her outer beauty—her lithe figure, shining eyes, and naturally radiant smile. Sure, he hadn't seen that smile much yesterday, but when she lifted her guard it was a boost to his spirit. She found a hidden path to his heart. Nolan hadn't been with a woman in years and had all but given up on the natural urges of a man. Unbeknownst to Anne, she'd knocked down those walls and forced her way through that barricade.

Nolan shook his head. He wanted to get her out of his mind. There was no way she would ever be interested in him. He was a lone force in the world. He had a destiny that few men shared. He knew it was his burden to carry, and to share it with another would only bring heartache. This was his lonely secret, his bane, and his curse. He bore it alone with the help of a few knowing friends. Otherwise he kept to himself and focused on his purpose in life—the love, care, and protection of horse culture.

This purpose found him early in life while growing up in the middle of horse country near the heart of Virginia. His father was a horse breeder, his mother a housewife. The two owned a prestigious farm just outside Middleburg where they raised Hanoverian crosses used for jumping and dressage. Nolan grew up on the back of a horse and was a natural. He and his sister, Tammy, learned the secrets of horse training from an early age. Nolan discovered his special gift, not unlike Samantha, when he was nine years old. Although, unlike Samantha, Nolan had a group of people around him who also knew about the yellow mist and what it meant. Nolan was nurtured along and his gift was cultivated and honored. He was destined to become a great horseman.

Then a string of unfortunate events turned his life upside down. The first involved a young woman named Catherine Medvedev, his first and only love. Catherine and Nolan met at one of the horse shows that were a constant fixture in Virginia throughout the summer season. Both Catherine and Nolan competed in eventing and stadium jumping. Nolan was the better rider, but Catherine was a strong competitor and turned into a good friend. They fell in love and had two years of bliss before Catherine fell ill with a rare form of liver cancer. By the time they found the disease it was too late; she died in a short four months.

Devastated, Nolan moved from his small town, leaving the family farm. He made his way across the state working at random jobs until Tammy called and told him about a job at the McPhadden horse farm, Coombs Hollow Stables. He was hired there to work with the colts, bringing them around to saddle. It was a dream job for Nolan, as he always had a way with the young ones. It was there that he learned how to communicate through the yellow mist and how it worked both ways. A young horse, a filly he called Silly, was under his care and coming along nicely. He worked this filly especially well, as the horse's natural abilities, intelligence, and talent were evident. It was late one night that the yellow mist was swirling in his inner vision and Silly's voice came through with startling clarity. Nolan worked on cultivating this gift in light of his new discovery. Soon he and Silly were joined as no horse and trainer had been. They were a true team.

Silly was three years old and Nolan already had her saddle-trained. She was in the groundwork stage of her training, doing the work to build muscles and agility. Nolan never had a horse of this caliber, the finest of conformation, the boldest heart, and a willing mind. Within and through the yellow mist the two, human and horse, were connected on a deep level of understanding, mutual trust, and partnership. Nolan truly loved this animal. More important than the bright competitive future of this horse was the fact that she was one who remembered. Xu's promise lived in this brilliant animal; it was alive and thriving, and she would bring others along with her. A new hope settled in throughout the Virginia horse community with those that knew, that small society of people who understood the sacred bond. Whispers of excitement echoed in the barns, show grounds, and meeting rooms, and the story of this new horse slowly spread. The bond was back; there was a new horse that carried the knowledge. There was a young man, Nolan Powell, who had the gift. This hope, this expectation, was shared by the few knowledgeable folks who understood this to be the beginning of a new era. The beginning of a time when Xu's promise could be brought back, cultivated, taught, and honored.

Then came the night that Nolan has relived every day since. Nolan had moved some of the horses from Coombs Hollow over to Carter's Farm for an equitation presentation. It was an annual event where the new horses from around the area were showcased for potential buyers and sponsors. Silly was already being discussed by several prominent trainers and high-level riders. There was true excitement surrounding this young mare. The Carter event was always well attended and was one of the highlights of the year within the Virginia horse community. It was an event that Nolan, try as he might, would never be able to forget.

Nolan had just finished with Silly. They did some ring work and general basic exercise. The sun was low and it was time to put the horse up for the evening. After a thorough brushing and some extra grain, Nolan left Silly in her stall. The barn was a marvelous structure built in the late 1800s. Large, hand-hewn oak beams held aloft a steep-pitched roof of wooden shingles and two towering cupolas. The interior featured 16 roomy stalls lined with walnut tongue-and-groove, a wide middle aisle, and several large tack rooms at either end. The barn was updated through the years with modern plumbing and electrical systems; the last work done some 25 years earlier. It was on the historical register and was a beloved landmark for the county residents.

The fire was unforeseen. It started in an electrical circuit overloaded by new equipment of the modern age. The seeds of destruction were sown years ago when, during a remodeling job of the barn's small office, a worker stapled up some chicken-wire lathe. It was underlayment for the new plaster wall being installed as part of the upgrades. One of the staples inadvertently pushed its way through a strand of newly installed electrical wire that supplied the offices new electrical outlets. The short in the wires went unnoticed for years and posed no real danger. That changed in modern times with the advent of computers, flat screen TVs, and other electrical devices that demanded, and drew, more power.

A week before the fire, the barn manager installed a new computer and a 42" flat screen television in the office. Until then the compromised electrical circuit served a couple of light bulbs. It was now called upon to deliver a much higher current for the new energy-hungry electronic devices. The small staple, hidden for so long, now became a grave liability as the short began to spark and the wooden structure beneath the wall smoldered.

As Nolan was putting Silly up for the night, he got a faint whiff of smoke, then it was gone. The thought of a barn fire didn't even cross his mind. He dismissed the smell as coming from the main house where, because of cooling weather, the Carters had one of their fireplaces burning. He closed the barn and shut off the lights.

Nolan was staying in one of the estate's many cottages. His was closest to the barn, within eyeshot. After settling in and having a small dinner, Nolan turned in for the night. He was restless and didn't know why. The yellow mist was swirling in his mind and wouldn't let him sleep. That's when he noticed the strange light on the ceiling of his bedroom, a dancing red and yellow light, flickering across his vision. He lay there and watched it for a few minutes until the reality of the sight sank into his consciousness. Jumping up, Nolan ran to the window where the ghastly sight of the burning barn seared into his brain. Flames were licking up the far side of the massive structure, bending over the roofline and working their way up the wooden shingles. Terrified, Nolan ran straight out the door dressed only in his underwear, his bare feet feeling the cool, wet grass below.

When he got to the barn, smoke was seeping through the cracks between the great sliding doors. He pulled open the one on the left and a massive billow of pent-up smoke poured into the night. Looking down the corridor, he saw flames at the other end of the barn. Immediately he started opening the stall doors that were holding back the frantic horses. One at a time he progressed down the corridor, each one taking a bit longer as the horses had cowered back into their stalls and had to be shooed out. The flames grew more frightening as he got closer to his real goal. Silly's stall was at the far end closest to the fire. Why hadn't he started at that stall? Why had he saved that one for last? He'd had to chase the last horse all the way out of the barn, the poor animal was so frightened it had lost its wits.

Turning back now, Nolan went after Silly. It was then that all hope was lost and his true nightmare began. The fire had burned through the main office wall into the adjacent utility closet that housed a gas-fired water heater. The heat of the fire quickly burned through the unit exposing the unfettered flow of natural gas. There was a small boom and the door to the closet exploded into the corridor along with a fresh and deadly plume of roiling flames. Within seconds, the entire end of the building was engulfed, including Silly and her stall. Nolan was knocked backward by the explosion. He lay in the corridor propped up by his elbow watching the terrible events unfold. His most vivid memory of the entire episode was the screaming of his most beloved horse as she burned alive. He heard the noise inside and out, through his physical eardrums and through his mystic connection within. He shared Silly's last moments of torment and pain. The horror of that night scorched his consciousness and burned his soul. To this day he can hear the screaming; he can feel the horse's dying agony as if it was his own writhing, his own last movements within the deadly flames.

They called him a hero. They said he was brave. He saved the horses from the fire. Inside Nolan felt like anything but a hero. His anguish over the tragedy overwhelmed his soul. Three days later, Nolan left Virginia for good. He traveled west and landed in Wyoming. For several dark years he kept to himself, in silent suffering, without hope. The farm where he worked allowed him a certain amount of anonymity; he did his job and went through the motions, ever suffering from the memories of Catherine and Silly. The yellow mist had died in his heart. He could no longer see it or feel it. He, for the most part, was dead.

For five agonizing years he lived this way, until he heard rumors of a wild band of horses that showed up at a ranch in Nevada. A ranch hand who worked at Ruud's cattle ranch told a story of wild horses—mustangs—that were using up the water resources and being a real nuisance. This story would not have interested Nolan, but when he heard it, the yellow mist returned to his vision in an awesome explosion of dazzling and disorienting colored light and sound. It was much more than he could manage to ignore. He immediately left for Nevada.

Nolan sat in the well-lit basement safe room rehearsing his past and thinking about Anne. It had been so long since he was interested in a woman. He had it in his mind that he would forever be alone, forever be lonely. It was the one thing he was certain about, the one thing he had accepted about his life. Now it was different, there was a small window opening in his heart, a slight fracture of a space opened up because of this woman. He sat and contemplated the meaning of these things. He didn't fully trust this feeling. He remembered old wounds, old lessons of life denied. His mind wanted to connect all of these experiences and drive out any hope of something better, but his heart was soaring, a free agent of hope and anticipation.

Above, in the rooms on the main level, Nolan heard the officers enter the building to conduct their search. The sounds of clomping footsteps held Nolan's attention as he sat breathlessly waiting. He wondered where Anne was, if she was hiding in some forgotten room like he was. His feeling of being responsible for the whole mess came back and haunted him. He had to find her; he had to talk to her. Only a faint hope deep inside his heart told him that she was still at the ranch, that she hadn't left for California. He still had a chance.

CHAPTER TEN

A nne lay sleeping on the couch. After her meltdown, she fell into a deep slumber brought on by stress, trauma, and pain meds. She was completely exhausted and lay in a dreamless state of suspension, far away from her pain, cares, and concerns.

Samantha covered her mother with a brightly colored crocheted afghan and sat beside her until the police returned to say their good-byes. Rosie spoke with Officer Parker out on the front porch with the door closed so as not to disturb Anne. The conversation was held with a thin veil of professional politeness, and was short, terse, and filled with tension. Parker gave the clearance for Anne to leave at will, but threatened Rosie about hiding any evidence connected with the murders at the High Star Ranch. Rosie did her best to conceal her contempt for this man, but both of them knew each other far too well to be fooled by appearances. The officers left Angel Ridge with no hard evidence of the crimes they were sent to investigate.

The afternoon sun was leaning westward. A cool breeze was blow-ing from the north and the farm took on a lonely cloak of apprehension, as all of its inhabitants knew the worst was yet to come. The farm op-erations continued unabated, but those charged with the work walked slowly, talked in hushed voices, didn't smile, and kept their heads pointed down at the dreary earth. It was as if a fog had fallen over the farm and smothered the clarity of life and future.

When Joe opened the hidden door at the clinic and descended the stairs into the basement, he found Nolan asleep on the military-style cot. The lights were still on, giving the space, a cold sterile glare. Nolan opened his eyes.

"Are they gone?"

"Yeah, they cleared out a while ago."

Nolan sat up. His arm was in the sling, causing him to wince as he brought himself upright.

"You hungry?" asked Joe.

Nolan sat still for a moment as his brain came back online. His eyes blinked and he rubbed his face with his one good hand.

"Where's Anne? Is she still here?"

Joe took note of the way that Nolan asked this question. There was an intention, a motivation that he hadn't seen in Nolan before.

"Yes, she's napping up at the main house."

Nolan considered the words as if they had some great meaning.

"I need to see her."

"Okay, let's go up there and see what's going on."

"Give me a minute," said Nolan, as he stood up and walked over to the sink and mirror. Within a few minutes he washed his face and ran a comb through his hair. Joe waited upstairs and chatted with the vet about some of the new arrivals. Before long, Nolan came clomping up the staircase and appeared in the room with Joe and the vet.

He looked at Joe. "What did she say?"

"Who?"

"Anne. Did she say anything?"

Joe saw a look of uncertainty in Nolan's eyes. He was searching.

"I haven't talked to her. I have been down here all day," Joe said with a slight smile. His eyes sparkled as he probed Nolan's intentions.

Nolan just looked at him with a straight face. "Well, I'm going up there. You coming?"

"You know, I need to finish up here. Why don't you go along and I will catch up with you in a few? Then we'll go get some grub."

Nolan nodded.

"How's that arm?" asked the vet.

"A little stiff, but I'll mend," Nolan said. He gave the vet a weak smile, turned and walked out. After being in the stuffy basement for several hours the cool fresh air felt good on Nolan's face. He started for the house with the intention of finding Anne and telling her how he felt about her. It was a strange mix of confidence and self-doubt that ran through his mind as he slowly walked up the hill. He knew that he had feelings for this woman, that he found in her a spark of life missing in him for all too long. Maybe it had been much too long. He had not pursued a love interest since Catherine died almost 10 years ago. The pain of that loss was faded now. But worse than the pain had Nolan gone through were the remnants of doubt that developed over the years. Nolan never faced the loss. He shut it away, turned it off. His imagination said he was over it, fooling himself into thinking Catherine's death, and his love lost, was just a faint memory, something that many people went through. It didn't occur to him to consider the fact that the energy still lived, still existed within ...transformed through the years of denial into a dark, brooding force; a force that kept him alone, apart, and separate. Quite unknown to him, this force lay hidden in his psyche, entwined in his thought patterns, wrapped around his self perceptions, his most inward beliefs. As Nolan got closer to the house, it was this brooding force that rose in his mind. With each step closer, his mood darkened and his feelings of self-pity came front and center.

In the past this mood would have driven Nolan back, running for shelter. He would have fled into his work with horses or withdrawn to his books. Those two things—horses and knowledge—were what Nolan found to keep his dark thoughts at bay. He could lose himself in the presence of horses. He could find solace in the thoughts of others written in countless volumes throughout the ages. As well read as he was, Nolan had only skimmed the surface of psychology and death. He was completely blind to the facts about his inner turmoil, his self-perceptions. He kept plodding up the hill trying to think of what to say when he saw her.

A gust of north wind bore down forcing Nolan to pull his jacket tight around his shoulders, difficult with his arm in the sling. As he walked up to the house, past the dining hall, past the paddocks, past the barns and arenas, he took note of the fact that the place seemed deserted. Everyone was either indoors or had their heads down concentrating on the task before them. He stopped for a moment to peek into the training barn. The stalls were empty except for three horses near the entrance. One of the horses, Coley, stuck his head out and gave Nolan a nod. Nolan could see the horse within the blue flower; there was a sense of sorrow that passed from the animal. Nolan smiled and gave the horse some kind words and turned back toward the house.

As he came into view of the main house, Nolan's heart began to pump. Normally a very confident man with clear values and transparent motives, Nolan was out of his element. But his heart nudged him toward his goal. His self-doubt slowed his steps but just as quickly, his bold intentions pushed him forward. He stood at the front door in a moment of hesitation, then knocked.

Anne could not have been more shocked when she opened her eyes to see Nolan sitting by her with his quiet gaze fixed on her face. In a moment of recognition she both rejoiced and recoiled. Rejoicing because, in her heart of hearts, she wanted to be near this man, to share herself, and to unlock the secrets of his soul. Recoiling because, in her self-reflective femininity, she knew her face was a nightmare, her hair a mess, and her breath foul. As she gained full consciousness she withdrew into herself. Nolan must have felt this energy being pulled back because his face altered from the current patient, thoughtful gaze to one of confused rejection. Anne put her hand over her mouth.

"Nolan!" The words came out sounding slightly angry. "What are you doing?"

Nolan read the expression on Anne's face as disapproval. His calm was rattled as he struggled to gain some balance of his reeling feelings.

"I …came to see you …to see how you're doing …I was afraid you might have gone."

"Umm …" Anne remembered she had been planning to leave. "Yeah, well, the cops wouldn't let me go. I am being detained …or something."

Anne looked around the room. There was just the two of them. Rosie and Sam were nowhere to be seen.

"Where is everybody?" she asked absently.

"Everyone went down to the hall for dinner."

"Oh," said Anne reflectively. "Why aren't you there?"

Nolan looked at Anne and smiled. It was a relaxed and satisfied grin.

"I wanted to be here with you." He kind of shrugged as if to say, "Why do you think I am here?"

Anne was quiet for a moment. She looked at Nolan's face, his chiseled good looks and his knowing eyes. Her self-conscious fears rose up and forced her to act.

"Nolan, give me a minute to freshen up, okay?"

"Of course."

Anne threw the afghan to the side and swung her casted foot onto the floor.

"How is it feeling?" asked Nolan gently.

Anne struggled to her feet.

"Sore; it's a bit sore," she said, as she limped out of the room and into the main bath just around the corner. She moved into the small space and closed the door. When she looked into the mirror, she was mortified. Her entire cheek from her eye to chin was covered with the most ghastly bruise. The area was ringed with varying shades of a disgusting bluish color mixed with yellow and red-brown patches.

"Oh, my God!" Anne gasped. "I can't let anyone see me like this."

Equally as bad was her hair tangled and matted from her nap. She glowered at her image. She finally meets a man she is interested in and this is how he sees her. Immediately, her self-confidence sunk to a new low. She wasn't one to make a huge fuss over her appearance, but she did have limits. Because, like it or not, she was subject to the media-induced opinions of the masses when it came to acceptable boundaries of beauty. She opened several drawers before finding a brush. She turned on the hot water and went to work on herself. At least she could present a more stable persona, bruised or not.

Nolan sat out in the living room listening to Anne shuffling around in the bathroom. He could hear the muffled sounds of running water, the gurgle of the drain, the opening and closing of drawers, her heavy footsteps. The dampened noise pushed through the thin walls and out to where Nolan waited and, against the backdrop of the silent empty house, seemed unnaturally loud. The noise only increased the tension Nolan was feeling. He sat on the couch going over in his mind what it was he wanted to say.

He thought back to the night before when he finally caught up with Anne out in the desert. The warmth that she showed him still lingered in his mind. He could still feel the way she had pressed up tightly against him as they rode back to the ranch with her gentle voice whispering into his ear. It was the subtle way that she had completely submitted herself to his leadership, opening herself up to him with such humble honesty, that had softened him. He saw to the pit of her heart and soul and was touched by the utter beauty that lay beneath that stern exterior façade. He longed to return to that space, that connection he felt with her. Sitting on the couch, waiting for her, he got a different feeling. His doubting mind bore a hole beneath his confident memories of what had happened between them the night before. The hole was made even wider by the tense reception he received from her, and before long the weight of the self-created doubts collapsed upon themselves sending his confidence crashing into the deep pit of ambiguity and hesitation.

"What am I doing?" he thought to himself. The answer did not come back. Instead his mind took him on a torrent of disjointed thoughts and old memories. He found himself thinking about Cloud Runner and the horrible moment of the passing of that great steed. He thought of the beautiful gift of the blue flower that was passed from the horse to him and the responsibility that came with it. He thought of his old horse Silly and how the pain of that passing still lingered deep within the recesses of his consciousness. He thought of Catherine and the love that had been so long lost, his heart grown cold and emotionless. His life was passing before him and the sheer loneliness of his days had been such a part of his existence it didn't seem wrong anymore. The connection he had made with Anne Harper was like a small, bright spark of possibility, a potential, a little light glowing against the dark heap of reality he had been living for so long. He longed to feel that hope again. He wanted to protect that small light, that spark, to keep it alive, to keep it from being snuffed out like so many hopes before. The doubts came again but so did something else, something unexpected—a steely resolve to reach out and grasp this possibility, to risk his heart and his honor, to stake a claim to his desires and go after what he wanted, what he deserved.

Nolan smiled at his own weakness. He was nervous. He had come for the girl and the possibility of rejection was tormenting him. In all other things he was confident, a master. In this matter, the matter of love, he was as weak as an inexperienced teenager, consumed by his first crush. The thought humored Nolan in a surprising comeback of his wit and will. He had nothing to lose here. Only something to gain, something he knew in his heart Anne was feeling as well. He would take the lead, he would make the first move. Nolan's newfound confidence crashed as quickly as it rose when he heard the bathroom door open and watched as Anne came out.

Anne clunked into the room, limping hard on her new walking boot. In a few short minutes she had managed to brush her hair, pull it back into a neat pony tail, wash her bruised face, and generally pull herself together. She looked beautiful to Nolan. He didn't see her wounds. He looked past the outer scratches and saw into her deep-pooling soul. Her hazel eyes appeared deep brown in the dim light of the living room. Nolan saw in them a light—not a physical light but the light of energy, of purpose, of life. It thrilled him and he smiled a goofy, tender grin that matched the feeling in his heart.

Anne came around the corner and saw Nolan sitting on the couch with a smile on his face. He was looking at her with an intention that made her both frightened and thrilled. Her heart had been a fortress in lockdown for many years, but now in this moment she felt the key to that lock was before her; she felt a shimmer of life softly rising in her spine. It was like her womanhood was unfolding from a tightly bound knot. All the years of deflection, of denial, and refusal of the attentions from countless men trained her spirit to reject these natural feelings. Her heart and love had been wound up tightly into a steely cold coil, a tension of opposing forces held in place by fear and self-loathing. When she came into the room and saw Nolan, that coil released itself and the energy held within the psychic spring burst apart, spinning wildly in all directions. The sensation produced a warm, cathartic shudder from the depths of her pelvic floor to the very crown of her skull. She felt this shock go through her body and when it reached its peak of intensity, she could not help but smile herself. The two, Nolan and Anne, in a moment of recognition, looked at each other with smiles of knowing gladness; their hearts danced together in the ancient patterns of understanding, kinship, and love.

Anne giggled. "You look like shit," she said playfully, breaking the tension.

Nolan only smiled wider with a flush of embarrassment. "You look beautiful," he said shyly.

Anne gasped in disbelief as she came closer. "Oh, really! Do you need glasses? Have you noticed anything particular about my face?"

"Well," said Nolan looking at the great bruise stretched across Anne's face, "purple looks good on you."

Anne plopped down on the couch next to Nolan. They both felt the connection. Nolan reached over and took Anne's hand.

"I heard you were leaving."

Anne looked at the floor. Her thoughts of running away now seemed like ancient history.

"I don't know what I am doing," she said as she squeezed his hand. "Everything that happened just freaked me out. I thought getting out of here would be best."

"But . . .?"

Anne turned her gaze to Nolan. His eyes were full of life, kind and knowing. She saw in him the hopes that had been all but lost in her life.

"But …well …I had second thoughts."

Nolan nodded. "I'm glad you didn't leave," he said. "I wanted to talk to you, to tell you how damn sorry I am for what happened. It's my fault. I feel really bad about it."

Anne's face took on a contemplative tone, her lips pressing tightly against her teeth. "You don't have to apologize," she said looking down. "I know what all this means to you …the horses and everything."

"That's not the only thing I care about," said Nolan as he leaned into Anne and gently kissed her lips. The kiss came suddenly and caught Anne off guard. She withdrew just a bit and the two sat face to face. Nolan, not backing off, looked into her eyes. His knowing heart pierced through Anne's hesitation and she surrendered herself to the moment. Pushing past her thousand reasons why this was a bad idea, Anne moved closer to Nolan and closed her eyes. The two embraced in a passionate kiss and in a rushing, endless moment they unleashed the awkward tension that built up between them over the last two days.

The kiss lasted only a few moments, but in those few moments Nolan saw the blue flower open its mystical petals arcing wide across his vision and reaching into Anne's heart and mind. The misty blueness swirled delicately and expanded into the room growing ever larger until it enveloped the two within an inviolable indigo cocoon. Anne felt this energy as a rushing sensation tingling down her spine. The energy moved down her entire body pushing through the floor into the earth. It came back up and through her crown, continuing up past the ceiling into the open air, then down again before settling just behind her navel in a warm, glowing sensation of wellness and power. Anne shuddered and pulled away. She looked at Nolan with an expression of open-eyed awe and a wide satisfied smile. Her face said, "Did you feel that? Was that real?" Nolan understood the look on Anne's face and smiled too. He gazed into her eyes for an eternal second before pulling her back into another longer and even more beautiful kiss. There was a fraction of a moment when all the worries, pressures, and memories of the past 48 hours melted away and the two sat embraced in eternal bliss, their souls dancing among the misty blue strands of light.

All too soon they pulled away and looked at each other in complete submission. Anne's bruised face was lit up with a glowing perfection; Nolan's face was a study of gentle love and masculine confidence.

"One more," whispered Nolan as he pulled Anne back, again kissing her with deep passion. Anne gladly accepted his advance and wrapped her arms around his battered body. This energy was something she had never felt before. It was like coming home; a glowing warm reception of complete understanding with no secrets and no restraint.

Across the compound down at the dining hall, Joe looked over at Rosie and gave her a knowing wink. His twinkling eyes and slight smile formed an expression that Rosie had come to know over the years they had been together.

"What now?" Rosie asked with smile.

"Oh, let's just say I am sensing some fireworks going on."

Rosie raised her brow, "Really?"

Through the years Rosie came to trust her husband's impeccable intuition. Joe had the gift, the yellow mist, but he also carried an extra ability. Rosie saw it many times in their 25 years together. It was an uncanny sense of order. Joe had an uncommon sense of how the disparate pieces of life fit together, how these pieces would eventually and naturally be arranged. He could see the order of things, how two things might react together, or apart. Applied to life on the Nevada range, Joe could predict the weather with certainty, even weeks out. He would know if a new employee would fit into the group or what conflicts would arise between the ranch hands. He knew which horses could live together and which ones would cause trouble. He was a master at card games because he understood the order behind the random shuffle of the deck. He knew the outcome of politics, which government employees would rise to the top, how they would behave in public service, and how the slow march of the corrupting forces of political power would affect each one in different ways. This sense of things that Joe had was just part of his regular thought process. He could neither explain it, nor even attempt to understand it. It just was. It was part of his being. Rosie knew this about him and had come to trust it explicitly.

Joe was silent about the details. He generally wasn't a man of many words. Rosie's curiosity was insatiable and she pried for more.

"So ..." she said. Joe understood that she was asking a question.

"Nolan and Anne," he said in a stage whisper as his eyes smiled.

Rosie was amazed. "Really?" she exclaimed. "That was the last thing I would ever have predicted. You should have heard what she was saying about him this morning."

Rosie sat back and pondered the development. She didn't even think to question what Joe was saying. She looked across the room at Samantha who was sitting with some of the female trainers at a table near the fireplace. Samantha was chatting away with a smile on her face as a round of giggles went up from the table. Rosie didn't know what they were talking about, but they were all enjoying the conversation.

Joe noticed Rosie gazing at Samantha. "It's the yellow mist," he said.

Rosie looked at Joe, "What do you mean?"

"The yellow mist. That's why she's here."

"You mean Samantha?"

"Yeah, that's why she came here. It's what brought her here." Joe paused and looked at Samantha. "She's here to learn."

Rosie smiled. She liked the girl and was glad to hear what Joe was saying. The mysteries of life and the comings and goings of people through her world always fascinated her. This seemed like a new chapter opening in her world, her life on the range.

"I am glad to hear that," she said to her husband.

"Me too," said Joe, as he jabbed his fork into his plate of food.

The mood at the ranch lifted somewhat as the crew sat down for dinner. It had been a long day captured by the dread anticipation of the unknown. Everyone knew what had happened, and all were speculating on what was yet to happen. The presence of the police rattled everyone's nerves. Now that tension released itself into an atmosphere of cautious optimism. The spirit was bolstered by the fact that the police went away empty-handed and that Nolan and Anne were, for the most part, okay. There wasn't any question that a showdown was imminent but there was a small, brief window of time where they could let down their guard and enjoy each other's company. Although muted and far from boisterous, sounds of laughter filled the dining hall.

When the front doors opened and Anne and Nolan came limping into the room, a peal of applause broke out and made its rounds across the group. Nolan smiled while Anne looked at the floor in embarrassment. Samantha got up and ran to her mother, pulling her over to the table where she was eating. Nolan came directly over to Joe and Rosie.

"Hey, cowboy," said Rosie. "How ya feeling?"

Nolan took a seat next to Joe. "I'll live," he said grimacing.

Joe looked at Nolan with smiling eyes. Nolan noticed the look.

"Hello, Joe. You look chipper."

Joe smiled, nodded, and said nothing. Joe knew he didn't have to ask any questions. Rosie would take that role soon enough. Nolan felt their eyes taking stock of his appearance, as if looking at him would give them some clue as to what happened between him and Anne. He felt their anticipation, their need for the details.

He looked at Rosie. "Okay, what is it, Rosie?"

"Well, how'd it go?" Rosie could barely contain her enthusiasm.

Nolan took a deep breath. He hated talking about his personal life, but these two friends wouldn't let him be silent. A slight smile spread over his face as he looked down and blushed.

Rosie saw the sign. "Really?" she said nodding her head. "What happened?"

Nolan knew he had to tell her straight-out or this conversation would go on all night. He looked Rosie directly in the eye and with boldness said, "We talked, we kissed."

Rosie bubbled over with delight. "I knew it!" she sang. "I knew there was something between you two."

Joe looked at her dubiously, but just smiled and said nothing.

"Okay," replied Nolan. "There it is, that's all there is. Now we can move on, right?"

Rosie hunched up her shoulders in glee, picked up her fork and went back to her dinner.

"Right," she agreed.

"Besides," Nolan got suddenly serious, "we have some more important things to talk about." He looked at Joe who nodded in agreement.

"What do you have in mind?" asked Joe.

"We have to find a connection back into the herd."

Joe nodded as his expression turned dour. He had no answer.

"We need to locate the band of stallions. I think that will give us the best chance," said Nolan. His words were confident and direct. "You need to help me with this Joe. I can't do it alone."

Joe understood what he was being asked. Rosie had some idea, but remained silent. Nolan continued.

"Right now the stallions are fighting over who will take Cloud Runner's place. If we get out there by daybreak, we will have some clue as to which horse that may be. It will take both of us to make the connection, make it stick. Right?"

Joe nodded his agreement; he was looking down at his plate.

"So you and I get out there, find out who's on top and then perform the ceremony."

Joe looked up at Nolan with eyes full of doubt. Nolan noticed a void in Joe's confidence.

"It's the only way Joe."

Joe spoke slowly, "I know you are right, your words are right. But it has been a long time, a very long time since anyone has done that."

Nolan was resolute.

"You know I have never done that ceremony, right?" said Joe.

Nolan looked directly at his friend. "Yes, I know."

"You know that there are certain risks, serious risks, right?"

Rosie perked up. "What are you talking about? What risk?"

Joe looked at her. His eyes suggested she not interrupt. She would know soon enough. Rosie got the message and remained quiet. Nolan continued.

"I don't know any more than what you told me that one time. But, Joe, I know we have to try. We have to take the risk. The stakes are too high; to fail would be a terrible tragedy."

Joe was silent. He was thinking about what Nolan was asking him to do. The ceremony was called by a name that couldn't be spoken. It had been passed down from ancient times through Indian culture. Coming first to the Plains Indian tribes, it spread to the west over the Rockies and onto the high plains. The ceremony was a powerful and dangerous rite and was guarded as sacred by the few real medicine men who remained in the land. Joe received the knowledge from his grandfather and was present one time to witness the extraordinary force of nature the ceremony drew together. The secret ceremony was as ancient as Xu's promise and tied man and horse together on a deeply profound spiritual level. It carried risks. The ceremony created such a powerful force that if one was not diligent about each step, if one was the slightest bit careless with his intentions, there was the risk of losing one's mind, the risk of spiritual blindness, and the risk of death.

Joe leaned back in his chair. His intuition told him the truth about what lay ahead. There was something dark and foreboding, yet around it danced a silver edge of possibility.

"It will take some time to prepare," said Joe, his voice slow and deliberate. "I hope you know what you are asking. Once we start down that path, there is no turning back. The only way to return is to go through the rite."

In fact, Nolan didn't know what he was asking. His unwavering commitment to the herd kept his mind from considering the details. He saw the path ahead as set as a matter of fate.

Across the room Anne sat next to Samantha watching her eat her dinner. Everything about her daughter seemed new to her now. She noticed her delicate hands, her shiny blond hair, her sweet disposition and her natural ease while surrounded by strangers. Samantha was talkative and light hearted. It seemed strange to Anne that she never noticed this side of her daughter. Anne remembered what Nolan told her the night before about Samantha and the yellow mist. Anne wanted so much to ask her about it. She was curious to know if it was real, what it really meant. She was curious as to why Sam had never mentioned it. Anne really didn't understand what the yellow mist was; it seemed like so much Indian magic. The way Nolan had described it made it easy for her rational mind to dismiss it as just a story, a kooky story. Yet something in Anne's heart nagged at that reasoning, tugging at her notions of reality.

Anne turned and glanced at Nolan. He and Joe were in, what looked to be, a serious conversation. Joe was shaking his head while Nolan spoke with considerable tension. Anne guessed they were speaking of the herd. Just then, Nolan looked over and caught her glance. Her heart fluttered as he gave her a tender smile before turning his attention back to Joe. She wanted to go over and be next to him but her maternal instincts demanded more. She stayed with Samantha, intrigued by the newness she found in her own daughter.

How would she tell Samantha about Nolan? What would she say? The only man Sam had ever seen her mother with was Simon, so long ago. A wave of embarrassment swept over Anne's mind. Her inner identity as a mother clashed violently with her idea of being a lover. Just then, as if knowing her mother's thoughts, Sam looked up at Anne and smiled. In that smile, Anne detected a calming assurance, a confident voice that whispered soothing sensations. Anne took Samantha's hand with a gentle squeeze and returned Sam's smile, although more awkwardly.

"I'm glad about you and Nolan," said Sam in a slight whisper, as if she knew Anne would not want anyone else to hear.

Anne's mind sparked. "What?" she stammered, trying to find words. Finally she blurted out, "How do you know about Nolan?" Anne's tone was one of motherly boundaries and shocked curiosity.

Sam looked past her mother in a faraway stare, "I don't know. I just do. Really, it's okay with me. I'm glad about it."

Anne was shocked. She just came from Rosie's. She and Nolan walked together arm in arm but everyone else was at the hall. She looked at Sam with a disapproving glare. Anne felt somewhat violated by the comment, but mostly felt a deep awe mixed with fear of the unknown.

"It's the yellow mist, isn't it?" asked Anne.

Sam looked up quizzically, "Yeah, I guess it is."

"You'll have to tell me about it. I am very curious."

Sam nodded in agreement and turned back to the table where one of the girls was telling a story about a recent shopping trip to Reno.

Anne again looked over at Nolan. He and Joe were still deep in conversation while Rosie sat close by, silently eating her dinner. The interlude with her daughter left Anne a bit spooked and she wanted to talk to Nolan about it. But judging from the talk going on between him and Joe, it would have to wait. Anne turned her attention back to her daughter and to the others at the table.

CHAPTER ELEVEN

Sheriff Daniel Parker sat in the MCU. The background noise was a low din of whirring computers, police radio chatter, and one-sided telephone conversations. Parker didn't notice the noise. He was staring at a stack of 8x10" photographs lying on the desk in front of him. He looked at each one of the photos several times and was beginning to draw some conclusions. One photograph that interested him, the one on top of the pile, was a photo with a person in it. It was a man on a horse. The man's face was partially hidden, turned away from the photographer, and the horse was a bit blurred, but it could possibly be identified with the right forensics.

Next to the stack of photos was the camera found in Bulling's truck and the report on the fingerprints obtained from it. The report indicated four different sets of fingerprints on the camera. One of the sets belonged to Striker, the other to Bulling, and the others were still unknown. Apparently, both Bulling and Striker had found this camera as interesting as did Parker.

The sheriff leaned back in his chair and looked around the spacious cabin of his command unit. The fluorescent light made the place appear flat and sterile. Next to him, Deputy Miller was on the phone to the county coroner preparing a plan to deliver the bodies to the morgue. On the other side of the cabin, the information officer was discussing details of the stories that would appear in the Reno papers the following morning; another officer was doing research on Anne Harper. The sheriff was proud of his men and the capabilities he had at his disposal. Being related to a senator certainly came with perks.

Along with those perks came an expectation from the senator that his will would be followed, that it would be satiated in all its desire. To fail the senator was not something Parker was prepared to endure. His mission was clear. He had to find someone to blame for the deaths and that someone had to be tied to Angel Ridge. Parker would never manufacture a false case against someone. But in this case, all of the evidence pointed to Angel Ridge, to Anne Harper, and to the man in the photo, this man on the horse. All the pieces were coming together; Parker was just waiting for the report from the K-9 unit on where the trail led from Striker's truck. This was the last piece he needed in order to finalize his plan. He was expecting the search party to return any minute.

The information officer hung up the phone and turned his chair around towards Parker. Parker looked over at the man with an air of expectation.

"It's all arranged," said the officer. "There will be a press conference at nineteen hundred. We'll do it at the Best Western; they've got the most room. I've got all the majors there so expect about 15 people. The stories will break in the morning and will likely go national just because it's the senator's ranch. Most of my contacts think this could rise and fall in a day depending on who picks it up for political reasons."

Sheriff Parker looked at his watch; it was almost five. He had two hours to get the rest of the pieces together and write some comments for the press conference. Plenty of time, he thought. He turned to Miller who was finishing his call with the coroner.

"How'd it go?" Parker asked.

"We're all set. We'll take the bodies down to the morgue while you're doing the press conference. We have a special order to seal the autopsies until the investigation is over."

The special order, obtained by a judge closely related to the matter, was to keep the records from the press. By the time they were released, it was hoped interest in the matter would have died, and the senator could be spared any uncomfortable questions about his ranch and what happened. All Parker had to do was handle the press conference and, with some luck, the firewall he had built around this incident would contain the ensuing chaos if the truth got out.

"Where the hell is that K-9 unit?" Parker bellowed.

"They are coming down the road now. Should be here any time."

Parker got up to stretch his legs. He went to the door and stepped out of the coach. The fresh air felt good and reinvigorating. The sun hung in the west, its light casting long shadows across the ranch. He looked up the road to where the search party would be coming. Seeing the dust plume rising in the distance, he knew they were close. He walked out to meet them.

Soon enough a filthy dust-covered truck came into view. It turned from the dirt road onto the asphalt and zoomed up to where the sheriff was waiting. As the truck came closer, Parker could hear several dogs yapping with excitement. In the truck's bed were three kennels holding the tracking dogs. The truck pulled up and came to a stop. In the cab were three ragged and dusty men. When Parker looked into the cab he was disgusted by what he saw. Trash completely littered the floorboards. The dash was crammed full of odd junk—an old clipboard, papers, boxes and rolls of half-used electrical tape. The entire interior was covered in a musty layer of grime and dust, old fast-food bags, cups, and used napkins infused with the smell of a roadside greasy spoon. Parker took a step back.

"Whadya find out there?"

The driver hung his head out the window and spit a full load of tobacco juice, most of which ended up on the side of the truck.

"Well, we followed the trail up until we lost it in Tanner Creek. Whoever was up there knew what they were doing. Made a clean break in the scent; we couldn't pick it up."

"How far up on Tanner did you guys get?"

"Up towards where it comes down from the ridge."

Parker thought he knew the spot. "Isn't that just a few miles from Angel Ridge?"

"Yeah, that's the spot. We worked the other side pretty well, but could find nothing. Like I said, whoever we were following must have known how to cover their tracks."

"So ...how many? Two? And one horse?"

"Yeah, that's pretty clear. It looked like one was walking, limping maybe, then the one on the horse caught up. They stayed in one spot for a while, then took off on the horse. Never stopped after that."

"Limping, you say?"

"Yeah, that's what the tracks looked like. Wouldn't you say so, Bert?"

The man in the middle craned his neck as he hung his head peering out at the sheriff. He nodded in agreement about the limp.

"Yeah, it was definitely a limp. You could tell by the weight of the tracks."

"Which leg was limping?" asked the sheriff.

"The right one."

The sheriff nodded. "Did you guys get the photos I asked for?"

The driver turned and started rummaging through the pile of crap on the dashboard. He fished out a small camera from under some paper.

"Here ya go. We took a photo every hunderd feet like ya asked."

The sheriff took the camera.

"Thanks, guys. Turn your slip into Miller at the office to get your pay. I do appreciate you boys coming out here on such short notice."

"No problem, sheriff. You have yourself a good day."

With that, the driver turned his attention forward, slipped the truck in gear, and zoomed off. The sheriff watched the truck move down the road, then turned and headed back to the MCU. He looked at the camera in his hand. These photos would be perfect to use at the press conference. As he stepped into the MCU, Parker handed the camera to the information officer and instructed him to get the photos printed ASAP. He had one more piece to put in place. His nephew, the younger Parker, was resting in the back of the bus after returning from the search of Angel Ridge. The sheriff found him with his eyes closed lying on a bench in the conference room.

"Jared," Parker said, nudging the young man with his knee.

Young Parker opened his eyes, but did not move.

"You said that Anne Harper had a cast on her leg."

"Yeah, she did."

"Which leg was it again?"

Young Parker thought for a few seconds, dreary from the edge of sleep.

"The right. It was the right leg."

Sheriff Parker smiled, turned and went back up front to his station. This was all he needed to put the case together and make some arrests. This would be the centerpiece of his press conference.

Joe's task was in front of him. He knew what needed to be done. He could see the end goal, the desired result clearly in his mind. The things he couldn't see were the steps required to get him there. With the passing of Cloud Runner, the connection into the herd was lost. Without that connection, saving the herd would be all but impossible. Joe knew from his interactions with Cloud Runner that the yellow mist was strong within the herd. He knew they remembered. He also knew that Nolan had been given the gift of the blue flower. What once belonged to Cloud Runner now rested solely in the realm of man. That power belonged to the herd and must be transferred back into the heart and soul of one of the horses, the rightful place for the blue flower to reside. Finding that horse, opening up its soul, and delivering the blue flower was both daring and dangerous. Daring because the required ceremony was a shadow in Joe's memory. Dangerous because of the risk to Nolan's own soul and mind.

Darkness descended on Angel Ridge. The sun set in a glorious display of red, purple, and yellow, playing off the layer of clouds stretching across the sky. The last rays formed a solid beam of crimson light just under the cloud layer, moving like a search beacon over the land as the sun dipped below the horizon of the great Sierra Nevada Mountains. Joe watched this kaleidoscope of nature from a perch up on the ridge opposite his ranch house. He was alone. He often went up to that place to watch the comings and goings of the day. In the past he found there both insight and inspiration. Today he found nothing. There was an emptiness that surrounded his thoughts as if a shield was brought down, separating him from his own self.

Joe made his way down from the ridge following the little dusty trail as the light faded and darkness enveloped the ranch. That same darkness enveloped Joe's mind as he struggled to remember the ceremony he witnessed so long ago. It was when his grandfather was still alive, his mother's father. Joe had been invited to be a witness of the ancient Indian rite—and the horse—the subject of that rite, was Cloud

Runner's father. It had been 25 years earlier and the memory had all but faded into the dimming past.

Joe walked slowly, deep in thought through the dim night. His aimless course took him up the ranch road toward the highway. Silence lay like a blanket across the darkened landscape. Joe was focusing his thoughts on his grandfather. Within Joe's imagination he could see the man's big brown hands, gnarled by a life of work, leathery, wrinkled skin shiny with old age. Joe could remember the smell of tobacco mixed with some spicy scents. He remembered his grandfather's small black eyes that shined and sparkled as if he was always laughing; the small round face, the smile, and the hair. Even though his grandfather had grown grey with age, Joe remembered him with the coal black hair of youth.

His grandfather's given name was Toh'a Mu'ha or White Moon. He was a full- blooded Piute born in the hinterlands of the Nevada range and basin. In the modern world among the white folk he was known as Tona. He lived his entire life in Nevada, married a mixed-blood Native American-European woman, had five children, and enjoyed a full life.

Tona lived this life in two worlds. He was old enough to still have one foot in traditional Native American culture. Born in the late 1800s during the last of the Indian wars, Tona grew up with a solid link to the past, as well as one foot planted in the modern day society. Tona spent most of his adult life working for the railroad in different capacities, which satisfied the modern culture's demand for steady pay and financial security. Even though Tona had fully embraced the changes brought on by the industrial revolution and the settling of his ancient lands by the white folk, he also kept and nurtured his own heritage. He was trained as a medicine man; it was his lineage from the misty history of his family's past. The knowledge was passed to Tona from his father who received it from his father and so on down the generations, back to the beginning. He practiced this medicine until the day he died in the mid-1970s.

With the break of traditions and the pressures of modern life, the knowledge had skipped a generation whereby Tona wasn't able to give the gifts to his own sons. Instead, the knowledge was shown to Joe, his daughter's son. Tona trained his grandson in the practical methods of healing and herbology. He also instilled in Joe the old stories, parables, and ceremonial dance. Joe was an eager student and took on the mantle of the family healer as his grandfather's vitality waned with age. Joe was 27 when his grandfather died.

Joe walked slowly down the dirt road. He had the picture of his grandfather hanging in his mind when, from far away in the darkness, came the scratchy cry of a lone crow. The sound broke the heavy silence in such an odd way that Joe accepted this sound as his grandfather's presence. Joe spoke softly, directing his words to the empty night.

"Grandfather, I honor you. I ask for guidance. Cloud Runner has passed. The chain has been broken. The work we have done may soon be lost. But there is a chance. If my intentions are good, then we have a chance. I seek the answer to my questions, I seek the answers ..."

Suddenly, the answer came to Joe in a flood of thoughts and impressions. In his soul the yellow mist swirled up in an angry, twisting spiral of light and energy. It rose from his feet up through his torso and shot out from the crown of his head. Anyone looking on from a distance would have seen nothing but an old Indian walking slowly down the darkened road. But inside Joe's consciousness, he was overwhelmed by the sheer excited energy of the yellow mist. Stronger than he had ever felt it before, it took his breath and, in his weakness, he collapsed to his knees. His eyes bulged as he was consumed by the misty yellow storm. The experience was so powerful, so imposing, it forced Joe to lie down prostrate on the dirt road. High overhead, in a place far out of time and space, he saw his grandfather's laughing eyes seemingly mirthful at Joe's present condition. Joe watched this vision in a state of awe. He saw the pieces of this profound message in intricate detail, all connected, all interworking, all as one. The vision lasted only seconds. After it passed, Joe lay on the road for several minutes, his face covered with sweat, his breathing heavy. The task was before him; the path would not be easy.

Anne and Nolan sat close together watching the dancing flames in the fire pit. The dark of night was kept at bay by the fire's orange and yellow light. Patches of shadow and light flickered over Anne's face as she listened to the irregular cadence of the crack and pop of the burning pinewood. Around the fire pit there were others; Samantha and Rosie sat across the pit with one of the trainers. Everyone was quiet, each lost in their own thoughts of the day's events and wondering about what was yet to come.

The cool air was closing in and hung heavy around the group in a foreboding stillness. Anne was struggling with her thoughts about the yellow mist, what it might mean, and how it related to Samantha. It left her feeling completely detached from her daughter as if Sam had been inducted into some special members-only club, complete with secret handshakes and sacred oaths. Anne felt like an outsider. She couldn't grasp the idea that her daughter had some special place in the world, a place where Anne couldn't go. Anne always saw her daughter through her own life's lens. She had plans for Samantha. This new wrinkle, this yellow mist was a game changer and the idea left Anne feeling desperate and alone.

These ideas welled up like dark shadows from Anne's deep places of insecurity, each one building upon the other, piling high into an overwhelming fear of the unknown. Anne didn't handle fear easily. She refused it in its present form, and with a little mental trick, quickly morphed the fear into resentment. Anne simmered as her resentment blossomed. She resented that only days ago Sam was a happy little girl with a well-planned life ahead of her. Just days ago! She resented that Sam was now part of some elite group of strange Nevada cowboy mystics, a group that Anne felt alienated from. She resented the fact she broke her foot in pursuit of some cause that really didn't affect her. Then she hit upon the crown of her disappointments, the peak of her fear. She resented her feelings for Nolan. This man swept into her heart and caught her off-guard. She had feelings for him and resented the whole affair. She blamed him. It was something she did not want, something she did not have time for, something oh, so inconvenient. She looked over at Sam who looked peaceful and happy staring into the fire.

Nolan was watching Anne and noticed her furrowed brow. He had his own demons inside, but Anne's face pulled him into the present moment. He looked at her with amazement; her exquisite and obvious pain put his own misery into perspective. She was lost in her thoughts and he could feel her desperation. The blue flower in his mind's sight let him see a bit more than he wanted to. He could tell Anne was struggling. He felt pity for her. Not in a high-handed, condescending way, but with truehearted compassion. He reached his hand over and pressed her arm.

"Are you okay?"

Anne was shocked, brought back from her internal arguments with a jolt. She looked at him with anger in her eyes. As soon as she saw his face, her heart melted and she felt ashamed. His face was so kind, so forgiving, so easy. She looked away.

"I need to know more about the yellow mist," she said quietly.

Nolan was silent, regarding her with compassion and a grace that she didn't understand.

"I want to know more about the yellow mist," Anne repeated. "I mean, what is it? How does it work? What does it mean? I just don't get it."

Nolan looked over at Samantha. He understood Anne was afraid.

"Okay, let's talk about that," he said, turning to Anne. "First of all, the yellow mist is a gift. No one knows where it comes from or why some people have it and some people don't. It seems to be connected through families, but not always."

"Why do you call it the yellow mist?" asked Anne with a smirk.

"That is how it looks. That is how we see it, in our mind's eye. It's a misty swirling yellow sensation. It's kind of hard to explain, but the yellow mist is a direct connection to horses."

"But not all horses," said Rosie.

Nolan nodded. "That's right, only certain horses seem to have it. This herd we are trying to save has it."

"So it is some kind of mystical power?"

"I wouldn't call it a power; it is a gift that connects man and horse. The stories about it go back to the legend of Xu. The idea is that it has been passed on unbroken through the ages. I have heard it called Xu's promise."

"Xu? The first horse angel?"

"Maybe you should tell her the whole story," said Rosie.

"Okay, let's start at the beginning. The other night Joe told the story of Xu, the first horse angel. That is where the story starts. Joe could tell this much better than I but the bond that Xu made with the horse Amrit was sealed with the yellow mist. The story goes that the light reflecting off the river where Amrit was trapped was a shining, yellow light which was infused into their connection, into their friendship. This connection spread into Amrit's herd and into the Butai tribe in those first years. Of course, because the Butai had the horse as a partner, the tribe became very strong and began to grow in number. This was all due to the horse. The power of the horse enhanced the power of the tribe. These early days were full of promise and the tribe thrived beyond their wildest expectations. The horse became very valuable to their survival and the yellow mist was the tool to unlock the potential of this man-horse relationship. These people spread out into the surrounding lands taking their knowledge with them. The domesticated horse spread eastward into Mongolia, south to Persia and on to the Mediterranean, west into what is now Europe, then across the sea into America. All along the way the yellow mist followed the trail. The bond of horse and man is sacred, and it has persisted ever since."

Anne wasn't satisfied. "These are just stories. You tell it like you believe it. Old myths? Come on, what do you really know?"

Rosie smiled.

"What do I really know?" repeated Nolan. "I know the day I received the gift. I know that Sam has it. I know that Joe has it and I know the horses that have it. That is what I know. The story of Xu has been passed down for ages. Sure, it's a myth, and like all myths the story encapsulates a seed of truth, something real. The story is a way to tell that truth; the details are really not that important. But throughout history we can trace the horse angels by their writings, their training methods, and their relationships with their horses. Take Xenophon for instance. You can read his treatise of horse training and find the yellow mist within those words. He knew; he tried to teach it. He was a great horse master who influenced an entire generation of horsemen to care about their horses, to be gentle, and most of all, to have respect. That is what I know."

Anne still didn't know any more about the yellow mist than before.

To her, it all seemed to move in circles. She wanted practical evidence. She wanted to see it in action. Everyone at the fire saw her disquiet, especially Sam who had known this aspect of her mother for years.

"So what's the purpose? What's the end game?" asked Anne with a hint of sarcasm.

Nolan looked at Anne, his face showed signs of understanding.

"The end game? The end game is to remember. We all have a deep and abiding gratitude for all the horse has done for mankind. Without the horse, our civilization would not exist as it does now. Without the partnership between man and horse, our world would be much different. It was the horse that gave us mobility, gave us the ability to excel in agriculture, helped us build our cities. The horse helped us shape our world and aided in our prosperity as a whole. We all owe a great debt to horses. That is the end game, to remember what horses have done for us. And now that our technology has replaced them, we need to honor them and care for them as best we can from here on out. That is the end game."

A chill went down Anne's spine. As she listened to Nolan's passionate words, she got a sense of the ancient bond between the horse and man. She recounted the innumerable instances across the arc of time where the horse was present in the great achievements of mankind. These thoughts came to her in a flood, rushing over her rational mind, quenching her resentments and defenses. She suddenly understood the reality of what Nolan was saying. She felt it deeply, in her conscience. Like a window opening upon a dark room, she saw the light of truth in this history. Her fear was gone. Now all she wanted was to be a part of it and live the truth of the gratitude owed by herself and all people to horses. She was suddenly a part of the club.

Nolan noticed the change in her.

"You get it?" he asked.

Anne smiled thinly, "Yeah, I get it."

Suddenly Nolan's face changed. His smile faded and a look of worry came upon him. He turned around and stared out past the patio onto the road leading up to the main house.

"What is it Nolan?" asked Rosie, noticing the alarm.

Nolan was silent. A few seconds later the sound of scuffing footsteps came floating down the road. The light from the fire cast flickering dark shadows out into the road and, as Nolan watched, he saw Joe walk out from those shadows like a specter coming into the light. Joe's gait was a tired stagger—slow and labored—as if he carried a heavy weight. As he came closer, Nolan noticed something about him; something almost imperceptible, something frightening. Joe walked up to the fire and sat down heavily on a seat between Nolan and Rosie. His face was pale. His hair was ruffled and dust was clinging to his shirt and pants as if he had been rolling in the dirt. There was a disconnected look on his face, far from the usual solid nature he generally carried.

"Joe? Are you okay? asked Rosie. "What is it? What happened?"

They all saw it. Joe had a faraway look in his eye; his hands were trembling. He looked around at the faces of those gathered as if he didn't recognize them. Both Nolan and Samantha felt the yellow mist swirl up and agitate. Joe was silent for a few minutes as Rosie sat by him rubbing his back and doting. Slowly the color returned to Joe's face. His black eyes were glittering and heavy with thought.

"Joe, what is it?" Nolan asked gently.

Joe turned to his friend and took a deep breath, letting out a long-winded audible exhale. "We must go. There is not much time," he said enigmatically. "It's the blue flower. We must go." As Joe said these words, he seemed to sink back into himself once more.

No one but Nolan knew what he was saying. Nolan discerned the purpose of Joe's condition; the reasons for his current state of distress.

"Is there a ceremony? Are we doing it?"

Joe looked at Nolan again. This time with a bit more coherence.

"Yes, there is a ceremony …we must go soon …there is not much time."

Nolan looked at Rosie. She had a strange mournful look on her face. Nolan tried to read her thoughts when she nodded over at Samantha.

"You're going to need the girl," said Rosie

Anne sat up straight. "What does that mean? What ceremony? What are you all talking about now?" Her anger was flaring again.

"It's the yellow mist," said Joe in a faraway voice.

"Here we go again with this yellow mist crap!" Anne was louder than she wanted and was quickly losing control.

Rosie understood how Anne was feeling.

"Listen, Anne. We are here for the herd. The ceremony is to form another connection from Nolan to the lead stallion. We need all those who see the yellow mist to participate. It isn't easy, so the more of those we can get, the more chance we have of being successful. Samantha must go to the ceremony."

"Then I'm going too," said Anne.

Rosie and Nolan looked at Joe for some kind of guidance. Joe was still staring into the sky as if he were alone. Anne's words hung in the air as everyone waited for Joe to speak. The seconds ticked by and Joe nodded his head.

"Yes, she must come too."

Anne was expecting some resistance. Now she volunteered and for what, she didn't know.

"Okay," said Nolan. "Let's get moving. We'll meet at the house in 30 minutes and go from there."

Joe again nodded his agreement, stood up, and walked off toward the house.

CHAPTER TWELVE

The press conference was hastily arranged at one of the few local hotels, the Best Western, in a small 30 x 15-foot meeting room designed to accommodate about 15 people. The walls were decorated with brownish-tan grass-cloth wallpaper that matched the neutral color of the time-worn carpet. All of this was half lit by the fluorescent overhead lights giving the place a dingy, old look. There were easily 30 people crammed into the room, including the camera crews, making the space feel even smaller. The sheriff's podium was set up in the corner next to a doorway leading out into the service area of the hotel. The cameramen used the small crowded room to make the event look much bigger than it really was. A bunch of reporters sitting tightly together surrounded the cornered sheriff. It was made for television, a great shot, dramatic, showing the immediacy of the story.

Sheriff Parker stood at the podium. He was flanked by several of his men. Speaking in front of an audience came easily to him and this was no different, although he expected less of a crowd. Somehow the word spread faster than even he expected. There were reporters from as far away as Salt Lake City, Utah and all the major national channels were represented. Someone was trying to make this a major story, a big deal.

The press conference progressed as Parker had imagined. Thus far, Parker had controlled the information flowing out to the world. He was very careful to reveal only the parts he wanted them to know. He hadn't lied, he just left out certain details of the event, certain parts of the story. He was laying out a story and subtly disseminating bits of evidence to ensure the reporters would write as he needed them to, as Senator Ruud needed them to.

He told the reporters that several men were murdered. He said they believed there were two people responsible for the killings and these two were currently at large. They were considered armed and dangerous. A statewide manhunt was in full swing and they tracked the team up to Angel Ridge Rescue Ranch. Parker wanted to get that name in there and he planted it perfectly. He also said that one of the fugitives was limping, probably had a broken foot, and that they found blood on the trail indicating one or both had some type of flesh wound. They rode out of the area on horseback. One horse. He concluded with the fact that the department was currently following several leads.

After the short presentation of his version of the facts, Sheriff Parker turned the time over to the question-and-answer period. There was a scramble of raised hands and Parker picked a man in front, one he knew from the Reno press.

"Sheriff Parker, are there any apparent motives for these crimes?"

The question was teed up perfectly.

"We found a couple of dead mustangs at the scene of the crime. I think these two were poachers or just out for blood sport. We think our men, er, the ranch hands, must have come across them during their killing of these wild horses."

Parker kept choosing the reporters he knew.

"How many horses were killed?"

"We found two at the crime scene. Killed by gunshot."

"How were the men killed?"

"That has not yet been determined."

The questions were coming quickly and Parker answered each one masterfully, always giving the shortest possible answer without giving too much information. He was spinning the story the way he wanted it. It was going perfectly; the senator would be proud. Parker was about to end the session when a man standing near the back of the room called out.

"Sheriff Parker? Steve Boche, KTVX Sacramento. Were there any other horses involved in this situation?"

Parker stopped to consider who this man was and what he was after.

"I am not sure I know what you mean," said Parker.

"Were there any other horses killed that you know of?"

"There were two at the crime scene. I think I already said that." Parker looked around the room for someone else with a question but the man at the back persisted.

"What about wild horses that were killed away from the crime scene?" he asked.

Parker paused again. This man knew something. He had to choose his words carefully.

"Well, the investigation is ongoing. At this point, we have found two horses that were killed."

"And what were your men, er, I'm sorry, I mean Ruud's men doing in the vicinity of the crime scene?"

"We do not have that information yet."

"Were there any survivors? Are there any eye witnesses?"

"No."

"Sheriff, you said you have not determined how many men were killed. How is that possible?"

Parker was getting irritated; he needed to end this thing but also needed to appear as if he had nothing to hide.

"We are not sure how many men were up there. We are trying to account for all the men at the ranch. This has not been accomplished yet."

"How many men are known dead at this time?"

Parker had to pick a number. He left himself an escape if this was ever to come up again, but he had to pick a number.

"There are four dead at this time," he said coldly. "We are withholding their names pending notification of their families."

The other reporters in the room were now sensing something more to the story. Why was this man asking these questions? What did he know? Suddenly Parker was faced with several other reporters coming back for another round of questions. The control that Parker had exerted over the press conference was slipping away. He was trying to keep this a story about a couple of wild horse killers being discovered on the range. Now some other more embarrassing questions started up.

"Sheriff, have you spoken to Senator Ruud about this?"

"Yes, we have been in contact."

"What was his reaction?"

"He was devastated by the news. He has a deep love for the wild horse herds and was shocked at the murders involving his workforce."

"Sheriff, you say the senator loves wild horses? Didn't he recently sponsor a bill to increase the numbers of wild horses taken off the Nevada range?"

Parker lost control of the story; he knew it. It was time to end this meeting.

"I don't know what that has to do with the ongoing investigation into the murder of the senator's ranch hands or the killing of wild horses. I am sorry. That is all the time I have as we are conducting an aggressive manhunt for those responsible. Thank you all for coming."

With that the sheriff turned and walked off the stage. He was livid. When he was safely out of the room and into the back service area he exploded on his communications director, Hank Lamb.

"What the hell was that?"

Hank waved his hand. "Oh, don't worry, that went just fine. You gave all the right information. You covered your tracks and you left yourself several outs. It's fine."

Hank was a chatty man and Parker didn't want to listen to it. His intuition told him something was wrong. Something was out there he couldn't see, didn't comprehend. Arguing with Hank about it would be a waste of time.

"Okay," Parker said, pretending to cool down.

"Did we get the bodies to the morgue?"

"Yes sir, everything went as planned."

"Well, let's get back to the ranch. I have some things I want to follow up on.

The sheriff and his cronies left the building and soon they all were headed back to the ranch and the MCU.

The sun had gone down. The last of the light gave up to the blackness of the wide-open Nevada range. A late-rising moon had yet to make an appearance, leaving the night dark and empty. In Joe's maroon Suburban with Rosie at the wheel sat Nolan, Anne, Samantha, and Joe. Anne took the front seat to give her room for her walking cast. Joe, Nolan, and Samantha sat in the back; the ample roomy interior making them all appear small. The truck was pointed southbound on the highway leading into town.

Anne was still feeling some trepidation but decided to force herself to go along with this next adventure. She was still not sure where they were going other than to some ceremony. Samantha, on the other hand, couldn't be more excited. She was exploring her newly named gift and knew something big was in store for the evening. As she sat in the back seat with Nolan on her right and Joe on her left, she could feel the yellow mist surging between the two men. They were having some unspoken conversation and she could feel the waves of shimmering yellow light flash back and forth between them. There was something else she sensed, something coming from Nolan only. It was being sent to Joe, but not the other way around. She did not understand but she could feel it. She sensed it as being very large, much older, almost ancient; a transmission being passed from Nolan to Joe. It was underneath the yellow mist—holding, supporting—like a deep and dark river. This insight made Samantha wonder and she tried to seek it out, but to her newly trained senses, she could only see the yellow mist. She sat back and enjoyed the feeling.

Fifteen minutes later they were at the outskirts of town just where the streetlights started to glow. As Rosie was decelerating to the posted speed she noticed Sheriff Parker's police cruiser speed by.

"Boy, he's leaving town in a hurry," Rosie muttered.

Anne took notice and caught a glimpse of the police car as it zoomed by. The sight of the two men inside the car made her shudder.

Rosie tilted her head up to look in the rear view mirror.

"Parker just went by."

"They must have finished the news conference," Anne said. "Yeah, look there." She was pointing to a hotel on the right where there were several news vans in the parking lot, one from KTVX in Sacramento.

"There's Gary!" Anne said. "Pull over! Pull in there. I need to talk to Gary."

Rosie looked at her with a frown.

"Just for a couple minutes. It won't take long, I promise." Anne pleaded.

At the last second, Rosie hit the brakes and turned into the parking lot, pulling up to the van with the giant KTVX logo painted across the sides. Two men were loading gear into the van's sliding side door. Anne rolled down her window.

"Gary!" she called. "Hi!"

Gary looked up from the black camera case he was lifting and with a confused look on his face suddenly recognized who was calling to him.

"Anne? What are you doing?" His voice had a deep, booming resonance.

Gary walked up to the truck. Tall enough to have to bend over to reach window height, he had deep-set features and a Cro-Magnon brow. He leaned down to the window and gave Anne a serious look, shocked by the bruise on her face.

"What happened to you?" he asked with genuine concern.

"Oh, it's a long story. I'll tell you later. But tell me, how did it go in there?"

Gary couldn't let it go. "Are you alright?"

"Yeah, I'll be fine. I don't have much time. Tell me how the conference went."

Gary glanced around at the faces inside the Suburban thinking how strange they all seemed, his big head almost filling the entire window. He turned back to Anne.

"Parker was pretty tight-lipped about the details, of course. I got him to admit a few things."

"Like what?" Anne was pensive.

"The number of men killed, the number of horses killed, that kind of thing."

"How many men did he admit to?"

"Only four known dead, is what he said."

"Okay, he is lying. There were at least nine men there at the time. They were all killed. We know that for a fact. You should check the morgue and the coroner's office to see what you can find. Don't let this one go. We are onto something big here. Trust me."

Gary looked at her beginning to put the pieces together.

"He said they were looking for two suspects, one walking with a limp, possibly wounded. They escaped on horseback."

Anne looked down, giving herself away. Gary now knew she was part of the story. Regaining her composure she looked up at him.

214

"Look, we have somewhere we need to be. But please continue checking this thing out and I will call you as soon as I can. I'll tell you everything then, okay?"

Gary paused for a couple of seconds thinking things through. Then he winked.

"You take care of yourself, Anne. I'll be expecting your call."

Anne rolled up her window as Rosie shifted into gear and pulled out of the parking lot back to the highway.

"Someone you work with?" asked Rosie.

"Yeah, that's Gary Streetland, one of our top reporters. He'll ferret out the truth. He's very good at what he does."

Rosie just nodded her head. The drive through town took all of seven minutes. A couple of retail stores, the local bank, everything was closed but a gas station/food mart at the farthest edge of the tiny town. Just before the station, there was an unusually large building, so big it looked out of place next to the rest of the hinterland buildings that lined the main road.

"What's that?" asked Anne.

"Oh, that's police headquarters."

"Why so big? Seems very unnecessary."

"Well, Ruud makes sure his people are well taken care of. It's how it is around here. Don't for a minute underestimate these people. That would be unwise."

Rosie was dead serious. Anne took a mental note. Soon they left the town's lights and were back in the darkness zooming south down the highway.

Another 15 minutes went by with nothing to see but the road stretching out in front of the headlights. It was completely black outside and completely silent inside. No one was talking; each was lost in their own thoughts about the circumstances that led them to this dark highway. Suddenly Rosie took her foot off the gas and the Chevy began to slow down. Anne looked out the window and saw nothing; no lights, no other vehicles, just the inky blackness of night.

"Mile marker 230, right?" Rosie asked.

"232," Joe replied. It was all he had said since they left the ranch.

"Oh, that's right." Rosie sped up and two miles down the road slowed to a stop, pulling off the main road onto a wide dirt patch. She put the SUV into park and left it idling.

Being so dark outside, it was hard to see anything beyond several feet from the truck. Anne searched the inky darkness for clues as to why they stopped. The slow, throaty sounds from the idling Suburban sounded like a lullaby.

"What are we doing?" Anne asked to no one in particular.

"Waiting," Rosie responded. It was obvious she didn't want to say anything further so Anne sat silently, and waited.

For five minutes nothing happened; no one spoke. Seemingly from nowhere, from out of the blackness, two men wearing white shirts and loose white pants, stepped out of the shadows like ghosts and came up to the driver's window. They were obviously Native Americans; each one had long black braids cresting both shoulders. One was carrying a large black bag, like an old-fashioned doctor's bag, yet much larger. The leather handles were perched on his shoulder. Rosie rolled down Joe's window; he was sitting directly behind her. Joe stuck his arm out and waved the two closer. They spoke in hushed voices. Anne wondered who they thought might be listening.

"We all ready?" Joe asked softly.

"You didn't give us much time," said the man with the bag, smiling slightly. "But, we are ready."

"Will you ride with us?"

"We will."

"Okay Christo, you can squeeze in here, and Lon can sit up front."

Joe opened his door and after asking Samantha to climb over to the third seat into the very back; he slid over to let the man in. Christo climbed in, pulling his large bag onto his lap. The one named Lon crowded into the front seat making Anne take the middle hump. Her casted foot still resting to the right, her left leg raised uncomfortably over the truck's transmission. Once everybody was rearranged and the doors closed, Joe made the initial introductions.

"Everybody, this is Lon and this is Christo. They will be performing the ceremony tonight. This is Anne, Nolan, and in the back is Samantha."

"Hi!" Sam called with enthusiasm.

Christo turned around and looked at Samantha. When their eyes met, Sam was completely overtaken by the yellow mist. It swelled up and squeezed her chest tight, forcing the air out in an audible moan. It was like she was looking into the eyes of the source of her misty gift, the pure energy, the original power. This all happened in a few seconds, a lingering gaze. Christo smiled at her as if pleased by her awareness. He said hello then turned back to face the front. Sam drew in a deep breath and felt a fascination with this man. He knew something.

"Is this the man?" Christo asked as he reached across Joe to pat Nolan's leg. He would have shaken his hand but Nolan's arm being in a sling rendered the gesture impractical.

Nolan turned up the corners of his mouth and nodded toward the Indian.

Christo studied Nolan's face for a few seconds then said, "It's nice to meet you." Lon turned around and was also focusing his intense gaze on Nolan. Nolan felt a bit like a zoo animal, these two men peering at him in the darkness, assessing his frame, his mind, and his soul. Nolan could see the mist and the blue flower agitating in the back of his mind. It was obvious these men also shared the gifts and Nolan wondered what else they knew.

Next, Christo turned his attention to Anne by putting his hand on her shoulder; Anne craned her neck around but couldn't look directly at the man. She exchanged his greeting somewhat awkwardly with one eye pointed towards his direction. Lon sat next to her, the silent observer.

Christo reached out and put one hand on Rosie's shoulder and the other on Joe's leg and spoke in a gentle and sincere voice.

"It is good to see you, my friends."

Rosie looked up at Christo in the rear view mirror. "It's good to see you Christo. We are all ready; just give me directions."

Christo nodded toward Lon. Without missing a beat, Lon pointed right.

"Follow this dirt road."

"Oh, it's so dark out there I didn't even notice there was a road," said Rosie in her familiar friendly voice. She pulled the gear shifter down into drive and moved the truck onto a small dirt road. At once she came to a gate and Lon jumped out to open it. Soon they were traveling across the expanse of the Nevada range heading slightly upward toward some unseen mountain in the distance.

In the police cruiser Parker was livid. Something was amiss. Some force was gathered up against him and Senator Ruud. He knew it was Angel Ridge. He needed to redirect the narrative on this situation away from him and Ruud and onto the perpetrators of the murders.

"It's time to make an arrest," he said. "Time to throw down the gloves." Deputy Miller sat in the passenger seat quietly, lost in his own thoughts.

Parker continued, "I'll call the judge and get the warrants. It's clear that we have a case against that Harper woman. Let's bring her in and see what we can find out about the guy she was with."

Miller was silent. Parker looked over to see if he was paying attention at all. Undaunted, Parker continued.

"We are going to have to find that horse, the one in the picture. Let's get a team up to the Angel Ridge, find it, impound it, and run some tests. Meanwhile, we will take Ms. Harper into custody, put her in the pressure cooker and see what we can find."

Parker looked over at Miller. Once again it was clear Miller had something else on his mind. Parker was aggravated.

"Well? What the hell is it? What's on your mind now?"

Miller looked out the window at the passing highway markers flashing green in the headlights. He spoke slowly and deliberately as if not too certain of his words.

"I don't know. Something just isn't right. I don't want this thing to backfire on us."

"What do you mean by that?" Parker pressed.

"I keep thinking about the crime scene out by the bowl. You know those men were trampled by a stampede of horses. In all my life I have never seen anything like that. I know you haven't either. Something else is going on and I can't help but think we're missing it."

"Yeah?"

"I just want to be sure we don't get caught up by our own blind spot."

"So what are you suggesting? We need to act now, before Harper leaves the state. We need to give the media a new trail to dog, or they'll come after us, sure as shit."

"Yeah, I know you're right, but I still have this nagging thing I can't explain."

"Well, when you get something concrete, let me know. Until then we need to proceed, savvy?"

"Yeah, I got it," said Miller staring out the window. The two zoomed off into the night, back to the ranch and the MCU. Soon the judge would be called, the warrants would be issued, and the chase would be on.

It was four miles up the dark dirt road. So dark that the black night seemed to suck the life right out of the headlights, absorbing the photons like a hungry sponge. The world looked very small in the limited space lit up just in front of the truck. Rosie was driving slowly as the road kept streaming into the lights giving an illusion that they were on some kind of endless treadmill or hamster wheel.

No one was talking, each person lost in their expectations of what events lie ahead. Nolan was nervous. Joe was concerned. Anne was anxiety incarnate. Samantha was curious, and Rosie was just trying to keep the truck on the road. The two Indians and the bag were calmly detached from any outcome. They were enjoying the ride.

It took 15 minutes to reach the end of the road. Abruptly, the hamster wheel stopped and the road veered hard left. A small low-slung building appeared in the headlights; a cabin as dark as the night. Rosie pulled the truck next to the front door, pushed the gear into park, and shut down the engine. For a moment everyone sat in the stillness, the complete blackness, before Lon opened his door and the interior vehicle lights broke the apprehension and got the crew moving.

As the others were getting out of the truck to stretch their legs, Lon moved quickly, opening the front door of the cabin and turning on some lights, both exterior and interior. The outside light flashed on to reveal a modest wooden clapboard exterior. In the current light it looked to be a shade of deep brown, although in reality it was a lighter blue. There was a small cement porch, complete with a gabled awning and two posts framing the door, two windows on each side, and a low-pitched roofline disappearing into the black night. That was all they saw. No landscaping, no pavement, just the dusty bare ground of the Nevada range pushing up against the foundation of the little house. All around them was a deep, deafening silence. One by one the group, without a word, entered the building.

Inside, the accommodations were spartan. There was a main room, a small kitchen off to the right and one door on the back wall that opened to an even smaller bathroom. Around the main room's perimeter were several low benches and some pillows. The room seemed neither dirty nor clean; the musky smell of sage-pine hinting slightly toward the latter. Across the old wood-planked floor were several large Piute-themed woven carpets; the largest one featured the huge head of a horse, stylized in the sharp-edged fashion of Indian textiles. At the left side of the room, opposite the kitchen, was an unadorned windowless wall with several stacks of blankets arranged in neat piles. Anne wondered what kind of spiders lived within the folds. In the middle of the room was a low wooden coffee table with some objects resting on top that were curious and looked to be of religious significance. When all were inside, Christo, still holding the bag over one shoulder, closed the door and turned to the others, his face was both friendly and serious.

"My friends, please make yourselves comfortable." The sound of his voice, easy and soothing, undulated between two or three very close monotones.

"Soon the ceremony will start and when we are ready, I will give you the first lesson. You are all here for a reason; there are no strangers among us. Each of you has a truth to bear and a responsibility for the outcome of our efforts to retrieve the *Wanekai Pohee*."

"The blue flower," Joe whispered to Samantha.

"This ceremony is very beautiful, but can be frightening as well as dangerous. It will be most important for you to follow my words and give your hearts over to the duty before us. Please find a place to sit while we make our preparations."

The five—Joe, Rosie, Anne, Nolan, and Samantha—stood at one end of the room in a state of groupthink paralysis. There was an overwhelming feeling of sacredness, making them reluctant to move into the room. Rosie broke the spell by finding a place on one of the benches. The others followed her lead. Lon had disappeared into the kitchen, which emanated with sounds of softly clanking pans and utensils. Christo joined him with his large bag.

The five sat near each other, all with a reverent disposition brought on by the sacred feeling of the bare and empty room. When they did speak, it was in whispers as if being in a church.

"So what is going to happen?" asked Samantha.

"I am not sure," Joe responded in an even softer whisper. "It has been many years since this ceremony was performed."

"What is dangerous about it?" Anne asked.

Joe looked at her and then to Nolan.

"When one is dealing with unseen forces there is always a danger—a danger of losing one's way, one's wit, or one's mind."

Anne frowned. Nolan sat back, looking away with a serious intensity.

"It's like what happened to me, right?" Sam whispered to Joe.

Anne's eyes widened. "What? What happened to you?" Her mother-instinct loomed large and terrible as no one told her about Samantha's entanglement with the seven dead horses.

Joe patted Anne on the leg, reassuring her to not worry.

"I will tell you all about it when this is over." Anne looked over at Sam for some clue of danger or distress. Sam gave her back nothing to worry about.

The whispers kept circling through the group as Lon and Christo prepared their potions and implements for the ceremony. Within minutes they both returned from the kitchen. Christo was carrying a large, shallow sage-green ceramic bowl. In the bowl was a pile of dried leaves, a stick, and two little cups the size of shot glasses. Lon carried a set of white clothes under one arm, identical to those he and Christo wore. In the other arm he lugged a hoop drum, a swath of rawhide stretched tightly over a round wooden frame, a drumstick, and a small towel.

As the two men set down their items, the rest of the group stirred in restless wariness. Lon walked up to Nolan and handed him the pile of clothes.

"Put these on," was all he said. Nolan took the clothes and retired to the small bathroom to change. The others watched as Christo laid his items onto the coffee table. Lon returned to the kitchen and retrieved some candles and several other items to complete the altar being assembled in the middle of the room. Soon, Nolan emerged from the doorway dressed all in white. Lon directed him to a spot in front of the table where he was instructed to sit on a large pillow laid down for that purpose. Next, Lon directed each participant to a specific place in the room. When all had taken their assigned places, Rosie, Joe, Anne, and Sam were seated at the perimeter of the room around the altar at the cardinal directions. Lon was opposite Nolan on the other side of the coffee table altar and Christo was standing just behind Lon.

There was a suspended moment of silence and expectation moving through the group. All eyes were on Christo as he spoke.

"Now then, we are ready to begin."

In the unseen world of spirit there are forces that the rational mind cannot, under any circumstance, perceive. It is at the focal point of the rational mind, the ego, where most of modern western culture has built its reality. A reality where things can be measured, looked at, held in hand, materialized, bought and sold. A reality where life itself is an ever-increasing collection of material experience. Where the thoughts of eternity are not entertained until that last dying day when the ego struggles against its certain demise by conjuring up the horror and illusion of finality.

Yes, this is where modern western culture has built its monuments, in the center of the ego. In horse terms, this is the $2 million gelding trained in dressage using the harmful and unrelenting methods of rollkur to force the horse into a shape that keeps the head down and the test scores up. Where getting the submission of the horse is more important than the animal's well-being, where a test score determines the worth of the individual rider and the value of the horse or its offspring.

The ego tends to bifurcate into both creative and destructive forces. The glorious rise of modernity with all the luxuries of clean water, unspoiled food, and 24/7 cable TV would not be possible without ego. Yet our endless wars, constant conflicts, and the sheer brutality of the rollkur is the ego at its dark edges. The duality of man's nature is by far the biggest hindrance to humanity.

Yet in the unseen world of spirit, there is no ego. The rational mind does not rule this ether. Check your ego at the door. No rationale allowed. The spirit world lurks just outside of our perception, taunting our egos with mystery and fear of the unknown. The spirit world, with its labyrinth of specialized truths moves like a deep river; powerful undercurrents affecting our daily lives unbeknownst to the casual observer.

Of course, just as deeply within our western cultured minds, this non-rational truth has been pushed aside in favor of that which can be seen, heard, touched, and spoken of. "If it ain't material, it ain't shit!" would be an appropriate bumper sticker on the back of the existential redneck's pick-up truck. Rationality, ego, remains a stumbling block for the western mind at the entryway to the spirit world.

This stumbling block was the focal point of the ceremony now in progress in the small cabin high up on the mountain in the Nevada range. The yellow mist was part of the non-rational spirit world but was near enough to the border of rationality to be experienced, communicated, shared, and practiced by those who had its gift. However, the blue flower, or *Wanekai Pohee* as the Nevadan natives knew it, existed at a much deeper level, less accessible by the rational mind. The whole ceremony was an exercise of getting the rational mind out of the way long enough to access the truth-structure of the blue flower, surround it by the will of intention, and to move it back to the lead stallion in the herd. The rational mind had to be shut off, the stumbling block removed. The non-rational spirit world would be laid bare, unprotected by the strong walls of ego. This was to be accomplished by administering to Nolan a strong cocktail of hallucinogens.

There were dangers, however, and precautions had to be taken. When the ego is anesthetized and the non-rational mind exposed—much like an operation on the physical body—there was always a chance of infection, unseen forces entering and taking root like bacteria in the body. The results of a spiritual 'bacteria' can vary in severity with the worst case being the premature death of the ego resulting in an incurable madness. The usual precautions would be a period of purification ridding the body of toxins and stress and preparing the person for the rigors of exposure to the non-rational. This would be analogous to sterilizing the operating room. In Nolan's case there wasn't time necessary for the purification rite. This was emergency surgery, no time for clean scalpels. To counter this very real danger it was decided to provide Nolan with a guide. Someone familiar with the spiritual landscape existing just outside the preview of ego. Someone to watch over him, help him to complete the task, and bring him back to the safety of ego intact. Stitched up with the precision of a plastic surgeon, leaving little or no psychic scars. This guide, it was decided, would be Lon who now sat across from Nolan with two little cups of black liquid as the ceremony began.

As Lon and Nolan drank down the thick, nasty-smelling black liquid, Christo gave the others the first lesson. "Do not give into fear; focus of the yellow mist," he said. It was plain enough for Joe, Rosie, and Sam, but Anne did not understand. She resisted her desire to ask obvious questions; obvious to her anyhow. Christo told the group he would teach them some simple songs. The singing was designed to occupy the mind, to keep fear at bay. Then they would use their imaginations to keep the yellow mist flowing through the room, surrounding Lon and Nolan to protect them in their journey. This group activity was the very important task to keep Nolan from sliding into the black void from where few men could ever return.

Nolan listened to Christo's words and had to admit to more than just a bit of nervousness. He had experience with the yellow mist. He had guidance early on as he learned to master the ebb and flow. He was skillful in the communication, the interpretation, the transmission of messages to and from the horse world, yet the blue flower was something completely different; it was much bigger, more potent, more demanding. Nolan did not know how to ride the waves of the blue flower. As he gagged down the thick potion of black sludge, he knew he was entering an unknown world. He had to trust the yellow mist to bring him back. His whole body shuddered as he forced himself to swallow. It was done; he had taken the first step. The aftertaste of that black goo would stay with him for weeks.

Christo stood behind Lon holding the hoop drum; he struck a low booming note and started a low chant.

"Zaaaaaaaaah…"

It was a low, droning sound coming from the bottom of his gut.

The vibration of Christo's voice shook the room in a very subtle way. Infinitesimal sound waves began moving the outer edges of each surface in the room, including the bodies seated around the table. Vibrations are the essence of life. To control and guide vibration is to control and guide life itself. With encouraging arms, Christo guided the others to join him. The yellow mist jumped and skipped and began to join the vibrations.

The mind is indeed a curious thing. As Nolan sat at the table, his senses collected the various inputs offered by the surrounding room. Foremost, his eyes gathered up the light. Just before him on the table were seven candles arranged in a circle. There the flames gently danced in the still atmosphere of the room. The candles illuminated the face of the man sitting directly across from him casting upward shadows from cheekbone to forehead. These shadows made Lon's face appear as a mocking visage, almost sinister. Behind Lon, and dimmer in the candlelight, stood Christo, erect with drum in hand. His brown face almost the color of the wall as the room drew away in the dimness.

Next, Nolan's ears were collecting the vibrations of the chanting and the drum beat. Seemingly simple, the sounds were beginning to build upon one another. The different timbre of each voice added a separate layer of vibration that collected in a mounting tower of unison sound. The overtones generated by the base tones started a subtle ringing in the room giving a sensation of a circular whirlpool of noise swirling around the center. Around Nolan.

Added to the sights and sounds was the sense of smell. Nolan's olfactory sensors drew in the different scents, each smell registering a separate memory and impression. Immediately in front of Nolan was the large ceramic bowl filled with sage and purple coneflower. It sent up a fresh, pungent fragrance that was more stinging than soothing. Then came the latent musty smell of the room itself—dust and dry mold, aging paint gases, and textile fumes. On top of that was the smell of human beings—sweat, body, breath, stale perfume, lotions, and toothpaste. Rolled together the smell was neither pleasant nor revolting, just the earthy and real sensation of life itself.

Nolan's sense of touch was registering the comfortable feel of the light-cotton clothing plus the slight chill of the cold room. As his breath moved in and out of his nostrils, he could sense his nervous system relaxing. He felt his heartbeat slow and his blood pressure decrease.

His fifth sense, the sense of taste, was completely overwhelmed by the nasty black-sludge potion he just consumed. Alternating between what might be described as the taste of a dirty sock fresh from the foot of a marathon runner and the rotting corpse of a decomposing rodent, the disgusting sensation flooded his tongue, cheeks, throat, and all the way down his esophagus to his stomach where the potion gurgled, grew warm, and expanded.

As Nolan's mind gathered all of his senses, his inner voice was busy chatting away in the endless procession of randomly connected thoughts and ideas. Like a stone skipping across a still pond, each thought touched his consciousness with a ripple effect, spreading out to form new ideas and new thoughts. It was the incessant stream of distraction brought about by the ego in its attempt to keep the dark forces of non-rationality at bay. Accompanying this internal chatter was the constant presence of the yellow mist. It danced around the room in short staccato movements ticking by like an oversized wrist watch. Nolan could see this in his mind's eye. The blue flower, on the other hand, had receded into the depths of his presence to a place unknown. Hiding out in some attempt of cosmic self-preservation.

Nolan attempted to focus on the chanting and on Lon who seemed to be saying some sort of prayer, the rhythm of which added a stimulating counterpoint to the simplicity of the chant. The more Nolan attempted to focus, the more his mind pulled him away into the stream of relentless chatter. The poison was starting to take effect, moving into his bloodstream, into his nervous system and up to the neo-cortex.

At first Nolan didn't notice the rising symptoms. His chattering mind kept up its analytical minutia wondering how long the candles would burn, what he had eaten that day, whether or not he and Anne would ever make love. The distractions kept coming into the quick-stepped pace of his active mind like high-pressure water from a fire hose. Nolan found his eyelids drooping as he tried to focus his wandering mind.

Then there was a stutter; a stutter in the chatter, an empty space in the stream of randomly connected ideas. It came unnoticed to Nolan's mind and only was evident when he realized the distractions began again. It was a subtle and frightening awareness that his mind had wandered off to somewhere unknown, a blank spot in his life-stream. As soon as this occurred to him, he realized that it had happened again. It was like he had been somewhere else and was now back, somewhere unknown and unremembered, an Alzheimer moment. It felt like a complete disconnect from the time continuum. His ego was in unfamiliar territory and struggled to maintain control. Nolan looked at Lon and saw the sinister shadows spreading further over his face. There was a color shift perception in the dim light and, for a split second, Lon's face flashed purple then green then back to normal.

Through all this hyper awareness, the yellow mist was thumping along with the beat of the drum. Christo and the others were chanting softly. Sound began to blend with the light and Nolan noticed a fascinating development unfolding on the table in front of him. The candle flames were moving in complete synchronization with the chanting and drum beats. One to the right, two to the left. Two to the right, one to the left. The flames danced with the sound of the drum—boom, boom, boom, boom. The rhythm was steady and gentle; the foundation of the earth, the rock of reason. It was the anchor to which Nolan tied his evaporating ego. The drum was the only stability in the quickly changing world. The beating heart—the life force—the only thing that was real.

Suddenly a forceful shiver splashed up Nolan's spine. He broke into a sweating hot flash. His nervous system sparkled with energy and he found himself rocking back and forth offering an outlet to the excess forces. Nolan watched the table; the candle flames were dancing but had assumed an even brighter appearance. The shapes were growing; tiny rays of light splayed out in all direction like mini-stars in a circular constellation. The light continued to diffuse until everything in front of Nolan was a blur. He noticed that his eyes were watering profusely and upon wiping them clear, the light returned to normal. His brain was starting to interpret the input from his corporeal senses with a hallucinogenic twist.

The room was vibrating. The sounds of the chanting swirled around. The dim flicker of the candles created more shadows than light.

The yellow mist danced along within the crevices of the slowly passing time. Lon kept up his counterpoint prayer. To Nolan the sound seemed to grow louder and more intense as the flicker of colors upon the images around him drew him in. He found himself staring at the ceramic bowl in front of him, seeing alternating reds, blues, greens, and deep purples. His neck felt weak and his head bobbled as his body kept rocking to and fro, to and fro.

The stutter happened again in Nolan's mind; this time he was disoriented and wondered where he was. The noise kept pressing into his mind—unrelenting and unruly. A small flame of fear grew up in his consciousness as his ego struggled to find its center of mass. The stutter came once again and Nolan felt the urge to get up and flee but when he tried to move he found his limbs unresponsive, dull and heavy. More fear as the ego felt its loosening grasp on self control. It was a losing battle, he was on a path that had its own rules, its own motives. Fighting seemed futile. Somewhere in his memory, Nolan drew up the reason he was here. He had to find the blue flower. This thought calmed him a bit and gave his spinning mind a focal point, a goal.

"The blue flower," Nolan thought, "I've gotta find the blue flower." His internal voice was loud and overbearing. He focused his eyes on the circle of candles. They had grown into seven powerful symbols. Each had its own name and cosmic address. They danced together in a seductive and suggestive movement calling Nolan closer into the flames. He looked and saw a face appear in the middle of the circle; a translucent visage flashing in and out of focus. The face grew clearer as the sound around him swirled chaotically; the dark black eyes in the face were searching the room, looking here and there. Nolan felt the urge to hide. The scene of the searching eyes scanning the room—like a dread beacon sweeping over the whitecaps of an angry, dark ocean—intimidated Nolan's sense of wellbeing. Instead of being able to hide, Nolan sat frozen in fear as the face in the circle finally spotted him. The dark eyes locked onto Nolan's being like a tractor beam. The face, it's expression heretofore a blank emotionless façade, now showed anger as it seemed to recognize Nolan and his special gift.

Nolan audibly screamed. Horror gripped his entirety as he felt his chest reflexively tighten. The chanting continued, the sweat poured out, the flaming circle grew larger and the face, now locking eyes with Nolan, began to chant with the others. There was a different tone to this chant; different words. Words as ancient as Xu. Words not uttered on the earth since the dawn of language itself. Nolan was now in the full grip of the potion. His mind collapsed upon itself and his ego was holding its last stand like General Custer at the Little Big Horn. As Nolan was captured by the baleful eyes of the angry face, the seven candles merged into a circle of light, turning slowly at first then ever faster like a spinning hoop of fire. The spinning hoop grew larger and larger and spun faster and faster. Nolan, feeling increasingly smaller and insignificant finally succumbed. His ego lay down on the battlefield and died with its boots on. The circle opened up like the hungry maw of a whale and Nolan fell into the dark, swirling emptiness being swallowed up whole.

Of course, Nolan had not gone anywhere. He was still rocking back and forth in front of the table, his jaw slack, his eyes glazed over and staring blankly at the candles, his face glistened with sweat. Lon looked in a similar fashion of mental disarray except his body was still and he had an inscrutable and slight smile on his otherwise blank face. The others watched from their different perspectives, still chanting and keeping the yellow mist aroused. The energy seemed to increase as Christo kept time with his hoop drum.

Inside of Nolan's dreamscape was a strange land of shifting shapes and an ever-changing color wheel. Nolan's ego fell valiantly at the doors of perception, the stumbling block temporarily silenced. There was a small window of time to find the blue-flower, surround it with will, and bring it back to be delivered to the herd where it rightfully belonged.

Nolan perceived himself on horseback; it was rocking back and forth carrying him through a landscape of dark terror. He heard the faint sounds of some garbled rhythm that seemed to be coming from the very land itself. A sharp terror gripped his innocent mind as he struggled to comprehend his surroundings. Disoriented and at the mercy of this horse carrying him, Nolan bent down to grasp its neck and held on tight. At that very moment the horse turned its head, unnaturally bending its neck around to look straight at Nolan. The sight was shocking but even more random was the face. The face was Lon's, dark and leathery, with an ancient wisdom chiseled into the deep lines. The dark eyes, seemingly too close together, beamed into Nolan's frightened consciousness.

"The blue flower."

The horse was talking, or rather the face on the horse was talking. Or was it Lon talking? Nolan's mind melted into a pool of clarified butter.

"The blue flower." The words came again, gently. The rhythm of which lilted against Nolan's terror.

"The blue flower." Nolan said out loud. "I've gotta find the blue flower." The thought fell over his mind like light from a sunrise. Suddenly the sky burst into a brilliant yellow canopy that shimmered and danced. Clouds of light pulsated above Nolan and the horse. The yellow mist had found its way into Nolan's psyche and was now lighting his path. Nolan looked down at the horse again; its face had resumed a more familiar appearance.

Nolan felt a comforting expectation of someone watching over him. He looked up into the yellow sky and saw only light but immediately noticed two almond-shaped clouds—bright and glowy. The clouds' shapes became a pair of eyes—Lon's eyes—beaming down from overhead, like a father peering into the crib of his newborn son. Nolan's tension lessened a bit and he was able to focus his intention although it wobbled like an out-of-balance tire.

In the room, back on the ego side, Christo and the others were chanting the continuous thrum of the ceremonial words. The sound was spinning in the room creating a reality in itself. The yellow mist was self-evident. Even Anne now could perceive it. She watched the vibrations move and dance, cluster then burst apart in some glorious display of glee and self-actualization. Christo, now standing behind behind Nolan, kept his eyes on Lon as the drum beat steady and purposeful. Christo was watching for a sign, an important clue as to how it was going on the other side. This was the critical moment in the ceremony; the point where the guide must connect with the traveler. Even now, in his hyper state of drug-induced stupor, Lon was searching Nolan's face.

His black, dark eyes watery and intense, drool spilling over his bottom lip, Lon probed, studied and puzzled over Nolan's face. He was mouthing some words that were inaudible within the noise of the group chant. Christo could see Lon's intention moving around the table, from the candles to Nolan, to the ceramic bowl back to Nolan. Suddenly with a cry that startled the entire group, Lon screamed out.

"Got 'em!"

Joe looked at Rosie with knowing eyes and nodded with a hopeful grimace. Worried, Rosie looked back to Nolan who continued his rocking motion, eyes empty, and mouth agape.

Christo's face loosened its tight grip and, while relaxing, showed the signs of relief. Lon had reached Nolan on the other side and could now help him move toward the goal, fetch it, and come back. There were still some challenges but this crucial first step was achieved and the goods delivered. Now Christo moved the group into the second phase of the ceremony. The drum beat sped up considerably. The chanting grew more harried and frantic. The pace increased as the yellow mist furiously skipped and bounced around the room. It was being pushed out like blood cells in a centrifuge, spinning faster and faster. Samantha noticed it first; the subtle beginnings of the edges of a whirlpool, with the center whirling around Nolan. The yellow mist was reaching some cosmic critical mass being pushed to limits rarely experienced. Soon it would reach gale force. Sam instinctively prepared herself for a storm.

Meanwhile Joe reached out the other way, toward the herd staged out on Ruud's ranch. Through the yellow mist, Joe made contact with the young stallion that would soon lead the herd. He could tell the young stallion was agitated by the pulsing, surging energy. Sure enough out on the range, the stallion began to whinny, nicker, and scream in that high pitched whine only horses can manage. Bucking, rearing, and pawing the ground, the stallion didn't know Joe and couldn't clearly understand the messages being sent by this strange human who interrupted his mind. It would take the blue flower for that. It would take a stronger power for the horse to understand the human messages coming over the cosmic wireless beaming directly into the stallion's guarded heart. But Joe had established a rudimentary connection with the animal that would serve as the conduit between Nolan and the horse, the connection and transporter of the blue flower.

Nolan was in deep; completely submerged in his hallucination. He was traveling on horseback through a strange and colorful land. Shapes were forming and un-forming, colors were wheeling through the hues, everything seemed to shift and shimmer. He seemed to be driven forward by the notion that the blue flower was just over the horizon. His problem was the horizon kept changing in both direction and distance. There was no fixed center in this fluid world; the only constant was the face he kept seeing in every object. It was Lon's face though Nolan just saw it as something that looked familiar. The guide was present and pushing Nolan along to the final goal, to finding the blue flower. Nolan saw the face in the mountains distant to the left; in a saguaro cactus that kept appearing and disappearing just ahead on the right. He saw the face in the rocks below his horse; in the sky clouds hung like pillows just overhead. The face—the guide—was ever present, giving Nolan a feeling of protection and well-being. The fear subsided and he kept pressing forward, on to the blue flower.

Suddenly the energy changed. The rhythm doubled, the landscape jumped, and the sky began to turn. Nolan noticed a faint yellow cast to his entire world. Instead of feeling rushed and hurried, Nolan fell back on the rhythm and the double time became an unlikely stillness. It was as if his senses were beaten into submission. Even though the world around him began to spin in a blurring vision of kaleidoscope frenzy, there came upon Nolan a deep understanding that settled upon his soul, a crystal clear vision of the perfection of the universe. The entire experience focused into a wisdom that overwhelmed Nolan's heart. In a split second he knew the secrets kept folded up inside the mundane-ness and minutia of everyday life, the cycles, and the circles. He held in his mind, for that one little fragment of time, the entire encyclopedia of universal knowledge. At that moment he was lifted up and shown the entire universe at once. The vast scope of combined cosmic hope and sorrow hanging in the astral balance. The sublime existence of his higher self was in complete control of every being, every object, every thought, and every desire. He melded with supreme consciousness as he was thrust into a serene timelessness. He lived a thousand years in a thousand different lives. He grew old and was reborn a thousand times. In that split second, he became the blue flower, existing in perfection and eternity, having no will and no desire. He knew he was home. He sat in sublime stillness and waited.

On the other side the yellow mist emitted a warning signal, the spinning edges stopped expanding and started to rise above the table in a whirling and snarling vortex. Even Anne could see the yellow tornado-shaped cone twisting above Nolan's head. The sight was so completely bizarre to her that she wouldn't have been at all surprised to see the Wicked Witch of the West flying by on her red bicycle. Lon broke his fixed gaze from Nolan and stared up at the rising yellow tornado, his eyes dark and wild. The sounds of the frenzied chanting were being drawn up into the vortex and spun around creating chopped up sounds that sputtered like a helicopter. The entire room looked like it was about to take off.

What happened next happened so quickly that even those in the room have several versions of the sequence of events. Each one saw something a bit differently, apparently because of their different perspectives from around the table. It was one of those events that fades over time. The convictions held by each observer, so pure and immediate at the outset become a series of foggy doubts while the brain realigns the truths to fit each person's outlook on what is real and what is fantasy. Just like the fervor of religious conversion seems to mellow when the convert moves back into the reality of his daily life, the events of that night, at least the memories of them, eventually dried up, changed color, and decayed like autumn leaves.

The only thing that was indisputable, to everyone, was the healing. The healing that mended the broken bones, torn and brushed flesh, and aching doubtful hearts. No one noticed when the healing actually happened, and no one foresaw or expected it. It just happened, unseen and unnoticed, one of those things that you realize after it has come and gone. The perfect gift, both surprising and much needed and completely unexpected. After the initial euphoria had faded, this was the only thing that remained intact and truthful.

It was indeed the healing that everybody remembered long after the matter was settled. But what did happen, happened fast. As the group was staring up at the violent snarling yellow mist tornado, Lon, in a moment of surprising lucidity, snatched up two of the burnt candles and thrust them into the ceramic bowl that sat on the table just in front of Nolan. The sage and purple coneflower flashed into flames, that rose up quickly and died out just as fast creating a thick, pungent, billowing smoke. The smoke was forcefully drawn into the violently twisting vortex and the once yellow mist now indeed took on the appearance of a real tornado, sucking up everything in its path. The force of the updraft caught Nolan's spirit and pulled the blue flower up and out and through the conduit established by Joe, across the miles of Nevada range all the way to the herd on Ruud's ranch, slamming into the young stallion with a force that knocked it to the ground, temporarily stunning the animal and those around it.

The blue flower had been delivered back to its rightful place in the cosmos. It was for the horse and the horse alone. The group watched as the yellow mist stopped twirling and the smoke sunk back to the floor, choking the participants with its black smudgy thickness. Christo stopped beating his drum and the group stopped chanting. Nolan fell over backwards and Lon struggled to his feet. Someone opened the front door to let some fresh air into the room; all were surprised to see the light of the new day growing outside. They had been there all night and it seemed like just moments. That is when Anne noticed the healing. Her foot wasn't aching. Her mind initially rejected the miracle when she noticed Sam looking at her in astonishment.

"What is it dear?"

"Your face, mom. The bruise is gone."

Everyone looked at Anne as she touched her face with nimble fingers. There was no pain, no tenderness.

"What just happened?" Anne said equally astonished. "What's going on?"

"A healing." said Rosie, "A healing has taken place."

"A miracle." Christo whispered in a church voice.

The group gathered around Nolan and helped him up. Joe pulled back the white cotton shirt and looked at Nolan's shoulder. The gunshot wound had been bandaged. Joe pulled back the bandage to reveal perfectly normal, healthy skin. Nolan's shoulder was no longer wounded.

"A miracle," Christo said a little louder, "We have witnessed a miracle."

"A healing." Rosie said again, "Oh, this *is* indeed glorious."

Smiles broke out all around as each person looked at the other with astonished eyes and giddy recognition. Nolan was coming out of his stupor; his eyes leaden with the after-effects of the potion. He looked up with faint recognition of his surroundings and smiled with the rest of them. The mood of the group was lighter than it had been, ever.

Anne brushed everyone else aside and crouched down beside Nolan. She wrapped her arms around his neck and kissed him roughly on the forehead. Squeezing tight with her cheek next to his she smiled.

"We did it, cowboy. We did it!"

CHAPTER THIRTEEN

Deputy Miller woke with a start. The soft whirring sounds ever present in the MCU helped him reorient his sense of location. He fell asleep in his chair in front of the computer monitor. Sitting up brought the familiar sense of stiffness and small jolts of pain through the base of his neck as he glanced at the clock to check the time: 5:23 a.m. He had been dreaming. He dreamed he jumped into a river to save a young child from being swept away and drowned. The current was strong and he was concerned about his own well being. He made his way toward the child who was stranded on some small island or maybe a piece of debris in the middle of the river. As he was about to reach the child, a giant boulder, or some massive object being carried along under the surface, rose up out of the raging water and smashed into him. As he was going under, the child looked over and with bright eyes and a weird smile yelled out to him, "I told you!"

Miller awoke with those words ringing in his brain, "I told you." He looked around the dim cabin of the MCU. Sheriff Parker must have gone to lie down in the bunk room; he was nowhere to be seen. There was an eerie calm about the place; that sublime flat energy that exists just before dawn. Miller was alone. He couldn't shake the feeling of powerlessness and dread—the strange mixture of feelings that only dreams can mash together. The curious part of the dream was the nature of the boulder. Every other part of the dreamscape was as realistic as life itself. But the boulder had a strange mystic quality, something deeper than just a rock in a river. It seemed alive, pulsating with animation and intelligence, like it was aiming for him. Hunting him. It had intention. The other thing that made the boulder curious was its color.

The boulder was blue.

Miller rose from his chair and stretched his aching back muscles. He moved the short distance to the front of the bus, opened the cabin door, and stepped out into the fresh Nevada morning. A faint light was stirring in the east. There was a gentle humming coming from the MCU's generator; an endless, droning purr that sounded unnatural in the stillness of the pre-dawn. Miller hurried from the bus, away from the mechanical noises that interrupted the natural silence offered up by the rising day. Soon he left the MCU behind and was strolling up the road, away from the ranch compound. He had to think.

Something about the whole affair with Angel Ridge sat a-kilter, straddling his common sense and his duty as a police officer. On one hand, there were 11 dead men to account for. On the other, there was Parker being pushed by Ruud to blame it on Angel Ridge. Most of the men died from injuries that couldn't be construed as murder. There were signs of foul play in the death of Striker and Bulling, but the facts were murky at best. Something wasn't adding up; there was much to this story that remained hidden. Had he known about the plans being carried out against the wild herd at the time of the deaths, Miller wouldn't be conflicted. It would have been very clear who was guilty and he would have, to his own demise, pushed to arrest all those complicit in the crime including Senator Ruud if he was involved. But Miller didn't know and didn't even suspect this type of high-level deceit. His natural desire to see people as honest and good had always been his blind spot, his weakness. Yet he knew something wasn't right. There was some part of the story that was missing.

Miller's conflict was centered on his sense of loyalty to Parker and the senator at odds against his troubled intuition. Miller had always been a company man, always followed direction. He was a team player, adding to the group and never detracting from it. His loyalty wasn't derived from some selfish desire to get ahead at any cost. He truly believed that in order to be an effective leader, one must also know how to follow. It was this honesty in his nature that moved his career ahead and engendered trust in those around him.

Now he was second in command at this small but significant operation. He was in line to become county sheriff. Even though it was an elected post, Senator Ruud had a way of being able to "predict" who would be elected. This kind of political manipulation didn't bother Miller as much as the feeling that he was expendable. He knew if he strayed from the company line he would be cast off, easily dismissed and banished from his comfortable life as a public servant. This was something explained to him when he first joined the force years ago. He thought he understood; he thought he could live within that system. As the years went by, he got to see firsthand what it really meant as men and women, friend and foe alike were routinely dismissed for the smallest infractions of the code. Yes, Miller learned what it means to be expendable and he kept to the program. He followed the law laid down by Ruud. As a result, he rose through the ranks. For the most part Miller could live with the code, but now there was this intuition, this feeling. He knew if he followed that nagging voice in his head, if he gave way to his doubts, it could very quickly lead to his demise. The consequence would be immediate. One didn't cross the senator unless you wanted an all-out war.

Within a few hours he would be called to join his men on a full-scale raid of the Angel Ridge Rescue Ranch. They had to bring in someone for the media to focus on. He and Parker stayed up half the night planning the raid, going over evidence, and building a case to take to the judge to get the arrest warrants. They focused on the Harper woman. It was obviously her camera they found. The tracks leading away from the scene of the crime indicated someone with a leg injury—she had a fresh cast on her foot. They were going to start with her and they were going to find that horse in the photo.

Soon, the entire force would descend on Angel Ridge and make a media spectacle of it. They had the proper news crews selected and briefed; they had the plan drawn up. Now they were just waiting for the warrants. It would not be long.

Yet all through the planning process, all through the night, Miller's mind was buzzing. Something was askew; he just couldn't put a finger on it. And now the dream; he could still hear that child's voice in his head, "I told you."

Miller ran his hand heavily across his face stopping to massage his eyes with his thumb and forefinger. He was tired, his muscles ached, his head was foggy, and he was losing his enthusiasm for the job at hand. Still, he had to press forward. He couldn't let these distractions affect his performance, his job, or his career. He forced his mind back to the task at hand, the arrest and prosecution of Anne Harper.

His watch read 5:40 a.m. In 20 minutes the men would start arriving to assemble into teams for the 7:00 a.m. sweep of the Angel Ridge Rescue Ranch. Miller was charged with coordinating the seven teams and their logistics. It was go time. There was no room for hesitation. He pushed away his doubts and focused on his mission. Walking back to the bus he charged on board.

"Okay everyone, it's go time! Get up and on your feet. Let's go!"

From the back of the bus he heard the men stirring on their cots. He would give this all he had; no turning back now.

The maroon Suburban rolled through the gloom of the pre-dawn highway. Inside, Rosie, Joe, Nolan, Samantha, and Anne were quietly riding along, each replaying the crazy events that just transpired. Lon and Christo were dropped off at the same point where they were picked up and disappeared like ghosts into the morning dawn. Anne and Nolan sat close together in the back seat next to Samantha. Rosie was at the wheel and Joe was riding shotgun. Everyone was exhausted, yet energized by the reality that had played out a few hours ago up in that little cabin.

As the mile markers swept by, both Joe and Rosie noticed something a bit out of the norm. There was more traffic than usual heading up the highway. As they neared Ruud's ranch a number of cars and trucks were pulling in. Joe counted six as they sped by on their way home. Rosie and Joe looked at each other.

"Something's up," said Joe.

Rosie nodded but said nothing. She was hoping to get back to the ranch and get some sleep before the day started in full, but when she saw the commotion at Ruud's place, something told her to forget that.

In the back, Nolan was paying attention. Although his head was still sputtering from the hallucinogen, he was mostly coherent. He saw the cars pulling into the High Star and knew the assault was coming. His intuition told him that it would be okay; he did not need to fight or resist. So he sat back and tried to relax. He knew the time for hiding was past.

Over the last two miles from the High Star to Angel Ridge, Joe counted another six cars. He, too, knew there would shortly be a visit from the authorities.

"The police are gathering," Joe said loudly as he looked over at Rosie.

"I think you are right," Rosie replied. "We should get Anne and Nolan out of sight."

Nolan shook his head, "No, not this time. We have nothing to hide. Let 'em come."

Rosie disagreed. "Nolan, you don't know Ruud like we do. He controls this town. He gets what he wants and when he doesn't, he makes people suffer. I don't think you want to cross him."

"I am not as worried about you, Nolan, as I am about Anne," Joe said.

"Me? What do you mean?" Anne interrupted.

"They have your camera; they know what you were looking for. You will be the main target."

Anne's heart fell. She looked at Sam and was glad to see she was fast asleep. After a long pause, Anne picked her phone out of her pocket and pushed a sequence on the screen. Holding the phone to her ear, she looked out the window with a very annoyed look on her face.

"Matthew? It's me …"

"No, I don't know the time, just listen."

"What?"

"Yeah, I am still up here …"

"Okay, listen. The cops are gathering for some action. We think that they are coming after me."

"Yeah, I imagine they still have the photos."

"They are going to arrest me." When Anne said this into the phone, her voice cracked and the others turned their heads and looked at her.

"Yes."

"No, I don't think so."

"I came up here to do a story, not be the story!" Anne's anger flared.

"Look, I need to know, do you have my back?" There was a pause in the conversation. Anne fidgeted while she listened to her boss talk, his puny voice was blaring from the small speaker.

"Okay, I had to ask. Don't take it so personally."

"I am sure I will be calling. Leave your phone on."

"Okay, bye."

Anne ended the call and put the phone down. She pulled her head back to look down at Nolan. He was leaning a bit heavily on her shoulder, but she didn't mind; his presence was intoxicating.

"Well, that's that," she said. "I have a team of attorneys available should I need them."

"Oh, my brother loves to play these games," said Rosie looking at Anne through the rear view mirror. "He's been screwing with Ruud for decades."

Anne wasn't impressed. She looked out the window at the gloom.

A few minutes later the Suburban pulled up to the main house at Angel Ridge. Rosie and Joe got out and Anne drove Nolan and Sam down to the bunkhouse where they were going to wait for whatever the police had in store.

There was a phone call waiting for Vicki Pearson, the Nevada State Director of the BLM. Most days, especially at this early hour in the morning, the roomy headquarters of the Carson City District Office would be dark and quiet. This day, this morning, it was buzzing with activity. In the main room—surrounded by the smaller private offices with glass fronts—there were four men huddled around a broad utility table pouring over topographic maps. Sitting at a nearby terminal, a much older woman was pecking on the keyboard with surprising speed. Another woman, nearer to the front door, was on the phone to someone calling from the Nevada range. She pressed the phone tightly to her ear to better hear the caller through the poor connection from the other end. Every button on her phone was illuminated; the mission was in full swing. The button on the very right was blinking. Holding. Waiting. That was the call waiting for Vicki Pearson.

Vicki Pearson—middle-aged with short-cropped hair and a pudgy denim-wrapped body—was outside the building giving last-minute instructions through the open window of a 2009 Chevy Silverado crew-cab. Inside, two helicopter pilots received the last bits of their pre-mission brief with serious considerations. When she was absolutely certain they understood, Ms. Pearson stepped back from the truck and clapped her hands together, not unlike a casino blackjack dealer when changing shifts, to signal the passing of the responsibility and relieving herself of control. The mission was now in the hands of the pilots who sped off toward the airport.

Ms. Pearson went directly into one of the private offices, shut the door, picked up the phone, and pushed the blinking button on the right.

"Hello?"

On the other end a male voice asked her to please hold for Senator Ruud. She waited only seconds.

"Hi, Vicki?" the voice of the senator was quiet but firm with authority.

"Hello, Senator, how are you?"

"Well, I will be doing fine once we get this matter settled."

"We are all ready on this end, Senator. I just want to be assured the final permits are in place and we have the go-ahead for the roundup."

"My office has everything in place," said the senator. "You will get some heat from the usual complainers, but it will all be legal and by the book."

"Okay, we'll get it done."

"Now, Vicki, I don't think I need to remind you that this is a one-time shot. We get one chance to get this right. I won't be able to get another round of permits put together, not with this administration. Not for awhile anyway."

"I do understand, Senator. You put me in this position for a reason, and I won't let you down."

"I know you won't." There was a slight pause. "Thanks for all you do. Goodbye."

"Goodbye for now, Senator."

There wasn't a moment to lose. Joe received the heads-up from his guy on the inside within minutes of returning home. The entire county police force would arrive at Angel Ridge at 7:00 a.m. Joe could handle it. Sheriff Parker did not ruffle any of the feathers in Joe's headdress. It was the second part of the message that had Joe scrambling—the part about helicopters and cowboys. The part about the impromptu roundup that was approved by BLM headquarters in Washington D.C. Of course, they didn't call it a roundup anymore. The politically correct term was "gathering." The wild herd running on the BLM expanse adjacent to Angel Ridge was to be "gathered" for inspections, immunizations, and for culling. Worse, a separate team of cowboys was staging on the High Star to push those horses up onto BLM range. There they would be collected and finally taken care of—BLM style.

Ordinarily the roundup—or gathering—would not be a problem. The folks at Angel Ridge had twarted this stunt before. All they had to do was open their gates and get the herd to come through onto their land. This would protect the band from being pushed up to the gathering place, on BLM rangeland where the government called the shots, and where the horses—the ones who remembered—would lose their protectors, their freedoms, and possibly their lives. Angel Ridge implemented this strategy twice before, much to the frustration of the BLM and Senator Ruud. Once the BLM finished their operations, the gates were reopened and the horses moved back to their chosen range.

Ruud got the jump on them this time. This time, there were no warnings, no public notices of the wild-horse gathering. This one came out of the blue. Even if it was illegal, there would be nothing to stop it; just several lawsuits after the fact—lawsuits that would drag on for years. Worse still, there was the second prong of the attack. In a matter of moments the entire county police force would be knocking down the doors of Angel Ridge. This would be the perfect excuse to keep Joe's folks from getting out to the range and pushing the horses onto their land. There wasn't a moment to lose.

It was times like these when Joe admitted that a cell phone might come in handy. As it was, Ruud had them all running but at least there were a few precious minutes left to try to save the herd. Joe called down to the barn and warned the manager to get several horses saddled and ready to ride. Now he had to find Nolan and get a few of the hands together to head off those horses and guide them onto Angel Ridge.

He was in his green pickup truck driving much too fast down the farm road towards the bunk houses. It was 6:55 AM. The sun was rising over the distant range throwing bright stabbing spikes of first light in through the front window of the truck. Joe shielded his eyes and kept the speed on. It wasn't until he had passed the second bunkhouse, that he spied the maroon Suburban parked on the backside of house number three. He came to a sliding stop and before the truck was even in parking gear, Joe had the door open and was halfway out. Urgency flew before him like a wild-eyed gypsy. Banging hard and rapidly on the locked door roused those on the inside. Sam opened it, and Joe entered to find a very startled Anne and Nolan.

"We must go! Quick! The herd's in deep trouble. We've gotta go! Now!"

Anne and Nolan looked at each other for some signal as to what was happening. They both drew blanks. Hopping up, they dragged their exhausted bodies through the front door, carrying their shoes and coats into the truck. In under two minutes the four of them were barreling back up the road directly toward the barn in the Suburban. Joe talked while they all put on their shoes and pulled their coats over their backs. Panic swept through the truck as each one realized what was at stake.

"Nolan, contact the herd and see what you can do to get them started this way." Nolan immediately relaxed and closed his eyes trying to establish a connection.

"Sam, Anne, I'll need you to come with us. I have eight horses being saddled up. We'll take four of my people and with us four we may have just enough to get the job done."

Sam looked at her mother. The look on Anne's face sent a little shock of alarm down the girl's spine. Anne sat frozen, with an overwhelming sense of foreboding, an intuition of evil, of chaos, and imminent danger. She knew the police were after her; she was the target. It was she putting the entire ranch at risk. Her tired mind, exhausted body, and traumatized psyche piled up all that happened over the last few days. She built an instant monument to the worst-case scenario. The thought of getting on another horse and riding out to the herd was too much. Anne was not ready for round two of gunfire, broken bones, kidnapping, and death. She couldn't put Sam in harm's way.

"Stop the car!" Anne yelled. Her face was resigned with defeat. "Stop the car!" She reached out and grabbed hold of Sam. Joe swiveled his head to look at the woman in his back seat.

"Mom, what's the matter?" Sam was frantic.

"Stop this goddam car, now!"

Joe rolled his eyes and hit the brakes. The vehicle skidded to a stop and Anne threw open the door pushing Sam out in front of her.

"What are you doing?" Sam was screaming, taken aback by the instant change in her mother. "What's wrong?"

"We don't have time for this," pleaded Joe.

"You two go right ahead. I'm done. The cops are here for me; maybe if I turn myself in it will give you more time for the horses. Maybe it will create a diversion." Anne was out of breath, adrenaline surging, in full-on fight or flight frenzy. "Either way, I can't take Sam out there, it's just too dangerous." She slammed the door and walked quickly away from the truck pulling Sam in tow. Sam looked back at the truck, tears in her eyes.

"No! I want to go!" she screamed, trying to break loose. Bursting into tears, she tugged harder. Anne did not let go and continued to drag her daughter away from the truck.

Joe and Nolan watched with mixed feelings. Joe shook his head and hit the gas. There was no time for discussion; maybe she was right, maybe it would help. Nolan was disappointed and obviously shaken by the way this was turning out. Joe tried to calm his friend.

"Listen, she'll be alright. But right now we need to focus. This is as urgent a situation as I have ever seen. We can't fail here. We can't fail."

Nolan nodded, closed his eyes, and tried to relax. The blue flower, his connection to the herd, was still strong behind his closed eyes. It was only seconds before he saw the swirling indigo petals forming a blue mandala turning in his mind. The harried nature of the moment kept him from making full contact with the horse but with all his might Nolan sent out his intention.

"Come to the gate …come to the gate …the gate." It was all he could get out before Joe pulled up to the barn and came to a jarring stop. They both jumped out and ran to the waiting horses.

Anne sat cross-legged at the roadside trying to think. Samantha stood over her with her hands on her hips, a defiant expression on her brow and a scowl on her lips.

"What are we going to do?" Sam demanded.

"Sam, the police will be here soon. They are going to arrest me. We're going to find Rosie, you can stay with her till I get back."

"What about the horses?" Sam questioned.

Anne did not answer. She knew the horses were important but her daughter came first.

"You know, mom. You should have a little faith."

It was an odd thing for Anne to hear her daughter talking about faith. She glanced up to see Sam looking older than her 12 years, with her stern face and fire in her eyes.

"What do you mean, faith?"

"Just look at your leg; it's healed. That can only mean one thing."

Anne felt defeated. "What's that?"

"It means God is on our side."

Anne looked down; she felt horrible. There was no way she was going to risk going back to Ruud's ranch, but inside she knew Sam was right. Confused and broken, Anne rose to her feet.

"Well, you may be right," she said. "Come on, we need to get back to the house."

"I don't wanna go back there," Sam protested. "I want to go help the horses. Come on. It's not too late."

"No!" Anne's retort was commanding, strong, and clear. "I *am* helping the horses. This is the only way I *can* help the horses." Sam frowned all the more and marched off in the direction of the house. Anne bit her lip and followed her daughter.

At that moment two squad cars came over the rise, road dust billowing from behind.

Anne cursed. Sam looked back at her mother, at the cops, then turned and bolted.

"You get back here!" Anne screamed.

Sam ran off in quick, lithe steps heading toward the barn. Anne looked up the road. The urge to run was quelled by her commitment to be the diversion. Anne stood steadfast, a look of resolute defiance on her face. The two patrol cars skidded up and four officers jumped out, pistols drawn. With speed and efficiency, they had their suspect on the ground, subdued, and in custody.

Running full speed, Sam made it to the barn. Huffing and out of breath, she ran into the breezeway only to find the others had already gone. The eerie silence seemed out of place. Stopping briefly to survey the scene, she noticed two saddled horses still tied to the bar down at the far end of the walkway. Sam immediately recognized one.

"Vandi!" Sam was pleasantly surprised to find her friend there waiting. She hurried over. Vandi, too, seemed happy to see Samantha. He quietly nickered as she approached. The yellow mist swirled up into her mind-sight as she quickly untied the horse, lowered the stirrups and jumped on. Sam whispered into the horse's ear.

"Vandi, we need to go help Nolan and Joe. We need to help the herd. They are in trouble."

The horse nickered again and then raised his head up and down. Sam felt the yellow mist moving like water in a small creek. She had a true feeling of connection like she was with her best friend. Like a missing piece of her soul had been returned and fitted into place, completing her, easing her tensions and inflating her confidence.

"Do you know the way?" Sam whispered.

From deep within, Sam heard the answer. She was learning to trust the yellow mist. She somehow knew that it would never lie to her, never betray her. She picked up the reins and turned toward the door. Just then, a police officer stepped into the barn directly in front of them blocking the way.

"You'll need to get off that horse, young lady," the man's voice was stern and frightening as he carefully approached the horse. Sam was backing Vandi up; looking behind her, she saw two more officers enter the far end of the barn. Turning around to face the officer in front of her, Sam felt a slight energy pulse from the yellow mist. Vandi was sending off a signal; it came through loud and clear. The message was simple—shoulder-in.

Just as the thought came into Sam's mind, Vandi leapt forward, turning his right shoulder and aiming it at the policeman. The forward momentum of the horse, coupled with its battering ram of a shoulder, knocked the policemen to the side like a bowling pin. Vandi did not miss a stride. In a full canter, the horse flew out of the barn and galloped away down the road. Sam could hear the angry voices of the cops yelling at her from the barn.

With the wind rushing past her ears, it wasn't clear at first, the sound of the horse giving chase to her. One of the cops had mounted the other horse and was coming after them. Sam and Vandi rode swiftly down the road leading to the range. The distinct three-beat ra-tat-tat, ra-tat-tat of the canter echoed across the steeply sloping land. Ahead, down near the bottom of the hill, Sam saw several police cars parked in front of the clinic. Without so much as a titter, Vandi left the road, veering off to the right onto a trail that led away from the clinic. It was then that Sam noticed the horse coming up behind her. Out of the corner of her eye she saw the motion, about ten yards back and closing in.

Turning her head, she came eye-to-eye with the officer, his short hair slicked back against the wind. He yelled something through angry lips but it was inaudible to Sam. She faced forward and again felt a short pulse of energy from the yellow mist. It stretched down the base of her skull, into and down her back. She followed it down into Vandi's core, where they were indeed connected. As the thought occurred to her, she attempted to connect the yellow mist to the other horse. Her intention stretched out toward the animal. She could sense the fear and loathing the horse had for the officer, but that was as far as it went. There was something more blocking a true connection. A psychic wall stood between Sam and the other horse. She pushed and strained to penetrate it, to move through it, all while at a full gallop. A deep, long inhale with an explosive, short and dramatic exhale and suddenly, without warning, her mind crashed through that psychic wall and she found herself inside the other horse as plainly as she was with Vandi. It was abrupt, crude and surprising to Sam's inexperienced mind. It caught her unexpectedly and she didn't really have a sense of what to do. Overwhelmed, Sam pulled it back just as abruptly. On the other side of the psychic wall, in the horse's mind, this unskilled and jerky commotion was too much for the poor horse to handle. In an act of self-preservation and fear, the horse came to an abrupt stop sending the officer soaring up and over the withers onto the trail. He landed flat on his back with a thud and a dusty puff. Seeing Vandi running off, the officer's horse jumped into a full canter and sped off leaving the officer groaning on the ground.

"Ha ha!" Sam was gleeful. She looked ahead. The trail kept her out of view from those at the clinic. She descended into a dry creek bed and made a wide arc back around to the road. Two minutes later Sam and Vandi, with the other horse in tow, were beyond the clinic around the bend where the trail connected back with the road. Walking Vandi slowly up to the junction, Sam peered over the horizon only to see a patrol car slowly moving towards her. Still below the road, she was yet unseen but not for long. Turning the horses, she quickly moved back down the trail and into the dry creek bed. This would have to do. She pushed Vandi into a canter and sped off down the gulch, not quite sure which direction she was going.

The four horsemen rode in a fury of swirling, dusty urgency. Actually there were three horse men and one horse woman. Running at full canter, each of the four held their eyes in a protective, hard-edged squint—hair streaming, hat brims bouncing, loose clothing flowing in the wake of their frantic run. They rode hard, with purpose; lives were at stake. A thick cloud of pumice dust trailed up and behind as they pounded rhythmically down the dirt road.

Joe and Nolan rode side by side. Behind them rode Jill and Danny, the only two ranch hands who were available on a moment's notice. Joe counted on Samantha and Anne joining the posse. He needed them to round out the duties. Anne's refusal was a glaring disappointment and could very well have decided the fate of the horses. As it was, Joe knew he needed a miracle to get the herd through the gates and onto Angel Ridge. Through his squinting eye slits he glanced over at Nolan who was himself lost in the misty glaze of the no-sleep, all-night spirit quest. Both of the men were now just running on adrenaline. Joe prayed that it would be enough to hold them until they could get through this. Time was ticking and the players were in motion.

They ran hard to where the remnants of the dilapidated shack tilted and defied gravity. It was the same place where just days ago Nolan and Anne rode up and over the south end of the ridge. Joe slowed the crew to give the horses a break. They all came to a stop as the dust cloud they created floated up, catching rays of glimmering sunshine. The air was cool. The sound of stamping horses and creaking leather was amplified by the stillness of the silent surroundings. Joe looked at Nolan.

"Anything? Did you get through?"

Nolan shrugged indecisively. He didn't want to tell Joe that all he was thinking about was Anne.

Joe looked ahead past the tilted shack, where the road ended and a narrow trail continued. The trail followed the fading ridgeline out to where the gate opened onto the rangeland where the land flattened out. Where the horses would be found.

"Let's get to the gate," Joe said coolly.

The four took to the trail single file. In a hurried trot they followed the track. It would take another 15 minutes before they reached the gate. Joe hoped that some sign of encouragement would appear and give him guidance. If they missed the chance to get the herd through the gate and onto his land, the fate of the horses would be grim. Even worse, the bond would be lost and the chance of revival pushed back another 100 years. Joe struggled against his mounting desperation.

15 miles to the south, a Bell 407 helicopter was airborne. It hovered at 2,000 feet as the men on board spotted the main body of the herd and were closing in. Radio chatter linked both air and ground forces. In one coordinated effort the ground crew and air crew were converging on the horses and would soon be driving them north. They were about 20 miles from the border where the BLM had complete jurisdiction. In less than an hour it would all be over. The horses would be placed in a holding pen until the transport trailers would carry them away to the long-term holding facilities in Utah and Idaho.

The herd gathered together near Upper Tanner Creek where the cottonwood trees stood like sentinels guarding the entrance to the gulch. There were 10 men on ATVs all speeding toward that spot. Several were coming up the creek bed; another group was converging from the south and the rest from the north. They would push the horses up out of the gulch and onto the flats. From there they would keep the horses moving to the northeast, skirting Angel Ridge on the west and

Fallon Ridge to the east. With 10 on the ground and one in the air, it would be a fairly simple task to get these horses up to the BLM rangeland and into the gathering pens.

Sherriff Parker sat in the command post near the front of the MCU. He had one communications officer and one operations officer at hand. Otherwise, everyone else was either on the roundup team or at Angel Ridge at the manhunt operation. Several screens in front of him gave Parker a front-row seat to the action. Video feeds were coming in from the helicopter, a couple of the ATVs, and from some helmet cams and police cruisers at the Angel Ridge compound. Parker loved this new technology; all paid for with stimulus money from the federal government thanks to Uncle Harry. It gave Parker an undeserved superiority complex. This was the biggest thing he had ever done. He had over 30 men under his command, along with a helicopter, a posse of ATVs, seven police cruisers, and, of course, his beloved MCU at the hub—all connected to respond to his every whim. He felt like the bona fide King of the County as he watched his operation unfold.

With the push of a button he could connect with any number of his men, getting an update or passing down an operational order. A small crackle in his earpiece let him know the circuit was alive. Pressing the magic button, he spoke with authority and flair. Parker was definitely in his element.

"Unit four, what's your status?" Parker reached up and adjusted a small black knob on a panel next to one of the video screens. "Unit four?"

A remarkably clear voice echoed back in the sheriff's headset. It was remarkable because it was coming directly from the helicopter. Courtesy of the federal government, the helicopter scout had on a headset with dual noise cancellation and a gated microphone. There was no background noise, just a clear, understandable voice.

"Unit four here. We have located the target; we are maneuvering into formation. Should engage the target in the next 10 minutes, about 15 miles from the border. Over."

"Copy that," said Parker, "Over and out."

He looked up to the video feed coming from the chopper. The

image was from a camera attached to the outside of the cockpit, just below the front windscreen. The camera was aimed downward at a slight angle. Parker squinted as if that would help him decipher the image. Try as he might, he couldn't see any horses. He pushed another button and grabbed the joystick resting on the desk just in front of the video screens. He pushed the joystick to the right and, sure enough, the camera followed his lead.

"Dang, this is cool!" Parker said to himself. Using the joystick he moved the camera from side to side scanning the range as best he could, but still didn't see any signs of horses on the screen. He started pushing buttons, scanning through the different camera feeds coming into the MCU. He switched between the helmet cams on the ATV riders, it was all jerky unwatchable video. Then he switched to the camera feeds coming from the action up at Angel Ridge. These feeds consisted of police cruiser dash cams and didn't reveal anything too interesting. He quickly realized that nothing useful was going to be found there.

Behind Parker at a station on the other side of the MCU, the operations officer was monitoring the communications coming from Angel Ridge.

"Give me an update," Parker ordered and, without turning around, the officer started reciting the facts as he knew them.

"We have searched about three-quarters of the ranch buildings. We have taken Anne Harper into custody. There is no sign of Joe Whitehorse or the man they call Nolan. We have two officers down."

"What?" Parker was taken back. "Explain!"

"No serious injuries reported. One was kicked, or something, by a horse, and the other was thrown from a horse. Both sustained minor injuries."

"Thrown from a horse? Do you know why he was riding in the first place?"

"The details are sketchy, but I believe he was chasing one of the Angel Ridge people trying to flee on horseback."

"A runner?"

"It appears so."

"Was the runner apprehended?"

"No sir; still at large."

"Huh," Parker reflected on the news.

"How long until the entire ranch is cleared?"

"Another 20 minutes."

Parker turned back to his monitors.

Joe and the others stared out at the lonely expanse of sagebrush and creosote bush. There was no discernable movement all the way across to Fallon Ridge; nothing unusual to see out on the range. The morning sun was up well past the mountains now, and the valley before them was lit with fresh dewy sunlight. Clear and quiet. The sweet earthy smell of sage hung delicately in the air. They sat four abreast on their horses and stared out at the range. An acute sense of anticipation settled in.

"Are we too late?"

No one dared answer the question. There was a pause and then Nolan spoke.

"No, they are being chased …just passed the top of Tanner Creek."

Nolan's connection to the new lead stallion was intense. Surprising even himself, he had a feeling, full-body and all-encompassing, welling up like a deep-creek spring, flowing into his consciousness. As the sensation spread over his mind, he was taken aback by the power and potency of the remaining link he had with the stallion. In a flashing moment, he saw a helicopter buzzing overhead and two or three ATVs moving in from the left. The vision startled Nolan.

"You okay?" Joe asked, noticing the energy flowing from Nolan's direction.

Nolan looked at Joe. Picking up his reins, he sat up straight in his saddle.

"Yeah, I'm okay. Come on; it's not too late. Follow me."

Nolan pushed his horse into a full gallop and rode out toward the middle of the valley. Within seconds the others were right behind him.

At that moment, Anne was sitting in the back of a police cruiser struggling against the handcuffs. She was not one to handle frustration gracefully. Just short of falling into a screaming hissy fit, she sat back and tried to calm down, forcing out a couple of deep breaths. All her worries tumbled across her mind, scouring her frail nerves. Probably the hardest thing she could do was to sit there while Sam was who knows where. She didn't notice Officer Gentry approaching the car and nearly jumped out of her skin when he opened the door.

"Come on out, Ms. Harper. The sergeant wants to have a word with you." By the tone of the man's voice, Anne could tell he was just here doing a job, a dispassionate public servant. As she swung her legs out of the car the man helped her stand up.

"Did you guys find my daughter?"

Gentry looked quizzically at Anne. Something in his eyes told Anne that he too had children, probably girls.

"Uh, not to my knowledge. Was she the one who ran off when we picked you up?"

Anne looked at the ground. "Yeah."

"What's her name?"

"Samantha."

"Hold on." He turned his head toward his shoulder and spoke into his radio.

"Hatch, come in …" A short pause then an affirmative answer.

"Hey, is there a girl with you down there? Her name is Samantha Harper. She's about 12 years old, five-foot-two with light brown hair."

"Hold on, I'll check." The radio clicked off.

Officer Gentry turned back to Anne, "Okay, I'll find out. She's probably down at the vet clinic with the rest of your crew. But now, come on; we're going into the mess hall."

He led Anne into the dining hall. A few tables had been pushed together for a makeshift command post. Jared Parker—the officer in charge, the same officer who had interrogated Anne just the day before—stood crouched over the table reviewing some papers. Several men surrounded him. When he turned and looked at Anne walking toward the table, he did a double-take. His face showed a clear look of anger as he turned his ire to the officer.

"I told you to bring me Anne Harper."

The officer stumbled on his words as he looked at Anne then back to Parker. "Uh, this is Anne Harper. Right? You *are* Anne Harper?"

Anne realized Parker didn't recognize her. Sensing an advantage, she kept quiet.

Parker walked up briskly, stopping just short of Anne, his face contorted, angry, and impatient. Anne could see the confusion in his eyes as he examined the flawless skin of her non-bruised face.

"Is this some kind of a joke?" Parker asked. "Just yesterday ..." His words trailed off. He looked down at her foot. No cast, no injury. Gentry didn't understand and stood nervously at Anne's side just as confused as Parker but for completely different reasons.

"Gentry, do you have her ID?"

The documents were handed over and Parker peered at them suspiciously.

"Who are you?" he asked directly, his words seething with spite.

"I want to talk with my lawyer," Anne said plainly, her spirits lifting a bit.

"I want to know your name."

"My name is Anne Harper. You have my picture there in your hand."

"Yesterday, you had a walking cast and a giant bruise on your cheek."

"If you say so."

Parker saw he was getting nowhere. He reassumed his role as commander-in-charge.

"Either way, Ms. Harper, you are under arrest for murder. You may phone your attorney after we book you. Gentry, get her down to headquarters and process her."

Parker turned and walked away. Anne was left feeling slightly duped by the whole affair. As she was being led back to the squad car, Gentry's radio buzzed.

"Gentry, we don't have any Samantha Harper down here. Nichols said she was last seen fleeing the ranch on horseback. Over."

Gentry looked at Anne. "Looks like she got away."

Nolan led the way. The wind whistled past his ears as his horse galloped full speed. Behind him, Joe, Danny, and Jill were keeping pace. They rode directly toward Fallon Ridge; directly out to the middle of the low, wide valley. In front of him, Nolan saw several jackrabbits sprinting off to the left. Then a herd of frightened pronghorn moved up from the right, passing in front of the four riders. The animals were being pushed ahead of the horses. Nolan knew that in a few short moments the herd would be in view. He pulled his horse to a stop and let the others catch up. It was time to listen.

On the range, depending upon the right atmospheric conditions, one can hear sounds from miles away. It was so naturally quiet that even small sounds of gnats were magnified. The four strained, listening for any clue as to what was coming their way. It wasn't long before they picked up the low frequency whup-whup-whup of the helicopter. It was faint but steady and coming closer. Another head of Pronghorn skipped by, coming up from Ruud's ranch.

"They're coming," said Nolan. He could feel the thoughts of the lead stallion, his chest tightened and grew warm. There was panic in the air. Looking at Joe, he raised his eyebrows looking for some plan of attack.

Joe's face was grim and stony. His black eyes fixed on the horizon.

"We're all going to have to do the work of three," he said. "Danny, you work the gate. Jill, you and I will stand in the middle and deflect the herd towards Danny. Nolan, you need to separate the herd from Ruud's drivers; they will be on ATVs. That's the critical part here. The ATVs will be driving the herd on both sides. You need to come between the drivers and the herd on this side. If you can, we'll be able to deflect them towards the gate."

A mile toward Ruud's High Star Ranch, the land arced away out of view. On top of this horizon a small cloud of dust rose up toward the sky. The sound of the helicopter was getting louder and now the four could hear the distinct whining of ATV engines.

"There they are!"

The four glanced at each other for any last words of encouragement. There were none. Danny turned his mount and galloped back toward his position at the gate. Jill, Nolan, and Joe walked their horses out to face the churning dust cloud that was moving their way. Soon they could make out the details of what was coming. The herd was out in front being led by Sun Cloud. Running full speed, the animals were kicking up dust that produced a giant trailing cloud. Flanking both sides of the herd, and partly hidden by the dust cloud, were the ATVs; both pushing and containing the horses to keep them running in a straight line. When the helicopter popped up over the horizon, the picture was complete. The whole menagerie was thrumming, buzzing, and pounding …and coming directly toward them.

Nolan pushed his horse into a gallop and aiming for the right side of the roundup, flew like the wind. Joe watched him ride away with mixed feelings of despair and hope. With no plan in mind, Nolan cast his lot in with fate. He took a chance on the slimmest of hope that he might be able to affect the sequence of events unfolding on that plain. There on that flat, sage-brushed piece of earth, nestled high between the two great ridges, Nolan laid down his intention, his desire, and his hope, outwardly expressed in an act of recklessness. He was all in, with a small, almost insignificant act thrown into the face of a raging and powerful machine, soon to collide in the wide arc of history that is horse and man.

Nolan was in a headlong gallop. As he looked ahead and saw Sun Cloud, the blue flower flooded his mind. It seemed strange to him that in this frantic desperation, he could feel at peace within the slow-motion twirl of the mystic blue connection. He immediately felt the presence of the young stallion. A short exchange of intentions occurred between the two. Nolan told Sun Cloud about the gate, "Take the herd to the gate." Nolan couldn't tell if the young horse received his message. The wind whistled in his ears, the sound of hooves pounded the earth; they were about a half-mile apart and closing in.

Between the two opposing forces, unknown to anyone on the plain, was a slight dip in the land, a swale. Cutting across the valley floor, it sank about 20 feet down and was almost 60 feet across. Invisible in the morning light, the swale lay hidden from those approaching on the ground. It proved to be that element of surprise that Nolan so desperately needed. The fly in the ointment. The sand in the Vaseline. A band of wild burros that spent the night in the bottom of the swale only added to this surprise.

The horses galloped ahead of the first ATVs. Nolan kept his eye fixed on Sun Cloud as they quickly approached each other. Suddenly from Nolan's point of view, Sun Cloud and the first horses in the herd disappeared into the earth. The first ATV followed the herd into the swale. The change in landscape caught the rider by surprise. Experienced as he was, he managed to stay on as he flew over the hill and into the gulch. Nolan could hear his engine revving as he momentarily left the ground. The rider would have been okay if it weren't for the eight wild burros directly in his path. The chaos in the gulch was just beginning when the rider hit the brakes and came off the machine, landing in the middle of the donkey gathering. The burros jumped into action and with wild braying, kicked and bucked, and flung themselves around in a fiery red-hot rant. The rider had no chance—he was trampled into the dry, dusty earth.

Simultaneously the next rider in the line flew over the hill landing on top of the first ATV that lay upside-down with its back tires spinning. There was a low, muffled crash and the second rider was down with injuries. By this time the other ATV riders were wise to this surprising topography and slowed to safely navigate the swale. The horses, however, did not slow down. Nolan saw them burst up from the swale into view and now all the closer. The burros joined them and the herd was approaching Nolan at breakneck speed. The thundering sound of the running horses both comforted and agitated him.

It was the break Nolan prayed for. The first two ATVs on the right side were out of commission and now the herd veered onto a new course. Nolan turned right and sped toward the outside of the herd. The next ATV was coming out of the swale and Nolan was going to cut him off. Nolan was on the right side of the rampage and headed directly toward the ATV.

At the MCU, Sheriff Parker was screaming at the video screen. He just watched the two ATVs crash in the gulch. With joystick in hand, he moved the helicopter camera in an attempt to get a view of what was going on.

"Didn't you guys get a fricking map of the route? What the hell's going on out there?"

No one was answering his anguished rants.

"Unit four! Come in!"

The radio crackled.

"Unit four here. We have two men down. Proceeding ahead. I repeat, we are proceeding."

Parker had the joystick. He could see a cowboy coming from the top of the screen seemingly on a collision course with one of the ATVs.

"Unit four, who is that rider? Is it one of ours?"

"Negative. The rider is an unknown. Appears to be hostile, sir."

Parker watched as Nolan galloped directly into the path of the ATV. In a game of high-plains chicken, the ATV veered off and rolled as Nolan's horse jumped up and over the ATV.

Parker was livid. "You are authorized to use force. You're authorized to use deadly force! Copy?"

"Copy that, base."

The horses were 400 yards out from where Joe and Jill sat nervously waiting. The chaotic sounds of low rumbling hoof falls were both terrifying and exhilarating. Any other day and Joe would have reveled in the noise, but this day was different. The entire herd was terrified, running at full speed. The result was a great billowing dust cloud that pushed up and outward, hiding the pursuing ATVs on either side. Joe could hear the thin whine of their engines rising and falling as the ATVs dodged the sagebrush trying to keep up with the horses. The helicopter, pushing in from behind, completed the horror that approached at high speed. The sight, sound, and smell all converged in the pit of Joe's stomach. He felt he was in the very path of an out-of-control freight train. Nerves tense, stomachs churning, the two could see Nolan on horseback darting around on the far side of the herd. There were three ATVs down now and it left a big hole in their operation. This was all the Angel Ridge crew needed to get the horses moving toward the gate. It was show time for Jill and Joe. Joe turned to find Danny far over by the gate and then turned back to Jill.

"We've gotta cover a lot of ground here. Let's split up some. Maybe you better run out that way a bit and then come around from the left."

"Okey doke," Jill said with strained confidence. "Good luck, Joe." She gave the old man a wink and pushed her horse into a gallop, away toward Fallon Ridge. That left Joe alone, sitting atop his mount, facing the great undulating mass of brown, white, and grey horses, their heads bobbing up and down as they ran. They were 50 yards closer now. Joe took a deep breath and kicked his horse into high gear. They jumped into a gallop and ran headlong into the fray. It was up to him and Jill to turn the herd toward the gate; how to do that was just a matter of instinct. Apply some pressure and the horse will move. Get Sun Cloud to move and the herd would follow. Joe was directing his pressure at Sun Cloud.

Joe approached the herd at collision-course speed. Out ahead, at the front edge of the growing dust cloud and past the main body of running horses, Joe caught a glimpse of Nolan on the other side of the herd. He was running counter to the horses, going after the ATV next in line. A split-second thought occurred to Joe—why was Nolan pressing his luck when there was clearly enough space now to move the herd toward the gate? Just as soon as this thought passed through his mind, Joe saw the helicopter pop up, rising above the herd, out of the dust cloud. It veered sideways directly towards Nolan. Joe's heart dropped as he looked up to see a man with a long rifle leaning from the cabin door. At less than 300 yards it was easy enough to see. The shots were silent because of the distance, noise, and movement, but the result was plain to see. Nolan and his horse went down hard. The last thing Joe saw of Nolan was the horse's legs flailing in the air as they disappeared behind the dust cloud and raging mass of horses. Joe let out a long piercing scream—the Piute war cry. Rage filled his eyes; an overwhelming sense of injustice consumed him like flash paper set ablaze. Worse, his sense of desperation was stoked by the desire to go help his friend but Nolan would have to wait; the horses came first.

The ATV zipped by the spot where Nolan and his horse lay covered in dust. Nolan was still while the horse's legs were twitching. Full throttle, the ATV took up position in the lead spot, right next to Sun Cloud. Now there were two ATVs driving the lead stallion, one on either side. They had to keep the herd moving forward and that meant controlling the leader. Yet behind Sun Cloud, on the left side of the running herd, there was no pressure to contain them. Three ATVs were down and there was a hole in their game. The instincts of the herd would keep them following their leader, that is, until some other force moved them away.

Jill and Joe were converging on the same point, coming in on Sun Cloud's right side. It was a dangerous attempt to push the herd away from their current path and toward the gate. They both galloped up as Sun Cloud and the first ATVs passed them on their right. Joe saw his chance and pulled his horse into a sliding stop. It was a clean 15-foot slide on the hardscrabble floor of that Nevada valley. Joe leaned back and his horse rose up on its hind legs pawing the air. A great shrieking cry came from both Joe and the horse, the yellow mist in all of its glorious intention pushed up from the ground in a flash of unseen brilliance. The power of the yellow mist surprised the main body of the herd and gained their attention. That burst of energy, coupled with Jill's headlong push into the main body, was enough to break them off from their lead stallion. The bulk of them broke away to the left while Sun Cloud continued forward.

The helicopter buzzed by overhead in formation with the ATVs, then banked hard to the left trying to stop the horses from moving away. This maneuver backfired, turning the horses even farther from the intended course. Now they were running directly toward the gate. Joe and Jill saw their chance, and leaving Sun Cloud to fate, charged after the rogue remnant, trying to keep the momentum toward Angel Ridge. Instantly the helicopter pushed back to the right. Jill moved ahead up the right side of the running horses and kept them moving straight toward the gate. Joe was right behind her—100 yards to go. The helicopter crew was relentless; the copter sped ahead and turned to face them, taking up a hover position blocking the route through the gate. The horses responded by turning to the left. Joe's heart dropped; there just weren't enough of them to get the job done. The horses were running to the south now, away from the gate. Joe knew they had been beaten; there was no way to get the horses turned around now. They had lost.

Tears of desperation streamed down Joe's dusty face. He stopped his horse and watched as the herd moved off toward certain doom.

"Oh, Lord, what now?" Joe's heart was pleading. All they fought for, the entire purpose of their ranch, their lives, their hopes, and their future—all of it was embodied in this herd of wild horses. Joe watched in disbelief as the herd ran past the gate and moved southward along the fence that marked the boundary of Joe's expectations—one side freedom, the other side death. Ruud had won. Joe saw his entire life's work spinning away, out of his control. Shoulders drooping, heartbroken, Joe lowered his tear-filled eyes.

But there was a pulse in the yellow mist, something bumped. Completely exhausted and beaten down, Joe ignored the impulse. He was done. He left all he had on the field of battle. He expended everything …and failed.

But it happened again, the yellow mist. Wearily Joe raised his eyes and in a split-second sat stunned by what he saw. The herd stopped and was bunched together along the fence line in a state of utter confusion. Joe saw the herd as a cornered animal, dangerous and desperate. Just then the herd reacted; it jumped and began running back toward the gate. Joe was startled and confused by it. He sat motionless in his utter exhaustion and watched the herd approaching. Then he saw the reason for the turn-around. Beyond the herd, and running up from the south were two horsemen. Joe looked hard through the dust and calamity. It was Samantha and Nolan.

Joe gasped in disbelief. His tears streamed full out now making it difficult to see. He choked back his emotional outpour, wiped his eyes clear, and took a deep breath. He knew they had another chance. Giving out another long, shrill cry, he kicked his horse forward, determined this time to get the horses through the gate. Jill was already ahead of him and halfway to the gate where Danny was waiting. The three of them held the line on the north side. The herd was running up on their left. Just one hurdle remained.

The helicopter hovered, above the gate like a dangling menace. It was the final challenge. All of the other men on Ruud's side rode off to the north, the helicopter remained as the lone obstacle. Sam and Nolan were pressing from the south. Jill, Joe, and Danny from the north and east, while the helicopter pressed from the west. The horses were being squeezed in-between. As the circle tightened, the pressure mounted. In this state of mind, the horse became very dangerous and unpredictable. Something had to give.

That something was gunfire. The sharp, popping rounds sent shivers down Joe's spine. He was close enough now to see the men inside the helicopter, and strangely he could not make out which one of them was shooting. A few more rounds cracked and Joe realized it was not coming from the helicopter. He looked around wildly but could not see who was firing. They were all converging on the gate; the horses were 50 yards out. More gunfire muffled through the noise of the galloping horses and roaring helicopter. It was clear now that the gunfire was coming from Joe's left. He looked over and sought out Nolan and Sam. Through the herd he finally spotted Nolan with his pistol drawn and pointed at the helicopter. Nolan fired a few more rounds. The copter shifted sideways, rose quickly about 100 yards straight into the air and flew off toward the north. A fatigued cheer went up among the horsemen as they moved the restless herd in and through the gate. One by one, the horses galloped past Danny through the opening. Joe, Jill, Nolan, and Samantha came up from behind to join him as the last of the horses passed through. They all lingered under the gate.

"Sam? It sure is great to see you!" said Joe. "You really saved the day."

Samantha smiled. "I found the horses in the barn after you all left. The cops chased me and tried to stop me but I got away. I followed the old river bed and when I came out, I found Nolan, trying to save his horse." Sam stopped short and looked at the ground. "Is she dead?"

"She's not dead," interrupted Nolan. They all looked over at him. "They were using tranquilizer darts. She'll be back on her feet in an hour."

The tension in the group eased a bit. Nolan looked at Sam.

"Sam, where's your mom?"

"The cops got her, I think. I just ran when they came up. I really don't know."

Nolan's eyes showed his concern.

"Why did you bring the extra horse?" Sam thought through the events at the barn.

"He ended up following me, I guess." Nolan shook his head in disbelief.

"Thank you, Sam. You really did save the herd today."

He looked up at the horses that came to a stop just ahead. They gathered and were all looking at the five people near the gate. Nolan could feel their agitation, their loss. Loss?

"Where is Sun Cloud?" Nolan asked, finally noticing the absence of the lead stallion.

"They got him …him and a few of the others." Nolan panicked.

"What? How? We've got to go get him. "

Nolan spun his horse, ready to ride off, but Joe stopped him.

"Nolan, no. Not now. There is no chance of getting him back. Ruud's got 30 men up there."

Nolan tried to grasp what this meant for the herd but his mind was exhausted. He could not think. He depleted every ounce of energy he had. The last thing he remembered was seeing an image of the blue flower. What once had been so vibrant and alive was now wilting, dull, and in rapid decline. Nolan slowly got down from his horse. Once on the ground, he collapsed.

CHAPTER FOURTEEN

Sheriff Parker was livid. He sat in the MCU shaking with rage. One of his true character flaws was his explosive temper. His temper was like a precocious child. It was beyond his control; flipping from calm to calamity in mere seconds, then back again. Although, when he really got angry it wasn't so easy to turn it off. When his gut-level anger raged, he was known to be dangerous, unpredictable, irrational. This was now his state of mind.

He watched the roundup unfold and fall completely apart. They managed to capture only seven horses. Seven from a herd of what? 200? He had three men injured, one critically. The helicopter came under fire. The pilots disobeyed a direct order and left the scene, allowing the herd to be pushed onto Angel Ridge and out of his reach. Again.

He would have to answer to Senator Ruud. What would he possibly tell the senator?

The manhunt had yielded one—that Anne Harper woman. But now he was hearing reports that even her identity was being questioned. The entire operation was falling apart. He called out most of the county's resources for two simple things: bring in the murderers and roundup the horses. On both accounts he failed. Parker hated failure. Ruud hated failure. It was time to rally.

Parker decided his best course of action was to personally interrogate the Harper woman. He needed someone to charge for the murders. If he found no one, Parker knew everything would fall on him.

Parker gave the orders for his men to shut down the MCU and take the bus back to headquarters. He stepped out of the coach, got in his cruiser, and sped back to town to meet Anne Harper. When he arrived at police headquarters things were quiet. Most of the men were still at Angel Ridge finishing up the manhunt. It would still be several hours before the men returned to the station, pumping some life into its now quiet and subdued atmosphere.

Anne had been escorted in, fingerprinted, photographed and set into a stark holding cell to wait for arraignment. Her concrete cell contained a small sink, toilet, and benches attached to opposing walls. The front of the cell was outfitted with typical jailhouse bars. It seemed odd to Anne that everything was so new and unused. Little did she know about the government largess that had been poured into this little town from its powerful benefactor, Senator Ruud. Almost half of the building remained empty.

Anne tried to sleep for lack of anything better to do. After the night at the cabin and the several days of adrenaline-pumping danger, she certainly was due for some rest. She was allowed her one phone call and managed to contact Matthew who assured her that he and two attorneys were already on their way. He asked her to sit tight and keep quiet. Feeling strangely safe, she was laying on one of the benches, eyes closed, trying to sleep. But her mind was reeling and wasn't going to let her escape that easy. Her scattered thoughts skipped randomly over multiple things, focusing on nothing for more than a few seconds at a time—Samantha, Nolan, the cowboys who tried to kill her, the dead horses, the yellow mist, Senator Ruud, her flight from the desert, the High Star Ranch—these small parts to the big story floated past her conscious mind streaming unconnected bits and pieces.

She came to write a story, to report on an amazing man, a horse angel. She came to expose the truth about the treatment of wild horses. A simple story, really. But things were not simple now. There had been a complete shift in her life course. Somehow, Nolan Powell captured her heart. Anne resented it. She didn't need this complication in her life. God, she had a daughter to raise. She had her career, her farm, her friends. Her friends …what would they say? A cowboy Anne? Really? A cowboy?

But Nolan, what a cowboy he was—undeniably handsome, great body, solid character, manly. He was certain, plain-souled and just plain good. He captured her heart. That was for sure. Suddenly, she missed him terribly. Her own life-pain seared at the thought of never seeing him again. I

If Simon were only still here. Her mind replayed, once again, that day on the jump course: the sunny, blinding twinkles of reflected light; the faces of the men, women, and children; the smell of cut grass. She remembered that sound. That popping sound of the exploding safety vest as it cracked open—the sound of death.

A familiar feeling of hollow anxiety swelled up in Anne's chest. She missed Simon. Not in an immediate way but more like the feeling of something she loved as a child. Something so long gone it's meaning changed from the reality of its true character to a mere fantasy. Nostalgic and sad, this feeling was something Anne was used to. It always led her to despair. It was in that familiar spot where something unexpected happened—the thought of Nolan cracked through the shell containing the hollowness. Nolan came into that empty space and was a light, a warmth, a friend.

Anne lay on the bench, amazed. She was feeling something she hadn't for years—gratitude. The sentiment made her smile. Here, in jail, facing murder charges, she was feeling grateful. Only love can do that. She smiled and shook her head at the irony. Nolan and gratitude were on her mind as she finally dozed off. Though not for long.

"Ms. Harper? …Ms. Harper? You need to come with me. Come on, get up."

The officer's voice was high-pitched and soft. Anne opened her eyes and looked at him. She was surprised to see a mere boy. He couldn't have been older than 18. Surprisingly clear headed, Anne sat up.

"Is my attorney here?" she asked.

"The sheriff wants to talk to you. I'm moving you to the interrogation room. Will you come with me?"

"Sure," said Anne as she stood and stretched. She felt strangely relaxed. Following the boy into the hall and around some corners, she was led into a small room and asked to sit at the table placed at the center. The chair was hard and uncomfortable.

"Can I get you anything?" asked the boy officer. "Something to drink, maybe?"

"Sure, a little water, thank you."

The boy disappeared and left Anne alone in the grey-walled room. She sat quietly at the table, waiting. She had no doubt she was being watched. There was a small camera mounted in the upper corner and a one-way mirror opposite her on the wall.

In fact, she was being watched. Sheriff Parker was standing just behind the glass taking stock of her appearance, demeanor, and attitude. Others were viewing the camera feed. The drive out from the High Star Ranch gave the sheriff time to cool down. Parker watched the woman, thinking to himself what a tough time he would have portraying her as a murderer. He picked up a file folder, left his viewing booth, and entered the interrogation room.

Anne cringed when Parker came through the door. The sight of him brought back the worst of that day on Ruud's ranch. His uniform made him look more threatening. Something about the power it represented was repulsive to her. It was just enough to kindle the fire of anger in her chest.

"Ms. Harper, I am Sheriff Parker."

"I want my attorney here before we do any talking," Anne said coldly.

"I understand," said Parker as he sat down across from Anne. "But let me show you something." He pulled out two photographs from his folder and tossed them in front of her. They were photos from that day out on High Star Ranch. One was her photo of Nolan and the other was Nolan's of her.

"These photos were taken from a camera we found next to the body of a man who was murdered four days ago."

Anne looked at the photos. The blood drained from her face.

"You were obviously there. I was hoping you could tell me what happened."

Anne easily could have told the sheriff she would wait for her attorney before saying anything. It would have been the prudent course of action. But Anne's anger grew from a small flame to a raging campfire on the verge of leaping over the containment and setting the forest ablaze. She could hardly help herself.

"What happened?" she blurted out. "Aside from the fact they were trying to kill me, those guys out there were killing wild horses. I was just photographing it. If you have these photos, you have the others. Where are the others? You can see for yourself what happened."

Parker was pleased that Anne was angry.

"Your camera was found next to the body of a man who was savagely beaten. His skull was crushed. It appears you had something to do with it. You and this man," Parker pointed at Nolan's picture.

"Did you hear what I said?" Anne volleyed. "They were out there killing wild horses."

"So you had to stop it?"

"Stop it? How could I do that? I was only photographing it."

"Yet there were several dead men at the scene."

"Yeah? And how many dead horses did you find?"

"I'm trying to find out what happened to the men, how they died."

"They died trying to kill wild horses."

"Did you see that? How come there are no photos of that?"

Anne remembered back to her flight across the rocks. She remembered the gunfire and the bullets zipping by as she ran. She didn't have a response to Parker's question. She looked at him silently, glowering.

Parker raised his eyebrows in expectation.

"No. You didn't see that did you? If you had, you would have certainly photographed it."

Anne's voice was flat, "I lost my camera when we came across the men rounding up the horses for the kill. My horse got away in a stampede and my camera was in the saddlebag. Otherwise, I would have photographed it."

"Stampede, huh?"

Silently, Anne looked away.

"How did this man die?" Parker asked as he threw a picture down in front of her. This picture didn't come from her camera. This one was taken by the investigation team. It was a grotesque photo of Bulling's body—covered with dirt and blood, his head caved in.

Anne glanced down not expecting the horror that was in front of her. She gasped and turned aside.

"What are you doing?" she said sharply. "Get that picture away from me. I don't know anything about that."

"So it must have been this man." Parker held up the picture of Nolan. What's his name?

Anne almost said Nolan's name out loud. She caught herself just as the word was forming. She stopped, and with a steely resolve, spoke slowly and plainly to Officer Parker.

"Listen to me carefully. I want to see my lawyer; no more questions until that happens. Savvy?"

Parker smiled, "Fine, Ms. Harper. Thank you." He stood up, moved across the room and, without another word, left Anne alone at the table.

Nolan opened his eyes. Through his searing fever the room seemed skewed somehow, as if there were no straight lines. Everything appeared to be slightly moving, slightly ajar. His mouth was bone dry, his tongue thick and pasty. He tried to sit up and was met with a stabbing pain that seemed to tear his shoulder clean from his torso. Collapsing back onto his bed, he lay in bewilderment. What happened? There was a dark sticky void where his memory used to be. He searched the room with his heavy eyes, trying to focus. It was dim and quiet. What time is it? Out of the shadows he sensed movement. A figure—large and dark— moved toward him. It was frightening and overbearing. Nolan let out a pitiful cry. Choked by his parched throat, the noise sounded like the voice-crack of a pubescent boy. He was truly petrified.

"Easy, pard." It was Joe. "It's me. It's okay."

Nolan squinted, trying to focus. "Joe?"

"Yeah, it's me. We're in the clinic."

Nolan heard the words but they didn't make sense. Clinic? His mind tried to connect the word with some meaning. It floated there, randomly, without gravity.

"Clinic?" Nolan's voice was raspy and weak.

"Here, take a sip." Joe eased a straw into Nolan's mouth. A few drops of cool water trickled over Nolan's pasty tongue, down his throat.

"What's going on? Where am I?"

Joe looked down at his friend. The sight touched him at his core. Nolan's face was white. His eyes were sallow and confused. Joe saw the fear in his friend's mind. Ripe and lush. Vicious and unrelenting.

Joe swallowed hard, choking back a sob.

"Nolan, it's me, Joe." Nolan's eyes were focusing and unfocusing. His mouth was agape and he was breathing hard.

"You're sick. The doctor is coming. Try to rest. You're going be okay."

Through the dark veil some thoughts began to come through. Nolan's mind struggled to connect the dots.

"Joe?"

A tear welled up in Joe's eye. "Yeah, it's me, Nolan. I brought you to the clinic. You're sick."

"What happened?"

"We saved the horses, Nolan. You saved them."

The memories were dripping through now. Nolan recalled the roundup, the helicopter, the gate. Though sticky and slow, the thoughts were moving.

"Oh …yeah …okay …" Nolan closed his eyes, a little more at peace. "So …what happened?" His voice was weak and strained.

"You came down with something in a hurry, friend. You have a fever. I don't know what it is. Like I said, the doctor is coming. He'll be here any time."

"The horses? Is the herd okay?"

"Yeah, buddy, we got most of 'em."

Nolan thought about the herd for a moment. He remembered riding his horse, chasing that one, the one named …*Sun Cloud!* His mind flashed bright white. He saw a series of rapid images popping in his mind's eye. Disturbing images of horrid suffering, unimaginable torture, and cruelty incarnate. These phantoms were unexpected and rushed into Nolan's consciousness uninvited like a late-night home invasion. He screamed.

Joe flinched. He reached down to calm his friend, but Nolan struggled free and screamed again. There was a frightening depth to his angst, something unnatural. Joe grabbed Nolan's shoulders and pushed him down to the mattress.

"Easy, Nolan, easy …"

Nolan's eyes flashed in confusion as he glance around the room. He looked up at Joe and just as the two men connected in a brief glimpse of reality, Nolan fell back into his dark sleep, going limp in an instant. Joe was left alone in the room with the body of his friend. He looked at the clock and wondered where the doctor was.

Anne fidgeted in her chair. She'd been in the interrogation room for a half hour and the hard chair was getting more uncomfortable by the minute. She suspected someone was watching her so she was completely still and uninteresting. Her nerves were getting the best of her as she began to grow impatient. Just then the door flew open, sending Anne up in a jolt. In walked a woman and a man. Anne didn't recognize either of them. The woman was in her forties with dark hair and even darker eyes. She walked with the confidence of a professional and wore a light-colored pantsuit, a plain belt and some low-heeled shoes. The man was equally professional. He looked slightly younger than the woman and wore jeans, a blazer, and an open-neck shirt. Anne eyed them curiously for a few seconds before the woman spoke.

"Anne Harper? I'm Sally Harkins. I'm a homicide detective from the Reno Police Department. I've been assigned to your case. This is my colleague Brad Robles. Mind if we sit down?"

Anne heard the word homicide and it brought into focus the seriousness of her predicament.

"I understand you spoke with Sheriff Parker and he showed you some of the photos in our possession."

Anne was motionless as she answered, "I have instructed Sheriff Parker that I will be glad to answer all of your questions once my attorney arrives."

"Well, that is certainly fine with me. I'm here to assure that you understand the charges against you."

"I haven't been charged with anything," answered Anne.

"Not yet, that's true. However, the evidence clearly shows you at the scene of a multiple homicide at the time the killings occurred. The crime took place on the ranch belonging to one of the leading senators in the country. We have both forensic and photographic evidence against you." She paused for great effect. "Charges will be filed."

The man sat cold faced and silent watching Anne's reaction.

Ms. Harkins continued, "There is a lot stacked against you. In Nevada, one count of premeditated murder gets you life in prison. A mass murder like this will probably yield a death sentence."

Anne was wearing down. She thought of Samantha and wondered who would ever step forward to raise her. The man noticed the change in Anne's eyes. He saw the fleeting bit of doubt.

"Anne," he said, "you're actually in a relatively good spot. You got to us first. We know about the man who was with you. He's moments away from capture. If you could help us a tiny bit, we're in the position to help you."

"You have a daughter, is that right"? Asked Detective Harkins.

Anne shuddered again. "Yes, that's right."

"Samantha?"

Anne glowered at the lady.

"I have a daughter too," said Harkins. "I'd do anything to protect her."

"What do you want?" Anne asked sharply.

"Well, two things. I want to know what happened and I want to know the name of the man you were with."

"And what do I get out of it?"

"Anne, if you cooperate we can cut you a special deal. We can make sure Samantha doesn't grow up without a mother."

"But I didn't do anything."

"Then tell us what happened."

Once again Anne was getting upset and she was about to respond when Detective Harkins' cell phone beeped.

It was a text message. Harkins looked at her phone, considered the message, and frowned. She looked over at Anne and spoke coldly, "Last chance. Tell me what happened."

Anne noticed some change in the detective's demeanor. Something happened that was not according to plan.

"No," said Anne flatly.

"No?"

"No, I want my lawyer."

Detective Harkins gazed at Anne in silence for an uncomfortable moment. Then she stood up along with Detective Robles.

"Have it your way." The two walked to the door, it opened, and were gone.

Almost immediately the door opened again and this time it was a familiar face. Matthew Clark moved through the doorway. After Parker and the other two, Matthew seemed like a savior. The relief Anne felt upon seeing her friend and boss brought her to tears. Matthew had two men in tow. All three were dressed casually, which belied the unmistakable aire of serious business.

"Matthew! Oh, my God!" Anne stood up and gave Matthew a hug.

"We got here as soon as we could. How you holding up?"

"Oh, I don't know …fine …I guess."

"Anne, this is Brad Jackson and Samuel Epstein." The two men nodded at her, neither showing any sign of friendliness.

"They'll get you out of here. Everything is going to be fine, trust me. You'll see." Matthew turned to Brad and gave him some kind of silent instruction. The two men turned and left the room without saying a word.

Anne looked at Matthew and smiled. She patted his shoulder warmly.

"I'm so glad to see you. You won't believe the things going on around here."

"Actually, I would. I used to live here, you know." Matthew was glad to see Anne in a light mood. It was more than he'd expected. It was very unlike her and it made him curious.

"Sorry about all this, Anne. I feel responsible for what you've been through. I want you to know I've got your back. I'm not going to leave you hanging. We have some evidence that will vindicate you and Nolan, just by dumb-ass luck for sure. But it will do the trick."

"What evidence? What are you talking about?"

Matthew broke out in a smile. He was obviously pleased with himself.

"I found something on your camera."

"My camera? How did you get that? I don't understand."

"I don't *have* your camera but we accessed it remotely, through WiFi. I had Marty do it. We actually downloaded your photos, even managed to erase the card remotely."

Anne shook her head. "I didn't even think about that, but it makes sense." She paused to reflect. "Damn technology, it's really getting away from me. But wait, they have the photos too. You blanked the card? How did they get the photos?"

"They must have downloaded them before I got to it, but never mind that. We found something else, after the fact. We almost overlooked it completely. It was Marty again. The guy's a genius."

"Matthew? What are you talking about?"

"Your camera, Anne. We found an audio recording on it. It's a full confession implicating Ruud as the mastermind behind all this. Clearly vindicating you and Nolan. We found it late last night."

"An audio recording? What? How?"

"Those cameras can record audio. Somehow that camera was in record mode when Nolan found the crew leader—the one who was killed."

Anne shook her head again. Her brow wrinkled. "What? I don't get it."

"I don't either, but Marty noticed the audio file after we printed all the photos. I played it for the attorneys and they said it would get you and Nolan off the hook. Solid gold."

"Okay, so what now? What do I do?"

"Sit tight, Anne, and we'll have you out within the hour."

A feeling of lightness came over Anne. Matthew noticed the change in her. It was subtle but there was something. Something deep. Something abiding.

The doctor methodically checked Nolen's vital signs. He went through the checklist: heart rate, blood pressure, and temperature. He thought he would surely find signs of internal bleeding, and he was surprised that nothing turned up. No bruises, no trauma, no sign of anything. Nolen's fever was 104. It rendered him lethargic, hallucinatory, and semi-conscious.

Joe stood back a few feet letting the doctor do his work. There was something strange about the whole thing. It came on so fast, so abruptly. Joe was searching his intuition for clues. He knew it could be a bug or some virus finally catching Nolan in his over-stressed state. That was plausible. Yet there was something else, something deeper and more sinister. Joe turned and left the room. He walked to the end of the hallway and picked up the phone. Dialing a number he knew by heart, he listened as the call connected.

"Hello?"

"Hi, Lon, it's me again."

"I figured you'd be calling back."

"Nolan's sick with high fever. The doctor's here but nothing is turning up. I want to get your opinion."

Lon was silent for a few seconds.

"Okay, give me a minute, I'll will call you back."

"Thanks, friend." Joe hung up and heard a pitiful scream coming from Nolan in the other room. Something was wrong.

Samantha sat in Rosie's living room. The clutter seemed to close in, making it hard to breathe. The old clock ticked menacingly. In the quiet of the house it sounded like a hammer, banging away the seconds. It was 3:00 in the afternoon. Rosie was away attending to some chores. Samantha sat alone.

The yellow mist flared in her mind. She struggled to understand what was happening. Almost always, the yellow mist was present only when horses were nearby. This time was much different. Sam was feeling called—drawn—to something she didn't know. Her short time at Angel Ridge confirmed her gift of the yellow mist. She was beyond questioning that. Now the mist seemed to be demanding something of her. There was something wrong. She watched the yellow mist swirl and dance with urgency, like a dog wiggling with excitement, unable to contain its energy. The mist was calling, pleading—something lay just beyond the reach of Sam's young mind.

Rosie had been away a short time. Sam was to stay in the house and wait to hear from her mother. Taken away by the police in handcuffs—the thought was shocking and unbelievable. Sam knew her mom would be okay. She was most concerned with Nolan. When they finally got him back to the clinic they actually had to carry him in. Before they disappeared into the front door, Nolan looked back and caught Samantha's eye. That *look*, that wild-eyed scary look. It was what started the mist swirling. It reminded her of …a frightened horse—wide eyed, head back, mouth open. It was a horrible sight burning in her mind. He looked like a frightened horse. The mist shimmered, seemingly confirming her intuition. Something was wrong.

Samantha walked out to the front porch. It was mid-afternoon. The sun was hanging leisurely in the western sky. The pre-evening shadows stretched out to greet her as she left the porch and headed toward the clinic. She needed to do something. Maybe Joe would have an answer. Forgetting entirely about her mother and the need to wait, Sam hurried down the road past the mess hall, past the barns and paddocks, out onto the long stretch of road that led to the clinic. Ten minutes later she was standing in front of the low, sage-green building. A few vehicles were parked outside. The yellow mist was pumping fountain spouts that seemed to splash down around her feet. It wasn't calm or easy, but volcanic, eruptive with a sublime violence that spoke to some higher urgency.

As Sam approached the front door, Joe came out and looked surprised to see her.

"Sam! What's going on?"

Samantha studied Joe's face. He looked haggard.

"Something's wrong, isn't it?" said Sam.

Joe's face relaxed as if contemplating a deep mystery. He looked away to the ridge as he spoke.

"I think it is Sun Cloud. I think he's in trouble."

"Is that why Nolan's sick? That's why, right?"

Joe looked back to the girl. He was amazed at her perception.

The yellow mist just then grounded itself where Samantha stood. It reached far down into the earth, connecting her like she had never felt before. It streamed down and disappeared from her perception, but still connected to her feet, up through her body to her mind's eye. At the other end of the stream she was suddenly connected with Sun Cloud. It felt as real as the sun on her cheeks. It was a sensation that sent a shudder through her entire body. The horse was indeed in trouble. She saw the soul of Sun Cloud and, through the stallion's eyes, perceived the grim surroundings of its pen. He was locked in a small stall. There was little air. A dim light overhead threw shadows through the slats in an old barn. Worst of all, he was dehydrated, weak, and very frightened. This vision passed quickly. It was a flash of intuition, a disturbing realization, like when Sam connected to the seven dead horses. This time her soul could bear it. She wasn't scared to face it.

Of course, Joe sensed the connection right away. His eyes widened and he saw something come and go, like a flash of lightning from the corner of his eye.

"What did you see?" he asked slowly.

"Sun Cloud, I saw Sun Cloud. He *is* in trouble. I saw him alone, being held in a barn somewhere …somewhere dark. He's sick. He needs help."

"Ruud's ranch," mused Joe. "I'll bet they took him back to Ruud's ranch."

Sam's emotions welled up, seeds from her mother.

"We need to go get him! We need to help him. There's not much time!" Her voice was frantic, alarming Joe's sympathetic nervous system. He thought about how that would look, driving up to Ruud's ranch asking for the horse back, or sneaking in and taking him. Either way the result was the same. Ruud was a senator; the cops worked for him. There was no way forward. The conflict was irresolvable in Joe's tired mind.

"There's no way, Sam. If Ruud has the horse, we won't get him back. I don't know what to do."

"We have to do something!"

Through the open door, Joe and Samantha heard a pitiful scream. Although muffled by distance and walls, Nolan's terror pushed its way out to menace them both. Sam looked at Joe with an expression that demanded a plan of action.

"Lon and Christo are coming over." Reassured Joe, "They will know how to help Nolan. I don't know what we can do for Sun Cloud. Maybe they will have an idea. Now, you run along back to the house. Have you heard from your mother?"

"No, not yet," Sam shook her head. She could tell that Joe was giving up. She turned and started back to the house. Joe called after her.

"Don't worry, Sam. It will all right itself. Things will turn out okay. You'll see."

Sam didn't turn around. She kept walking, tears streaming down her face. She walked up the road, her mind blank, her heart breaking.

The thought of abandoning Sun Cloud was too painful to consider. The yellow mist was pounding at her soul. Unrelenting. Unforgiving. She approached the barn, the same one where she gave the cops the slip. Without thinking, she walked in and scanned the stalls. There were 10 horses in the building. She picked a white-and-brown paint about 15 hands. Quickly she haltered the mare and led it out, over to the tie rack. She had the horse saddled and ready to go within minutes. As she was completing her task, one of the staff walked into the barn with a questioning look on her face.

"Hi!" said Sam, a bit too cheerfully. "Joe said I could take this one out for a ride."

The woman looked suspiciously at Sam.

"Do you need any help?" she asked.

Sam shook her head, "No, I got it."

The woman walked up and inspected the tack.

"Well, it looks like you know what you're doing," said the lady.

"I've been riding for years," replied Sam, hiding her true emotions.

"Well, ol' Whimsey here will treat you right. She's a good and gentle horse."

"My name is Margret. Didn't I see you at dinner the other night?"

Sam was impatient, "Yeah, I'm Sam. I'm here with my mother … and Nolan."

"Oh, is your mother all right? She was arrested, right?"

Sam didn't know what to say. Margret sensed the girl's agitation.

"I'm sure things will be okay, Sam. Are you alright?"

"Yes, I'm fine. I want to get going now."

Sam untied Whimsey and jumped up into the saddle.

"See you later," she said as she turned the horse towards the door.

"Wait just a minute!" the lady said and Sam stopped, her heart pumping with fear.

"You'll need a jacket. It'll get cold in a few hours."

Margret threw Sam a riding jacket that was hanging on a nearby coat rack.

"This should fit."

Sam breathed a sigh of relief. She took the jacket and thanked the woman, rode out of the barn, and headed down the road toward the range. In a short 20 minutes Samantha and Whimsey left Angel Ridge and were riding on the open range towards the High Star Ranch.

Sam noticed the yellow mist in its acute presence. She could clearly see the swirling in front of her as she rode south. Letting go of her intentions, she decided to follow the yellow mist. It seemed to be guiding her toward her goal, Sun Cloud. After 15 minutes, Sam and Whimsy came to what looked like an old road—a track really—grown over with weeds but still visible. The yellow mist was already ahead moving down the cow track drawing her closer to Ruud's ranch. Sam hurried the horse along. The track began to show a bit more use as the weeds gave way to bare ground. Cow prints and cow pies appeared along the trail. Further down the track it widened into a full-fledged road. There Sam saw tire tracks from some vehicle that passed on a recent visit to the outer edges of the ranch. Still she rode onward, the yellow mist beckoning her forward. In her mind's eye she could see Sun Cloud more clearly as she neared the place where he was being held. She followed the road for another 20 minutes until she topped a small rise, which gave her a clear view of the High Star Ranch down below. The sight was startling. Sam turned the horse around and bounded back down the hill. After securely tying the horse to a desert tree, she crept back up to have a look.

Below her was the compound of buildings, barns, corrals, and silos. The cattle operation was in full swing. She could see several men moving around the place attending to various duties. It didn't occurred to her over-eager mind that she would have to actually sneak into the place and find Sun Cloud. A wave of disappointment flooded her mind as she crouched at the side of the road taking in the view.

The yellow mist didn't let her despair for long. The inner-vision flared up, moved out toward the compound, and rested over a small building on the outer edge of the ranch. The sight reminded Sam of the Star of Bethlehem and the thought actually brought a quick smile to her troubled face. She plotted a course down to the small building. She would hug the ridgeline to the left until she got close enough to get to the building unseen.

"Where's Sam?" asked Anne with obvious urgency. Rosie looked flustered.

"She was here in the house when I saw her last. She said she was going to wait for you. That was the plan. Maybe she's down at the clinic. Let me call down there and find out." Rosie went into the kitchen to use the phone. Anne followed.

Rosie dialed the number and spoke with Joe for a few seconds then hung up.

"She was at the clinic about 20 minutes ago. Joe thought she was coming back here."

Anne did not like the sound of it. "I'll go look for her. Maybe she's at the barn."

"I'll go with you."

The two women left the house in a hurry. Taking Anne's car they made a quick stop at the barn. They found Margret attending to the afternoon chores and discovered Sam took one of the horses and had been gone about 30 minutes. This news worried Anne even more. Her motherly instincts were on high alert. Next stop was at the clinic to check on Nolan and talk with Joe.

As they pulled up, Joe was standing outside waiting for them. Anne parked the car and hurried up to get some news.

"Anne, it's good to see you," Joe said, like he had too much on his mind.

"Joe, Sam took a horse out for a ride. We just talked with Margret. Do you know where she might have gone?"

Joe's eyes widened as he pressed his lips tight. "When she left she was worried about Sun Cloud."

"What? What do you mean?" Anne's voice cracked.

Joe shook his head like he couldn't believe what he was saying.

"We think Sun Cloud is at Ruud's ranch, she wanted to go and bring him back. She was begging me. Of course I told her no, and she said was going back to wait for you. That was about, I don't know, not too long ago."

"Margret said she left 30 minutes ago. Do you think she was really headed to Ruud's?"

"I'm sorry, Anne. I just don't know. We'll roundup some folks to find her right away."

Anne suddenly thought of Nolan. "Where's Nolan? What's going on here?"

"Oh, man," Joe said under his breath. "You better come inside, just for a sec."

As Anne walked into the room where Nolan lay and his appearance shocked her. She rushed over to him, knelt down beside his bed, and put her hand on his blistering-hot forehead. Nolan rolled his eyes open long enough to see her. A faint smile appeared on his lips, then he again closed his eyes.

"What happened?" Anne asked quietly.

"We don't know," answered Joe. "Doctor's been here and thinks it must be a virus but something tells me it has to do with that horse."

"Sun Cloud," whispered Anne to herself. She leaned down close to Nolan's pale, glistening face. "Hang in there, it's going to be okay." Nolan didn't respond.

Anne quickly stood to face Joe.

"We have to go after Sam."

Joe looked bewildered as he thought through his options.

"Anne, I have to stay here with Nolan. Christo and Lon are on their way over to help. I have to be here for that. I can't leave or Nolan is finished. Take a horse, a rifle, and one of those radios. I'll show you the map and the shortest route there. Sam can't be too far ahead. She doesn't know where she is going and is probably lost by now. As soon as Lon and Christo get here I'll follow up with the crew. I'll be right behind you."

Anne didn't stop to think. The idea of Sam at Ruud's place was beyond dangerous. In less than 15 minutes she was in a full gallop, heading out to the range following Sam's trail. They loaded Anne up with the few electronic gadgets available at Angel Ridge. She had a radio, a map, even a GPS device. In the scabbard attached to her saddle, she had a lever-action Winchester, loaded and ready to fire.

The ride out to Ruud's place was quick and direct. Not the route that she and Nolan took a few short days ago. Anne saw the hoof prints of another horse on the same trail. She suspected they were from Samantha's horse. As time went by, the memories of her last experience out here made her tense and alert. She rode the entire route without seeing anyone. In less than an hour, Anne came across Whimsey, tied to a low desert tree. Samantha had to be nearby. Anne did not get off her horse, but headed over to the edge of the ridge to take in the view.

Ruud's compound was spread out before her. There were a few men visible here and there but it seemed surprisingly quiet with not much going on. Anne looked down and noticed Sam's footprints. Clearly visible, she could see the prints heading down the sloping hill and over to the small barn at the very left of the compound.

"Sam, what are you doing?" Anne thought to herself.

Anne pushed her horse into a walk and followed the line of footprints down the ridge. She wasn't going to leave her horse; it would render her too vulnerable. Within minutes she was at the barn. She managed to avoid being seen and tied her horse to the back of the structure away from the view of the main compound. The only door into the small wooden structure was at the front. Anne crept around the far side and peeked out toward the main buildings. Two men were walking from a cattle corral across the main road. Anne waited until they were gone. When she was sure she wouldn't be seen, she moved to the barn door, opened it, stepped inside, and closed the door behind her. She stood in the darkened interior. Slowly, her eyes grew used to the dim light coming in through the spaces between the weatherworn planks that served as walls. It was completely silent. She was able to make out three small stalls along one side of the building. The first two were empty with the doors swung open. The third one, back in the darkest part of the barn, had the door closed. With her heart pounding, Anne moved over to the closed stall door. In the dark it was difficult to make out anything.

"Sam, are you in here?" Her whisper cut through the stillness like a small breeze.

There was no response.

She slowly creaked open the stall door and the sight in the dimness broke her heart.

The first thing she noticed was a dark-brown horse lying on its side breathing much too quickly. Then she saw the frightened eyes of Samantha looking out from the farthest corner of the stall.

Samantha heard the barn door open and was sure she was caught. She thought she heard someone call her name but she was so scared she couldn't answer. Now she saw her mother standing before her, but that didn't make any sense to her trauma-infused mind.

"Sam? It's me, Sam. It's me!"

"Mom?" Sam couldn't believe it. She stammered again, "Mom?"

Anne rushed in and took her daughter in her arms.

"Samantha! Oh, sweetie. What are you doing here?"

Tears welled up in Samantha's eyes. She didn't realize how much she missed her mother.

"This is Sun Cloud. He is sick. We need to help him," Sam whispering.

Anne looked down at the panting horse lying on its side. Crouching, she felt the horse's head, rubbed her hand along his shoulder and neck, looked into his eyes, and opened his mouth to check his teeth.

"This horse is severely dehydrated."

"This is why Nolan's sick." Sam said.

Anne wrinkled her brow and looked squarely at her daughter. The urge to tell Sam she was being silly came on suddenly and compulsively. Anne caught herself, stopped, and looked back at the horse. She had witnessed so much over the past three days. Though she didn't understand it, the yellow mist was real. She saw it with her own eyes. Sam could see it. Anne took a deep breath.

"Tell me about that, Sam."

Sam was surprised at her mother's reaction. There was an understanding there that Sam hadn't seen before.

"They're still connected. Nolan and Sun Cloud. We need to save him to help Nolan."

Anne heard the words and her heart sank. Could it be true? Was Nolan's life in danger? She was suddenly frightened to the core. Nolan can't die. She pushed the thought out of her mind but it came rushing back like a torrent of black water. In a flash of gruesome memory she heard that noise. That popping sound of the two-point vest. The sound of Simon's death. The thought made her shudder.

"We need to find some water, right now," Anne said. "See if there's a bucket. See what you can find."

Samantha got up.

"But be quiet! The people here are dangerous."

Sam left the stall while Anne continued checking over the horse. Sam scouted around the small barn. The place was empty, like it hadn't been used for years. Light streamed through the wide gaps in the old plank board walls. Sam could see through the gaps to the outside. Across a small alley was another building, a cattle barn or something. She noticed a spigot at the edge of the building just 30 feet away. Lying below the spigot were two green plastic buckets, one large and one small.

Carefully, Sam opened the door wide enough to get her head out and take a peek. With no one in sight, she pushed the door open and slipped through. Creeping over to the spigot, she took the large bucket and began filling it with water. It was deep afternoon now and she was in the shadow of the building. The full bucket was too heavy for her small frame. Taking the smaller bucket she filled it from the first. Sam crept back to the barn, through the door and back to the stall. Sun Cloud was calmer now. The yellow mist told her that. She could also sense that her mother was calmer too.

Sam set the bucket down in front of her mother who was kneeling near the head of the great animal. Sun Cloud's eyes were open. His breathing had settled and he lay in a state of confused relaxation. Anne dipped her hand into the bucket and splashed some water over the horse's neck. She poured a little into the horse's mouth. She kept this up until the bucket was dry. Sam went out for another refill.

When Sam returned a second time, nothing had changed. Sun Cloud had not improved. She knew time was running out.

"He won't drink unless we can get him up," said Anne in a low whispered tone.

She looked at Sam inquisitively. "Can the yellow mist help?"

Sam was a little embarrassed. Her mother had never recognized her unique talents and Sam was hesitant to open this part of her life up to what otherwise could end in ridicule and shame.

"No," she said shyly. "It doesn't work that way."

"What are we going to do?"

"We have to save him, Mom. We have to."

"I don't know how, Sam."

A feeling of desperation overtook them as the horse closed his eyes and groaned.

The sound of a vehicle approaching shook them both from their anguish. The grumbling of tires on the gravel road grew louder, and as the vehicle pulled to a stop in front of the barn, their attention turned from the horse to their own mortal survival.

Anne bolted up to her feet and quietly but quickly went out to get a look at the vehicle through the ribbon-wide gaps in the walls. Her heart pounded as she recognized a county police cruiser.

"Shit!" Anne hissed, her fear flaring into panic as she found herself looking wildly around the space for a decent place to hide.

The car door opened and the sound of boots on the gravel signaled their imminent discovery.

"Hide!" Anne whispered as loudly as she dared.

Sam had already moved into the first stall and was crouching in the front corner completely out of sight.

The car door slammed shut, then footsteps, a steady crunching sound of leather on crushed stone. It sounded like only one person. Anne considered the possibility of having to defend herself. Her mind flashed to the rifle mounted on her horse. It might as well be three miles away. She rushed into the stall and crouched down next to Sam.

"When we get a chance, run," Anne whispered. "My horse is around the back. I have a gun." She couldn't believe she was saying this to her daughter. Her brain was coursing straight to fight or flight and she couldn't fly and was deathly afraid of a fight.

"If I have to, I'll distract him while you get away. Do you understand?"

Sam nodded, eyes wide, mouth agape.

Anne's heart was pounding in her ears. The footsteps neared the barn door and stopped. She peeked out over the stall boards, and through the gap could see the grey and blue of the cop's uniform. That made it all the worse. Her fear tap-danced over her entire nervous system.

The barn door was thrown open wide. The sound was screeching metal on metal and, in Anne's hyper-sensitive state, could have been sheets of rusty steel being torn apart by a large and evil brute.

Anne crouched lower but stayed on her feet in case she needed to act fast. Sam was sitting in the corner holding her legs tight to her chest. The yellow mist danced around her inner-vision quite lazily, in direct opposition to the outward threat.

"That's weird," Sam thought to herself.

The policeman entered the barn and closed the door behind him. He paused at the front of the barn, then walked slowly back to the third stall. Looking in, the officer noticed the water buckets and fresh water. He turned to more closely survey the interior of the building. Slowly, automatically, the man pulled his revolver from his holster.

Sam sat hidden and pondered the yellow mist. She wasn't scared; she wasn't worried. That was the remarkable part. Something was happening here that didn't match up with the apparent danger. She could feel the horse's presence; he was dying. She could make out her mother and the fear radiating in all directions. With a slight pause she decided to trust her instinct, to trust the yellow mist. With that split-second decision she stood up.

The cop wheeled around and drew his revolver, pointing it directly at Samantha. It was the quick, reflexive move of a highly trained policeman. The young girl stood calmly.

"What's going on here?" the officer shouted through the dimness of the barn.

Anne couldn't believe what was happening. Her instincts, too, were reeling although in a much different direction than Sam's. The card had been played. Anne stood up with her hands raised, the universal sign of submission.

"Officer, I can explain everything ..."

There was a slight pause. "Ms. Harper?"

Anne's mind jolted. This man knew her. She peered through the dusky light and indeed recognized him. It was Deputy Miller.

She sighed a resigning breath of defeat. All she could manage was "Oh, god."

"Are you two crazy? What are you doing? Don't you know what you're up against? I can't believe you'd come back here. What are you doing?"

Miller's tone did not sound threatening. Anne noticed something about him that was curious.

Sam spoke up, "You're here to help, aren't you?"

Miller lowered his gun, paused, and holstered the weapon. He glared at the two. "You don't know how dangerous this is."

"You're here to help us, aren't you?" Sam asked again. Her voice was confident, almost challenging.

"I'm here to help the horse, yes, and you too," he quickly added.

"I don't understand," Anne's words came suspiciously.

Miller didn't look happy. "We don't have time to go into it. Let's just say Joe is a friend. Right now we have about 20 minutes to get this horse out of here, otherwise he's dead for sure."

Sam sprung to life and moved out of the stall and back to Sun Cloud. Miller joined her as Anne lagged behind, not knowing whether to trust this guy or not. She stood back looking on as Miller bent down to have a look at the animal. Thirty seconds passed.

"Okay, I can get this horse up but we're going to have to trailer him out of here."

"Trailer a wild mustang?" Anne injected.

Miller stood up and looked at Anne.

He shrugged, "I know, right?"

"I can do it," said Sam, quite matter of fact. She was still at the horse's side. When Anne and Miller looked at her in astonishment, she looked back, smiled, and said, "Really!"

"I'll be right back. I'll go raid the vet clinic and get what we need. You two keep up the water bath, this won't take long. If anyone comes in here, keep them here 'til I get back. Hopefully that won't happen."

As Miller opened up the door, Anne called after him.

"Miller?" The deputy turned around. "Why are you doing this?"

He looked down, thought a moment, then said, "Because it's the right thing to do."

Miller got into his car and drove away. The sound of retreating tires left Anne feeling vulnerable. Her suspicions of Miller and his real motives worked over her conscious mind, increasing her anxiety. Looking over at Sam, who continued trying to re-hydrate the horse, Anne found a little comfort in the strength and courage Sam was showing. Sam was here for the horse. She wasn't going to back down. She had a purpose. Anne found this to be amazing and, in her heart, realized she didn't really know her daughter as she thought. The girl crouched down by the horse. Her whispered, soothing tones had a surprising depth, holding mysteries that a few short days ago Anne would have balked at. A sense of pride washed over Anne's motherly soul. It was the kind of feeling allowed only to parents. A deep satisfaction of knowing that one's child is a decent, loving, and valuable human being. Anne stood outside the stall watching Sam, letting the fleeting feelings of warmth and goodness keep her anxious mind in check.

Ten minutes later, they again heard the sound of tires. Anne bolted to the front of the barn and look out through the slats. It was a truck towing a small trailer used for transporting cattle.

"He's back," Anne said almost absently.

The rig pulled around the barn's far side. Soon Miller came through the door. He was carrying a small bag in one hand and some plastic medical tubing in the other.

"Do you know how to start an IV?" he asked as he handed the bag to Anne.

"Yeah, I can do it."

She took the bag and tubing from the officer and went back to the stall.

Miller was pacing.

"We don't have much time," he said. He turned and strode up to the front of the barn and looked outside he checked to see if anyone was coming. He turned again and paced back.

Anne quietly administered the IV into the horse's neck while Sam watched. Sam had one hand on the horse and was making soft, quiet, soothing noises. Within minutes, the drip was started and nourishing fluids began to flow into Sun Cloud's body.

"Okay, done," said Anne. Miller paced back and looked into the stall.

"We have about five minutes and then we'll have to get him up." Sam stayed with the horse while Anne got up to chat with the cop.

"So, what's really going on here?" she asked.

Miller was hesitant.

"Can you tell me anything?" she pressed.

Miller took a deep breath. He was obviously into something he wasn't proud of and merely talking about it caused him an overwhelming sense of shame. The deep conflict was evident in his face and eyes.

"This thing has gotten out of control," he said.

"This thing?" said Anne.

"Orders came down from Ruud to clear the horses from the ranch. It was supposed to be a simple roundup and removal. Well…a couple of the ranch hands got carried away and something went wrong. Some of the men started firing their guns and the assholes ended up killing some of the horses."

"That's a federal crime," Anne said.

"We were told to keep it quiet."

"We?"

"Who do you think runs this town? I work for one man, or at least for his organization."

Miller was looking down at the floor. He didn't like what he was saying.

"Anyway, then things got worse." When he said this he looked directly at Anne. "I don't know what happened but 11 men died out there. I am very sure you had something to do with it." He let these words hang in the air. Anne bit her tongue and said nothing. Miller wasn't looking for a confession, and Anne wasn't talking, so he continued.

"Anyway, now we have this mess, and it's a big mess. The press is asking questions. There's talk in the town and Ruud wants the problem to disappear. The last roundup attempt was a complete failure. The whole operation is coming unraveled. Ruud is looking hard for a scapegoat and, honey, you're it."

"So, why are you doing this again?"

"Look, I grew up around here. I've been here all my life. I've been working for Ruud since I got out of high school. It's been a decent living. I've got a family to support. But now Ruud is pushing this thing too far. He's made this about the Clark Family, about Angel Ridge. He's letting that stupid old family feud dictate his actions. In my mind he has crossed the line. Joe and Rosie at Angel Ridge are good people. They're doing good things, not harming anyone. They've been around here as long as anyone. I can't be a part of destroying them, just can't do it. I'm being asked to do things that I frankly can't do. Right is right and what's gone on here is foul, and wrong. Plus Joe is a friend of mine. I've known Joe for 30 years. Enough's enough."

Anne didn't know what to say. She felt Miller's compassion. She could see he was not the monster that she had figured him for.

Miller continued, "Joe called me about this horse, said it was vital that the horse survive. I told him I'd do what I could. I went to the holding pens to find him but he wasn't there. I released the other horses and found this one had been brought here. I don't know why or what or how, but there is something bigger going on here. I really believe that."

"Yeah, I'm beginning to believe that too," said Anne.

"You're a reporter, right?"

"Yeah, I was sent up here to do a story."

"Well, when this is over, I'd be happy to give you the story. I know a lot about what goes on around here. Things have got to change, and if you want, I'll tell you everything."

Anne was shocked. She'd forgot why she came to Angel Ridge in the first place. Now everything was coming full circle. This story would win awards—it was that big. For an instant she was transported into a daydream of receiving accolades and national recognition. Her ego burst onto the scene and stroked her self-esteem. It lasted about three seconds. A long, painful groan came from the stall—back to reality.

The two looked over and saw the horse struggling. Anne rushed in and grabbed the drip bag, keeping the tube from getting tangled. The horse rocked back and forth a few times and came upright, pushing its front feet out for leverage. Miller came in and helped to steady the animal. Sam was on her feet with a look of sheer joy. She was engulfed within the yellow mist, actively communicating with the stallion. With a mighty grunt, Sun Cloud pushed himself up into a standing position. He wobbled a few times as Miller saved him from falling over again. All three looked at each other with wonder.

"Wow, that was fast," Miller said as he threw a lead rope around the stallion's neck. "Okay, let's get him to the trailer."

All three surrounded the horse as they walked him out to the front of the barn. The horse took small, halting steps. His head drooped low. Miller looked out the door and saw no one. He pushed the door wide open and they moved as a group out and around the side of the barn.

The trailer was open and ready. Miller, holding the rope, walked the horse up to the ramp. Sun Cloud stopped at the ramp and refused to budge.

"This is what I was afraid of," said Miller, as he tugged on the rope.

"Let me try," said Sam. She came up and took the rope. Miller looked at Anne who nodded her approval.

Sam instinctively knew that Sun Cloud was in very bad shape. It was the only reason he was being so easy to handle at the moment. This whole time at the High Star, she'd been engulfed in the swirling mysteries of the yellow mist. Using both to her advantage, Samantha reached out to the horse in that mystic connection and gained his trust. Sun Cloud was very uneasy around Miller and Anne, but the small one, the young girl, he could see. In his horse's mind and soul there had always been a misty calmness. It was the way of his herd. When a human approached and could reach out through the yellow mist, it meant they were part of the promise. It meant there was nothing to fear. Sun Cloud knew the girl was there to help, to keep the promise. He did not fear her. In his mind he could hear her singing. She was singing the ancient song, the ageless melody of the promise. It was music that all horses knew, some more consciously than others. It was Xu's promise and it kept the balance alive.

With this trust Sam took the rope and she walked slowly into the trailer. Sun Cloud raised his drooping head and saw the girl within the promise. He knew she was his path to freedom. He took the steps forward and walked into the trailer.

Miller was awed. He looked at Anne who shrugged it off.

"I don't understand," Miller said.

"Maybe one day we can tell you about it. Let's just say that Sam has a gift."

"I'll say."

The trailer was closed and ready to roll.

Sheriff Parker pulled his cruiser into the entrance of the High Star Ranch. It had been a tough couple of days and it was getting worse. He just received a phone call from his Uncle Harry. The dressing-down was both humiliating and threatening. Parker failed on almost all accounts—completely unacceptable to the senator. Ruud said he was definitely considering a replacement for Parker. The press was flooding Ruud's office with calls. The negative publicity was something Ruud didn't need at the moment. When he heard the stallion was brought to his ranch, he nearly popped a vein. The cursing coming from Ruud's end of the phone sent chills of fright down the sheriff's spine. It was communicated in no uncertain terms. The stallion must be disposed of quickly and quietly. Any screw-up at this point and Parker might as well leave the county. His career would be over. Turned off like a light bulb. Parker was raging with frustration.

Pulling up to the compound, Parker noticed Miller's police car in front of the main office building. Parker's brow furrowed.

"What the hell is he doing here?"

Parker pulled next to the other police cruiser, got out, and walked swiftly into the office. There were a couple of workers in the room; both looked up as Parker stormed in.

"Good afternoon, Sheriff," came a pleasant greeting.

"Where's Miller?"

The greeter lost the smile when met with the brute manners of the sheriff.

"You mean Deputy Miller?" the man asked.

"Of course I mean Deputy Miller! Where is he?"

The man, who did his best to avoid conflict, hesitated for a moment, pretending to be thinking. He could tell Parker was getting more anxious with each passing second.

"You know ...I don't know," he finally said, speaking slowly for effect. "He was here about 15 minutes ago. Is his car still out front?"

Parker said nothing, turned on his heel, and walked back outside. He knew the horse was down at the end of the row in the small day barn. He would take care of this matter personally. He jumped in his car and headed towards the barn.

It was Sam who first spotted the approaching police car.

"Someone's coming," she said urgently.

Miller peeked around the corner and his face went ashen.

"It's Parker. Not good."

Anne thought quickly through the options. Sun Cloud's safety was the highest priority.

"Come on, Sam, to the horse." She turned to Miller.

"We'll create a distraction. You get this horse over to the clinic at Angel Ridge."

Before Miller could say anything, Anne disappeared behind the barn, mounted up, and pulled Sam up behind her.

"Hang on, honey." She sprang into a canter and burst out onto the road, riding straight toward Parker.

Parker was more than surprised to see a woman galloping directly towards him. He immediately recognized the woman as Anne Harper. He couldn't believe what he was seeing. His rage flared with this realization. Reflexively, he sped up with an evil intent of running her over. Anne kept up the canter and, at the last minute, swerved off toward her right. She bounded up the dirt road towards the open range. Parker hit the brakes and skidded to a violent stop. He looked out at the barn and could see nothing of importance. Miller with the truck and trailer were out of sight around the back of the building. Parker looked over at Anne running up the road and noticed the girl on the back.

"Okay, that's it!" His words spit from his head like fire from a dragon's jaws.

Next to the corrals lining the road were three ATVs. Parker exited his car and hopped on the closest one. He fired it up and took off after Anne and the girl. The stakes were high and Parker needed a win. He thought about what Ruud said, about the press asking questions. His biggest foe was Anne Harper—if she ever made it back alive. She had seen the stallion; she had seen the horse kill. She knew too much. Yes, that damn judge let her go based on some questionable audio recording, but she wasn't off the hook yet. If she died out here on the range—disappeared—the story would die with her. Such was the thought process of this crazed sheriff. He gunned the quad and followed Anne up the road. It wouldn't be long before he overtook the horse.

Deputy Miller watched the whole thing from his vantage point. Anne's plan worked. She drew the sheriff's attention away from the barn. Once Parker was over the hill, Miller climbed into the truck and drove undetected out of the High Star Ranch. Within 10 minutes he would be at the Angel Ridge clinic. One thing was sure—the stallion would survive. He wasn't so sure about Anne and Samantha. They had a good head start but the speed of their horse was no match for the ATV.

Anne directed her horse back to the path she took from Angel Ridge. Sam hung on to her mother with her head down and eyes squinted shut. The horse was running smooth and sure, but there was no telling how long he could keep up the pace. Anne knew she was in trouble. She looked back and saw the dust cloud kicked up by the ATV.

"He's following us!"

Sam opened her eyes and looked back. The ATV was coming up fast.

"He's gaining on us!" Sam shouted. The wind whistled in her ears as the hoof beats kept the fast-paced, three-beat rhythm. Sam kept her eyes on the ATV as it drew closer.

Anne's mind was reeling. The pit in her stomach told her big trouble was in store. Her last encounter with Parker confirmed he was bordering on psychopathy. Out here all alone there was no telling what he was capable of. Her mind searched for an escape. The road she was on continued for several miles until it petered out in the rangeland. She knew she would not be able to make it that far before Parker overtook her. She could leave the road but that would slow her down considerably, forcing her encounter with Parker that much sooner.

The road crested on a hill and then plunged into a swale. Anne kept the horse at full speed. The animal was puffing hard under her direction, but holding up steady and sound. The road made another upward swing and, when they reached the top, the ATV came blazing over the crest behind them. They entered the hilly patch between the High Star compound and the open, flat rangeland. If Anne was going to make a move, her best opportunity was while she was out of sight down in the swale. But there proved to be no opportunity to lose his trail and, before she reached the top of the next hill, Parker came roaring back into view. He was 300 yards behind now and gaining fast.

"Sam?"

"Yeah?"

"I think you should try to get off and hide. I am not sure what is going to happen."

Sam didn't hesitate, "No way, mom. Just keep going."

Anne's heart was heavy; she was losing her wits. It was all too much. The drama over the past three days hammered on her nervous system. Should she stop and face this maniac? What could he really do? That is when she heard the gunshot. She looked back; Parker was 200 yards behind. He had a pistol out and was taking pot shots in her direction. Her heart skipped a beat. She kicked the horse hard and screamed for him to speed up. The poor horse was running as fast as he could and beginning to tire. Sam reached out within the yellow mist to comfort the animal and to communicate the necessity of speed. Still Parker was gaining on them, closing the gap between safety and reckless endangerment.

Another crest and the road went down. There were no trees or any type of cover. Anne just kept going. As she reached the bottom of the swale, Parker zoomed over the crest. He was now about 100 yards behind. She heard several rapid gunshots and heard one bullet whiz by over her head. Anne burst into tears.

"Sam! What are we going to do?"

Sam was feeling the same panic.

"I don't know," yelled Sam in desperation.

"He's going to kill us!" The words came out of Anne's mouth almost automatically. Desperate thoughts ricocheted around in her empty brain. She looked down and noticed something that completely skipped her attention. She had a rifle. She could fight back. A sense of relief, though wrapped in utter fear, smoothed over her addled mind. She quickly formulated a plan.

"Okay, Sam, here's the deal. When we get over this next ridge we have to stop. I will take the rifle and shoot him as he comes over the ridge. Catch him by surprise. When we stop, I want you to run as fast as you can away from the road. Understand?"

Sam was horrified.

"Do you understand?" Anne's voice was frantic.

"Yes," Sam said weakly.

The ridgeline loomed ahead. Parker was 50 yards back now and continued to fire at them. Several bullets screamed by. In just moments Anne could come to a rapid halt, get on the ground, get Sam away, aim, and shoot. She began to draw the rifle but stopped, thinking that it might warn Parker that something was up. She resisted the urge and put her entire hopes on the top of the hill. Two more shots came across, as the whine of the ATV grew ever louder. The top of the ridge was 20 yards out.

"Okay, Sam, are you ready? This is going to happen fast! Once we're over the top I will stop, you jump off and run as fast as you can. Run away from the road, okay?"

"Okay, I'm ready," said Sam, though she didn't feel at all ready. Another bullet flew by. The ridgeline was imminent, and Parker was closing behind. They crested the hill and Anne got ready to halt the horse. She had about 15 seconds to pull this off.

Thirty yards behind, Parker watched Ann and the horse disappear over the hill. He would catch them at the bottom of the next ravine. His mindset deteriorated into blind rage and he focused on one thing only. He was dead set on killing these two interlopers, burying their bodies, and forgetting the whole thing. This would set his world right again. Ruud wouldn't have to know anything except the problem was solved. The press would go away; the story would die along with that miserable Harper woman. Parker would keep his good job, his good life. Just over the next hill he would dispense of this problem once and for all. It would be quick and easy. His clip had four rounds remaining. He had an extra clip in his belt, but wouldn't need it. The ATV ran at full throttle. He approached the ridge with gun in hand; his mind filled with wretched thoughts. Thoughts that banged on the front of his skull. As he crested the hill he readied himself for the last chapter in this horrid saga. But in an instant the whole plan changed.

His heart jumped to his throat as he encountered Joe, Nolan, Lon, Christo, and several ranch hands riding up the trail towards him. Taken completely by surprise, Parker panicked and hit the brakes, sending his ATV into a sideways skid. Instinctively he turned his wheels into the skid, but not soon enough. He hit the side of the dirt road and flipped end over end. The last thing he saw as he flew through the air was Anne and Samantha galloping down the road toward their friends. Parker hit the ground head first followed by the 530-pound machine. He died almost instantly as the fall severed his spinal cord. The machine continued to roll several times and came to rest wheels up in a cloud of fine, powdery dust.

Anne and Samantha didn't see the wreck. When they came over the hill prepared for battle, Anne's heart also jumped to her throat when she saw the posse coming up the road at full speed. Her relief gave way to tears as she rushed down the hill to certain safety. Behind she heard the metallic sounds of the ATV crashing through the sagebrush. She didn't turn around until she joined the group and knew she was out of danger. Anne and Samantha were safe.

Anne jumped off her horse and collapsed on the ground. She exploded into hysteric sobs; the sound of her bawling echoed around the swale. As those around her watched with compassionate hearts, all of her tension and fears released into a flood of salty tears. Nolan came to her side with a strong, comforting arm. He still looked gaunt and pallid, but Sam was right. When they saved Sun Cloud, they saved Nolan. He demanded to come with the rest of the crew regardless of how they thought he was feeling. Anne held him tight with both arms, crying all that much louder. The two embraced until all of Anne's pent-up anxiety was cried out. They mounted up and, without speaking, headed for Angel Ridge.

No one mourned Parker's loss. They left his body as it lay. Someone would find him soon enough and the group from Angel Ridge had nothing to answer for. After retrieving Sam's horse, they all retreated over the same route and in 40 minutes were back at the rescue farm.

CHAPTER FIFTEEN

Nolan opened his eyes trying to wake from a dream where he was flying in a plane fueled by rose water—some kind of mixture of two different distilled roses. They were running low on fuel and the pilot said they needed to find a place to land. He looked out the window and saw endless fields of roses.

In the real world, the sun was up and by the looks of the light streaming in through the small window, it was probably mid-morning. Nolan lay in his bed in a dreamy fog. He was at that sublime threshold between sleep and wakefulness where the dream lingers but receives the added layer of lucidity. That lingering after-effect which sometimes lasts well into the day was one of beauty, well-being, and peacefulness. Nolan felt whole. Complete. Protected. He lay there letting the feeling of peace wash over him. There was nothing urgent calling him from his slumber. He was under doctor's orders to rest up for awhile. He gladly accepted the opportunity.

Soon his mind drifted off to think about Anne. She and Samantha spent the night at the main house, no doubt sleeping just as soundly. Nolan wanted to see her. It was the one thing he would force himself out of bed for. He swung his legs to the floor and sat up. His entire body moaned with a dull yet immediate pain. From head to toe, Nolan's body was crying out; the last three days exacted a toll that would take time to heal.

Nolan quickly washed and dressed then headed up toward the house, walking slowly due to his stiffness. He was confident this time Anne would be glad to see him.

When he arrived at the house, everyone was at the kitchen table chatting over a breakfast of eggs, toast, and bacon. Anne slid over and offered Nolan a seat next to her. Samantha beamed her approval.

"How'd ya sleep last night, Nolan?" asked Rosie.

"Like a log. Still not quite awake."

"Here, have some coffee."

Nolan took the cup from Rosie and nursed the brew.

"Any word on Sun Cloud's condition?" asked Nolan.

" He'll be fine," answered Joe. "John's got him hydrated. He's eating and his gut's working. He'll be ready to turn out in a couple of days."

Nolan considered the words quietly.

"What about the sheriff? Anyone asking about him?" Nolan quizzed.

"We haven't heard a word."

"I don't think we have to worry about that," said Anne. "Deputy Miller is going to spill the beans on the whole operation over there. The senator is going to have a bigger problem on his hands."

"What? Deputy Miller? How did that happen?" asked Nolan.

"I think he has a conscience," Anne said. "That's why he helped us get Sun Cloud out of there. He's had enough and doesn't want to be part of that group. Poor guy. He is about to experience a level-five shit storm."

"Mom!" Samantha was embarrassed by Anne's words. Anne looked at Sam and went on. "Anyway, I am meeting with him later today. He promised to tell all. Should be a great cap to this story."

"Finally," said Rosie. "After all these years of having to take it from Ruud, he will finally get what he deserves."

"Well, we'll see," said Anne. "Matthew is going to go all out on this, that's for sure. He's got affiliates lined up. He has back-to-back promos going 'round the clock, a teaser campaign. He will make certain that people see this and know about it. It's going to be a big story and Matthew is out there selling it. But you know the nature of politics. Ruud could still come out looking clean. He's got all the right friends in all the right places."

Rosie just looked at her plate. She hoped for the best, but the thought crossed her mind that all this could backfire on Angel Ridge in some fateful sleight of hand. Ruud was that powerful.

Joe sat there thoughtfully regarding his coffee cup. His eyes were puffy and bloodshot. Suddenly he stood up from the table.

"That's it," he said.

Rosie furrowed her brow. "Where you going?" she asked.

"Nap time."

"Nap time? It's 10:30!"

"It's been a long week," said Joe. He smiled and walked out of the room.

Rosie looked at Sam. "Are you ready for your next lesson?"

Samantha smiled and nodded. She and Rosie got up, cleared their dishes to the sink, said their good-byes, and headed for the stables.

Anne sat next to Nolan, feeling grateful they had some time to spend alone. She leaned over and kissed his cheek.

"How you doing, buddy?"

Nolan's hand slipped around her waist. He pulled her a little closer.

"I am worn out ...almost completely," said Nolan. He gave a weak little smile. "But I'll bounce back. Like Joe said, it's been a hell of a week."

Anne's heart throbbed as her mind searched for words to express her true feelings to Nolan. After six years of being alone—on her own with no support—it was a strange mix of emotions that grabbed her. She had known this man for a short three days yet her soul connected with a solid, familiar link to his. He was as honest a soul as she had ever known. Yes, she knew little about him but the idea of plumbing the depths of his life was exhilarating.

Someone else clouded her train of thought—Samantha. It is always in the heart of a widowed mother to find a replacement father for her children. This eternal longing haunted Anne for years. Of course, no one could ever replace Simon; that goes without saying. But no one ever measured up to the role. Not by any means. Now there was someone who was suitable for both Anne and Samantha. There was a connection between all three. It was something Anne couldn't just dismiss—it was everything.

Then there was the yellow mist. Although Anne had only a vague concept of this mystery, she knew it was key to Samantha's existence and Nolan was one that could help her develop this gift, this crazy power. To what end, Anne did not know. Something in her being told her to quit trying to control everything and just go with it. Her intuition was voicing its approval of this man and of how everything was coming together. It was calming to her. It was different. She didn't feel embattled, like she needed to fight. She felt at ease and confident; a strange feeling after all the years of being alone.

With a great, deep feeling of love and appreciation, Anne began the conversation that would change her entire life.

"Nolan, I am going to have to go back to Sacramento soon."

Nolan was silent while he waited for her to finish the thought.

"These last few days have changed my life. Something big happened here; something amazing between you and me and I don't want it to end."

Nolan intently listened.

"I don't know how to go on from here," Anne continued. "This hasn't happened to me for such a long time, I really don't know what to do."

Nolan listened to the words and felt his soul stirring. His life after Caroline was a blur of countless lonely days. There was no real love, no real living. He filled the void with endless hours of work and toil. There was never any restfulness. Sitting by Anne, he felt completely at peace. This was a strange feeling to a man who was on the edge of isolation year after year. He didn't want this to end. The thought of another separation put him on the brink of desperation. He wasn't a desperate person. Quite the contrary. It was the thought of letting a true soul connection like this slip past him, out of reach.

He smiled and let out an ironic laugh.

"I can't believe this is happening," Nolan started out. "This was the last thing I would have ever bet on." He was smiling as if he really did appreciate the irony of the situation. "A cowboy and a dressage queen."

Anne frowned, "Are you mocking me?"

"Not at all," objected Nolan. "Tell me, Anne Harper, what do you want out of life?"

Anne was distracted by the way Nolan was avoiding her question.

"Well, I want …" she paused. This was something she hadn't thought about for years. What she wanted most was to get Samantha to the Olympics. She had to go with that. "I want Sam to ride in the Olympics for the U.S. team and to win the gold medal."

"That's pretty specific," said Nolan with eyebrows raised. "Anything else?"

"I don't know. I have been in survival mode for so long I haven't really thought about it." There was an awkward silence.

Then Anne said, "I want you, Nolan Powell. I want you in my life." She looked away toward the end of the table. "I want you in Samantha's life."

Nolan could feel Anne letting her guard down.

"I've fallen in love with you, Anne." Nolan's voice came across smooth, and sure, and strikingly honest. Anne put her arm around his shoulder and pulled him in close.

"Me too, cowboy."

Nolan's voice softened even more. "I think you and Sam should stay here." Anne looked into Nolan's eyes. "Sam has a gift, something that is rare and special. She needs help to develop it. She needs Joe, Rosie, and me. In five years she will be able to work with any horse in the world. It would be a horrible talent to waste on the mere Olympics."

Anne sighed, "Uh, no. I can't live out here. This is as dreary a place as I have ever known. I mean, what would we do for fun?"

Nolan smiled his knowing smile and shook his head.

"Those distractions you call fun? Tell me, are they really that much fun?"

Anne reflected on what Nolan was saying. She had no fun. She worked at the station; then worked at home. There was no fun. There was only the vague dream of Samantha's glory to keep her motivated. And now, suddenly, it all seemed so hollow, so useless, but in that vulnerable place her ego flared.

"I have fun," she said coldly, defensively.

Nolan nodded like he understood. Then he gave her another loving squeeze.

"Well, we don't have to decide anything right now, that's for sure. What's your plan for today?" He suddenly took on a cheery disposition.

Anne sat in deep thought for a few moments then came back to the conversation.

"Oh! I'm meeting with Deputy Miller in a few hours. We're going to have the interview of my life. No big deal, right? I am just going to get the biggest story of my career and then I am going to write. That's my plan. You?"

"Nothing that life-changing for me." Nolan said. "I'm going to take it easy, give myself a break, maybe read a little." They parted ways with a gentle and prolonged kiss with the promise of meeting up for dinner. Both Anne and Nolan looked forward to the night ahead.

At 1:30 p.m. that afternoon, Anne sat with Deputy Chris Miller in the dining hall at a table in the corner next to the fireplace. The room was quiet. The only people coming in and out were the old cook and one of his helpers. They took no notice of the policeman, now wearing civilian clothes, sitting next to the woman from California. Anne and Miller had plenty of privacy while the interview took place.

During the three-hour talk, the deputy laid bare all the facts he possessed about the High Star Ranch, the town's entanglements, the police force, the BLM, and how Senator Ruud ruled the county from his office in Washington, D.C. Anne had a recording device, plus she was furiously taking notes as Miller jumped from point to point in the long tale of greed, corruption, and manipulation. In all her days as an investigative reporter, Anne never imagined some of the things she was hearing. Even the most cynical observer would be shocked at about how easily Senator Ruud could turn things his way.

Anne's main story of interest concerned the wild mustang herd that Ruud had threatened. Miller knew all the details. His young nephew worked at the High Star for several years and he had inside information about what was going on there. Miller told Anne where the carcasses were buried. He also knew all about the men who died out there, where the bodies were taken, how the county coroner kept the incident quiet and how Ruud planned on paying off the families of those killed. This part of the story came with real evidence—names and places. This was where Anne focused her energy. She soon had the entire outline of a story that would blow Ruud clean out of the water. She and Miller finished up just after 4:00 p.m.

Matthew Clark, Anne's boss, returned to Sacramento the preceding day. He waited for Anne to call and when she finally did he was amped up with excitement to hear the details of the Miller interview. Anne did not disappoint him as she highlighted the main parts of Deputy Miller's story. This was exactly the kind of story Matthew waited his whole career to report. He was ecstatic as he knew the tremendous amount of political capital this story would drain from Ruud. But at the same time, he was playing the skeptic. He could not run with a story based on one man's testimony. The facts, times, and places had to be corroborated. There was still much work to do before the story went to press. He listened until Anne finished and then started his editorial review. By the time they were done, Anne had been on the phone for an hour and a half. She had enough material to start a rough draft. Matthew would find people in the area who would back up what Chris Miller told her. There was also another gruesome task—digging up the seven horse carcasses to prove the allegations of the horse kill. The two made a plan and then hung up the phone. It was 6:00 p.m. and Anne was anxious to see Nolan.

Even though she had hours of writing to do, Anne decided to give herself a break and wandered down to the dining hall to see if Nolan was there. Sure enough, she found him sitting with Rosie, Joe, and Samantha. As she approached, Nolan stood and gave her a hug. He was clearly happy to see her.

"How'd it go today?" asked Rosie with raised eyebrows.

"Oh, you will not believe the story I heard."

"Can you give us some details?" asked Joe.

"Yeah, I don't know why not. I don't think there is any chance of any of you taking this story to our competition."

Anne proceeded to recount the interview with Miller. Each of them sat slack-jawed at the audacity of the senator and the complicity of the township. Many pieces of the story added to what Rosie and Joe already knew. They looked at each other from time to time, nodding like they finally understood some mystery that had been bothering them for years. Anne continued with details, names, places, as well as information on specific financial transactions. She talked until she exhausted all that she knew, all that Miller had told her.

"Sounds like Ruud is going to get a wake-up call," said Rosie.

"It's not as easy as that," said Anne. "We can't run with this story until we verify every detail of this information. We need at least two sources. More would be better because we are dealing with a senator."

"I can help with that," said Joe. "I know all of those people you were talking about. This is a small town. I've been here my entire life. Some will help us, others won't. But I will call the ones who will help. You just tell me what to do."

"Me too," said Rosie.

And so it started there—Anne and her investigative team. They plotted a course of action that would confirm the worst of what was known about Ruud. They would focus on the horse kill and then, as time permitted, get confirmation on the other allegations. As they all got up and left the table, each carried a renewed glow of hope that justice would be coming soon.

Anne returned to her room, opened her laptop, and started writing. She was distracted throughout the evening by the thoughts of Nolan and what their future would bring. A warm glow burned softly in her heart.

Anne was up at 6:00 a.m. the next morning after sleeping only four hours. She was 90% finished with the first draft of her story and needed another hour to work on it before she sent it to Matthew for review. As soon as she finished, she emailed the document to her boss and went downstairs to find Joe at the kitchen table. Rosie and Samantha were still in bed.

"Morning, Joe."

"Anne."

"How's Sun Cloud coming along?"

"Oh, he's doing well. Should be ready to release back to the herd tomorrow."

Anne thought a moment. "That's perfect."

She poured a cup of coffee and sat down across from Joe.

"What did you find out last night?" she asked.

"I called all the people on the list you gave me. I spoke to all except two who were out of town. The ones I did talk to were willing to go on the record to support what Miller is saying. There seems to be a tipping point in the town. These people are tired of Ruud and his operation. It was easier than I thought."

Anne was surprised.

"Wow! Okay. That was easy …good. I will follow up with these folks today and get this thing wrapped up."

Joe smiled. He liked Anne. He could see through her steely façade and knew she had a good heart.

"Then what are you going to do?" Joe asked.

Anne knew what Joe was thinking. He wanted to know if she and Nolan were going to try to grow their budding relationship.

"I don't know, Joe. This thing with Nolan came out of nowhere. I won't be able to just leave and forget him. This is getting complicated."

Joe sat and listened. He was very good at that.

"We both want to work something out, but Nolan belongs here and I …" she stopped and gathered her thoughts. "I …don't know where I belong anymore. That is the thing that is bothering me the most. The time I have been here has changed my entire life. It is like my life has been turned upside down, shaken out, wadded up, and thrown to the side."

Joe smiled. "Your life is a grocery bag?"

Anne rolled her eyes. She knew Joe was playing.

"Up until now I had a very good idea of my goals—who I was and what I was doing."

"What changed?" asked Joe.

Anne thought it through and then it dawned on her.

"Samantha changed. Well, at least my understanding of Samantha changed. I finally think I know her."

Anne sat stunned at her revelation.

"And I thought this was about me and Nolan, when it is really about Samantha." Anne grabbed her head and ran her hand through her hair.

"God, I'm selfish," she said reflectively. "I just think about myself. That poor kid, to have a mother like me. My life has changed because I know the truth about Samantha. Not because I'm in love with a cowboy."

"Love?" Joe asked with a smile.

Anne stopped and looked at Joe. "Well, that just fell out now, didn't it?"

Joe laughed. "I could see that growing between you two," he said. "And do you know what I think?"

"What Joe?"

"I think your confusion is as much about you and Nolan as it is about Samantha. There has been a seismic shift in your life. Big changes. Something moved that has been stuck. It has changed your heart, your mind, your imagination, and your love. That is what I think."

Anne sat there thinking about it.

"Joe, you are right. I am not the same person who came here last week. How is it that things can change that fast? What does that say about the person I have been for the last six years?"

"Oh, you are the same person, Anne. But I would say you are more of who you really are than you used to be. You are more legitimate, more authentic."

"Well, I feel more alive than I have in years, that's for sure."

Anne sat quiet for another spell then spoke.

"I need to talk with Samantha. She has a voice in all this. I want to find out what she wants to do."

Joe nodded his agreement and sipped his coffee with a loud slurp.

Anne spent the rest of the day talking with the sources Joe had roused up. She confirmed most of what Miller told her. There were variations, of course, but the main story about Ruud was corroborated by more than one source. In most cases, three or more.

It was up to Nolan and his crew to go out and dig up the horse carcasses and collect that evidence. This burial site was far out on the range and there was no conflict from anyone about digging up the grave. It was gruesome work but the case was being built and the grimness of the job was made easier by the fact that everyone knew this would fall hard on the senator. It took most of the day to collect the bodies.

Meanwhile, Rosie went to visit the county coroner. She knew the man for 20 years and was confident she could get some information from him about the men killed on the ranch. She was correct in her assumptions, her friend confided the details about the deaths, the numbers, the cause of death, and all other details Anne's story might need.

All of this information flowed in and Anne took each piece, expertly arranged the details, and tied them together in a smart and intelligent narrative. By the afternoon she sent the entire piece to Matthew for final review.

After several lengthy phone calls between Matt and Anne, it was decided that a film crew would be dispatched to Angel Ridge and Anne would do a live report from the field. The crew would be there first thing in the morning and the shoot would coincide with the release of Sun Cloud back to the herd. It was the perfect dramatic visual to tie the story together for the viewing public. Concurrently, the story was being written up for simultaneous publishing across all media channels—newspapers, Internet blogs, websites, and social media. This would be a highly coordinated media event and Anne would be right at the heart of it. This was her chance to shine.

The day ended with a bittersweet sense of satisfaction, as this life-altering adventure was coming to a close.

That night Anne stayed awake thinking about her future. Samantha was asleep and the rhythmic sound of her breathing was calming, like summer waves on a midnight beach. Anne lay still while the dance of fame and glory tugged at her ego. She could see herself being hired away from KTVX to one of the big stations in Los Angeles, or even New York. The accolades would come pouring in as would the money. Additionally, the prestige of breaking a story like this would be over the top. She could see the headline, "Senator's Ranch Involved in Wild Horse Kill." It would be sensational—literally. In her mind she played over the video shots she would get—a helicopter view of the High Star; the shot of the horse graveyard; maybe even the carcasses; close-ups of Sun Cloud; and then the shot of that wild stallion returning to the herd after the heroic efforts of the crew at Angel Ridge Rescue Ranch. She was confident this story would go viral. There may even be congressional hearings at which she would be called on to recount the events that led to the uncovering of such a horrific crime. It was all so unbelievable, but still within the realm of possibility. Tomorrow her life would change—yet again.

The word "again" rang in her mind. Her life already changed dramatically. The idea of the wealth and fame that lay ahead made her wonder if the current situation with Nolan was just a foreshadowing of the real changes to come. Big changes. She refocused her thoughts back to the story; but each time she saw the shining light of glory, there was a shadow cast from the glow—that shadow was Nolan. His presence was everywhere in her thoughts. A symbol of opposition. A stumbling block to her egotistical joy ride. Her heart buzz-killing her head dreams. Nolan had climbed into her conscience and sat atop her motivations and her aspirations.

Anne turned over on her side and tried to sleep. It was no use.

"Samantha! Are you awake?" Anne whispered loudly.

The girl stirred but said nothing.

"Sam, wake up!"

Sam sat up in her bed, not sure what was going on.

"Sam, are you awake?" Anne whispered again.

"What? Yes, I'm awake. What's the matter?"

"I need to ask you a question."

Sam looked at the clock—2:37 a.m. She looked over at her mom and gave her a protesting frown.

"I can't sleep," said Anne. "I need to ask you a question."

"What?"

"What do you think about Nolan?"

Still half asleep, Sam struggled to understand the question. "Nolan?"

"Yeah, what do you think about him?"

"I like him."

"He thinks we should move here."

Sam's face lit up. Her drowsy attitude sharpened into focus.

"That would be cool!" Sam said with mounting excitement.

"Really?" asked Anne. "You would like that?"

"I would like that a lot," said Sam.

"You would want to live here?"

"With Rosie and Joe and Nolan? Yeah, I would love to live here."

"Why? What about your friends?"

Sam thought about it for a moment. She did have some good friends at home, but none of them knew about the yellow mist; none of them knew about her reality.

"My friends know nothing about my new life …about my gift, as Nolan calls it. It was Rosie and Joe and Nolan who helped me see it."

Anne laid back down. She felt a strange tinge of defeat.

"So are we moving here, Mom?"

"No, sweetie, I don't think so."

"I think we should. I think it would be cool to live on a rescue ranch."

"Okay," finished Anne. "I just wanted to know what you thought about it."

Sam put her head back on her pillow, but now was unable to sleep herself. The idea stuck in her mind and fired up her imagination.

The morning came too soon. Anne barely dropped off to sleep when the alarm brought her back to consciousness. She popped up quickly and with purpose. Letting Sam sleep, Anne rushed to get herself ready for her big day. In 45 minutes she was looking sharp at the kitchen table having a quick coffee.

The video crew was a half-hour out, giving Anne some additional time to refine the schedule, work on her script, and rethink some of the shots needed to get. The minutes zinged by. Before she knew it, the crew arrived and she was standing in front of the house briefing them on the day's schedule. It would be hectic and the schedule was tight. It was decided late the prior evening that the release of Sun Cloud would be live at 6:30 p.m. It was timed to get the most traction out of the story when it aired during prime-time news hour. In short, they had a lot of work to do.

Anne and her crew hit the ground running and soon were off to do the pick-up shots needed to interweave with the live broadcast.

Nolan was in charge of getting Sun Cloud ready to release.

The day flew by. There was a certain excitement in the air. A kind of expectation, like waiting for a birthday party. Everyone felt it. The dark cloud that hung around Angel Ridge lifted and, for the first time in months, there was reason for hope.

Anne filled each minute with details of the story. There was no time to stop, chat, rest, or dream. It was a day filled with tasks, one after another. As the sun traveled its course, Anne expertly assembled the pieces she would need—video, interviews, shot locations, script tuning. The entire day was devoted to the story.

As the day came to an end and early evening settled upon the ranch, everyone took their places for the big show, culminating with Sun Cloud's release. The release was to take place down at the farm's edge where the herd still grazed within the safety of the Angel Ridge perimeter. Once Sun Cloud rejoined the herd, the animals would be led back out to the open range where, for once, they would be safe.

Everything was ready. The entire ranch crew was out where Sun Cloud was to be released. Down in the folds of the expansive pasture the rest of the herd could be seen grazing lazily out of harm's way.

Rosie and Joe parked one of the farm trucks strategically and were sitting up on the cab for the best view. Sam was there, too. Nolan was up at the barn working with Sun Cloud, assuring the horse would be able to make the walk from the barn, past the spectators, and out to the herd. It was all perfectly scripted.

Anne freshened up and was milling around with the crew making the final preparations. She ditched her usual attire of a chic power suit and was looking relaxed in jeans and a work shirt. Confident, professional, and completely in charge, Anne was the consummate reporter.

Back in Sacramento the station was buzzing. The link was established; the producers were in their chairs. The support staff—from technicians to key operators—were all in place. The time had come.

"Now we go live to Angel Ridge Rescue Ranch with Anne Harper …Anne?"

The little red light on the camera blinked on. Anne was live on the air—the moment had come.

"Nevada Senator Harry Ruud has been implicated in a bizarre and heart-rending story concerning the killing of wild horses out here in Western Nevada. I am standing here at the Angel Ridge Rescue Ranch. This is an operation that saves unwanted or abandoned horses, owned by Joseph and Rosalind Whitehorse."

"Angel Ridge borders the High Star Ranch, which is wholly owned by Nevada Senator Harry Ruud. There are rumors of wild horses being killed by the ranch and I came here to find the truth. As you may know, killing wild horses is a federal crime and one does not make this allegation lightly, especially against a U.S. Senator.

"I have personally been to the kill site and witnessed the workers at High Star Ranch in the act of killing wild horses. Workers at Angel Ridge retrieved the bodies of seven horses that were killed and disposed of just east of here. The horrific scene was indescribably morbid and I am going to show some video now but be advised, sensitive viewers should probably not watch this."

Anne stopped talking and the video rolled. She had set the stage perfectly. Of course everyone would watch the video. Who doesn't look at the car wreck as they go by? The video was 35 seconds long. Anne waited for the cue. Scanning the scene, Anne saw everyone but Nolan who was preparing Sun Cloud for the release. Anne feared the timing would be off. Nolan should have been on his way down by now.

"Anyone seen Nolan?" Anne shouted.

"He'll be here," responded Joe.

The short break was up. The red light blinked and Anne was back on.

"As you can see, the evidence is compelling. Our phone calls to the senator have not been returned. The senator will have to answer to these charges since the case is now with the district attorney."

Anne looked up and saw Nolan walking down the road. He was leading Sun Cloud, the wild stallion, peacefully down the road in complete control.

"This story does have somewhat of a silver lining," Anne continued, "Three days ago, Senator Ruud ordered an illegal roundup and his men took the lead stallion back to the High Star Ranch. I was personally involved in retrieving that stallion from the senator's ranch. The horse, known as Sun Cloud, has been recuperating here at Angel Ridge, and this evening he will be released back to the herd where he belongs."

Anne continued. "Nolan Powell, a highly skilled horseman, has been working directly with Sun Cloud to make sure the horse is healthy enough to return to the wild. Nolan and Sun Cloud will be here shortly. Please keep in mind this is a wild mustang and is not by any means tame."

"Everyone please stand back and give Nolan and the horse a lot of room. Here they come now! You can see the beautiful bay color of this magnificent stallion—"

Just then Sun Cloud let out a loud screaming neigh. Anne didn't miss a beat.

"Sun Cloud is calling to his herd, which is just out of sight down that hill. Nolan's about to remove the halter and let the stallion go."

Nolan led the horse past the small crowd. The entire crew of Angel Ridge was there along with some of the townsfolk. Nolan stopped ahead of the camera. Sun Cloud reared up, calling to the herd again. The image was perfect drama for Anne's broadcast. Nolan didn't flinch. He raised a calming hand and brought the animal down, patting his neck to reassure him.

The visual was perfect. The great American cowboy handling the wild mustang; the rangeland in the background side-lit by the waning sun. The light was gleaming pure and brilliant. Nolan and Sun Cloud were standing proud, in partnership.

Only a select few could see the yellow mist swirling there, connecting the horse with Nolan. Only those few saw the reality behind the outward spectacle.

Nolan slipped the halter off Sun Cloud's head and the horse bolted away, kicking up small puffs of dust as he galloped down the hill toward the herd. The camera followed the horse until he was too far to be seen and then it panned back to Anne. She had a tear running down her cheek.

"I cannot tell you how emotional this is," she said to the camera. "Just days ago I rescued that horse from certain death. He was brought here, rehabilitated, and now back where he belongs."

Anne went to say something else but paused. There was an awkward space of silence, the kind that seems like hours on live television.

"Speaking of being where one belongs…"

Back at the station Matthew was watching the monitor. He knew this was unscripted. The producer looked at him with wide eyes, silently asking if he knew what was going on. Matt shook his head no. He was gripped with panic.

"This reporter has decided that this will be my last broadcast."

Matthew audibly gasped. He wanted to pull the plug and end the live feed, but it was too late. He listened in a state of shock.

"For years I have worked at this great station and have been surrounded by many wonderful, supportive people. But now I have found where I belong. I have decided to stay here at Angel Ridge and join the valiant efforts of these brave people. We owe the horse—all horses—a great debt and I have found in myself the desire to pay back my share. This is my final broadcast. Thank you to all of my friends and colleagues for making my time here at KTVX some of the best years of my life. This is Anne Harper signing off."

Samantha was the first to squeal in glee as she dismounted the truck and ran to hug her mother. Rosie grabbed Joe's hand and laughed, her happy eyes twinkled. The video crew stood stock-still with gaping mouths and blank eyes. Back at the station, the news anchor was back on air and sat speechless for a few seconds while trying to adlib a segue.

Anne turned to find Nolan next to her. He was smiling.

"Well, is that your final answer?" he joked.

Anne looked into Nolan's eyes. Her heart was pounding. "I don't know if it makes much sense," she said, "but it sure feels right."

Nolan put his arm around her shoulder and pulled her in tight. Samantha stood in front of them smiling. They all turned to look out to the range where Sun Cloud had joined the herd. For the first time in recent memory the herd was safe. The people at Angel Ridge succeeded in keeping the promise, in holding up their end of the bargain. The bond between man and horse was renewed and reaffirmed. Kept alive for another generation of horses and horsemen.

Nolan pulled Anne even closer and turned to give her a tender kiss.

"I am so glad to hear you are staying."

EPILOGUE

The next day Anne sat with Nolan at the ranch house. There was nowhere to go, no hurry, no stress. She never felt this complete sense of tranquility before. It was an amazing beginning to her new life. Samantha was completely at ease with the change of direction and the new life plan. The young girl was excited about the opportunity to develop her special gift with a group of capable people who fully understood. To Anne, things just seemed perfectly balanced for the first time in many years.

As she thought about her future, one within the partnership of horse and man, it wasn't lost on her that man and horse had been partners for thousands of years. This partnership was responsible for much of the progress mankind achieved through the centuries. Now that the horse was no longer a vital part of the evolutionary tract of mankind, what kind of future could the horse expect? What would horsemanship be in 100 years or even 500 years from now? This last question burned in her consciousness for days.

THE END